D0742245

San Diego Christian College
Library
Santee, CA

American Blood

810.9355
J12a

American Blood

The Ends of the Family in American Literature, 1850–1900

Holly Jackson

OXFORD
UNIVERSITY PRESS

OXFORD
UNIVERSITY PRESS

Oxford University Press is a department of the University of Oxford.
It furthers the University's objective of excellence in research,
scholarship, and education by publishing worldwide.

Oxford   New York

Auckland   Cape Town   Dar es Salaam   Hong Kong   Karachi
Kuala Lumpur   Madrid   Melbourne   Mexico City   Nairobi
New Delhi   Shanghai   Taipei   Toronto

With offices in

Argentina   Austria   Brazil   Chile   Czech Republic   France   Greece
Guatemala   Hungary   Italy   Japan   Poland   Portugal   Singapore
South Korea   Switzerland   Thailand   Turkey   Ukraine   Vietnam

Oxford is a registered trademark of Oxford University Press
in the UK and certain other countries.

Published in the United States of America by
Oxford University Press
198 Madison Avenue, New York, NY 10016

© Oxford University Press 2014

All rights reserved. No part of this publication may be reproduced,
stored in a retrieval system, or transmitted, in any form or by any means, without the
prior permission in writing of Oxford University Press, or as expressly permitted by law,
by license, or under terms agreed with the appropriate reproduction rights organization.
Inquiries concerning reproduction outside the scope of the above should be sent
to the Rights Department, Oxford University Press, at the address above.

Portions of this work are reprinted with permission from the following sources:
Holly Jackson, "'So We Die before Our Own Eyes': Willful Sterility in *The Country of the Pointed Firs*,"
The New England Quarterly, 82:2 (June, 2009), pp. 264–284. © 2009 by The New England Quarterly, Inc.

Holly Jackson, "The Transformation of American Family Property in *The House of the Seven Gables*,"
ESQ: A Journal of the American Renaissance, September v. 56 (3rd quarter, 2010), pp. 269–292.

Holly Jackson, "Another Long Bridge: Reproduction and Reversion in *Hagar's Daughter*," *Early African
American Print Culture*. Eds., Lara Langer Cohen and Jordan Alexander Stein (Penn Press 2012),
pp. 192–202. © 2012 University of Pennsylvania Press.

You must not circulate this work in any other form
and you must impose this same condition on any acquirer.

Library of Congress Cataloging-in-Publication Data
Jackson, Holly.
American blood : the ends of the family in American literature, 1850–1900 / Holly Jackson.
pages cm
Includes bibliographical references and index.
ISBN 978-0-19-931704-2 (acid-free paper)
1. American literature—19th century—History and criticism. 2. Families in literature.
3. Families—Political aspects—United States. I. Title.
PS217.F35J33   2013
810.9'355—dc23   2013008402

1 3 5 7 9 8 6 4 2

Printed in the United States of America
on acid-free paper

For Sari Edelstein, Jane Jackson-Edelstein, and all unruly genealogies.

CONTENTS

ACKNOWLEDGMENTS

For me, exploring the meaning of family is a lifelong project, and it has been an immense privilege to devote the first years of my professional life to writing *American Blood*. Many people have enabled, encouraged, and improved my efforts on this book; to say that they have been a kind of family to me would be an underestimation indeed.

Surprisingly, the first people I knew to disprove the myths of family blood were my parents, Percy and Karen Jackson. I am eternally grateful for the sacrifices they made unflinchingly for my education and for their unequivocal support from the very beginning. I thank the English department at Simmons College—especially Renee Bergland, Pam Bromberg, and Kelly Hager—for their early encouragement toward a career they so admirably modeled. Many current and former Brandeis faculty members shaped my progress, including Paul Morrison, Caren Irr, Sue Lanser, John Plotz, Aliyyah Abdur-Rahman, Tom King, Dawn Skorczewski, and Pat Chu. Faith Smith contributed vitally to this work and also offered crucial advice on my first publication. Most of all, I want to recognize my mentor and the director of the dissertation project from which this book stems, Michael T. Gilmore, in the hope that this project reflects his immense influence on my thinking.

I am grateful to Linda Simon for shepherding me through my gratifying time at Skidmore College, a job that taught me so much. Jennifer Delton, Mason Stokes, and Susan Walzer, my colleagues at Skidmore, are the kind of friends anyone is lucky to find once in a lifetime. At the University of Massachusetts, Boston, I have found extraordinary support and respect not only for my scholarship but also for a larger vision of a satisfying life, truly a rarity in the academy. Even beginning with my campus visit, Betsy Klimasmith and Shaun O'Connell made suggestions that improved this book; I am thankful to them and to all my new colleagues.

I am honored to recognize a number of esteemed scholars who have contributed indispensably to my professional development solely out of personal and intellectual generosity, especially Robin Bernstein, Shirley Samuels, and

Elaine Showalter; the Nineteenth-Century Women Writers Study Group, including Ellen Gruber Garvey, Gail Smith, Elizabeth Stockton, and many others; my comrades at the School of Criticism and Theory, 2006; Lara Cohen, my friend and aspirational peer; and Julia Dauer, formerly my student, now my friend and colleague, who provided assistance with research and manuscript preparation. For the past ten years, Danielle Coriale has been a cherished source of conspiratorial humor and support. My special thanks go as well to Ashley Shelden, my longtime confidante and playmate, whose verve and style made even graduate school feel glamorous.

Finally, my professional secret weapon is also my greatest joy: my wife, my treasured friend, my true partner and collaborator, Sari Edelstein. Without you to impress or simply keep pace with, there would be no point in accomplishing anything. Thank you so much.

American Blood

Introduction

I. THE NATIONALIZATION OF THE FAMILY

"In America the family," in any traditional sense of the term, "does not exist."[1] By the time Alexis de Tocqueville penned this account of democracy's corrosive effects on established forms of kinship, it was common knowledge that the eighteenth century had been an age of revolution in the family: "It has been universally remarked, that in our time the several members of a family stand upon an entirely new footing towards each other; that the distance which formerly separated a father from his sons has been lessened; and that paternal authority, if not destroyed, is at least impaired."[2] The institution of the family transformed as economic and ideological shifts undermined the patriarchal lineal family and analogous hereditary sociopolitical structures like monarchy and aristocracy.[3] By the middle of the nineteenth century, the modern domestic family had emerged, replacing the conventional economic functions of kin relations with the psychological, sentimental ties of the nuclear unit and theoretically detaching the family from wage labor and politics into distinct gendered domains.[4]

Even as our reliance on the "separate spheres" theory of nineteenth-century history has waned, this framing narrative of the family's transition from genealogical verticality to conjugal domesticity endures in American literary studies, underlying the prevailing view that the nineteenth-century novel's representation of this institution centers in sentiment, sympathy, and disciplinary intimacy.[5] *American Blood* attempts to redirect readings of the American family by foregrounding a culture-wide struggle over its definition and value, arguing on the contrary that the nineteenth century was in fact the heyday of genealogical thinking in the United States.[6] This study offers a new vision of the American novel in this tumultuous period, highlighting works that protest the overvaluation of kinship in American culture, depicting the domestic family as exclusionary, deleterious to civic life, and antagonistic to the political enterprise of the United States. Far from venerating the family as the nucleus of the nation, these novels imagine, even welcome, the decline of this institution and the social order it supports.

While scholars have extensively documented the founding generation's use of the rhetoric of consanguinity and the importance of the "republican family" in representing and transmitting the new nation, an opposing strain of eighteenth-century thought has been ignored: many Americans viewed the family as a powerful conservative institution that inhibits social change and might undermine the project of the republic.[7] Revolutionary rhetoric was broadly distrustful and disparaging of genealogical paradigms, relying on the Enlightenment critique of parental authority to justify the break from England and theorize a social order disconnected from inheritance.[8] After the Revolution, early Americans passed laws for the express purpose of disempowering the family and prohibiting hereditary systems of power from taking root, curbing the dynastic impulses that potentially lurked in each domestic family from stratifying American society along bloodlines.

Despite this foundational concern that unseemly regard for ancestry or posterity might return to taint the new republic, the familial rhetoric of nationalism was deployed so energetically throughout the nineteenth century that reverence for the family came to seem like a core American value instead.[9] With the rise of nationalism, blood-borne status triumphed over Revolutionary ideals, and antipatriarchal republicanism was replaced by filial piety in American politics.[10] The 1820s were the fulcrum of this transitional period from the 1790s to the 1850s, marking a watershed in Americans' relationship to genealogy and also in conceptions of individual citizens' relationship to national history.[11] For one thing, the 200th anniversary of the Pilgrims' 1620 landing at Plymouth serendipitously preceded the fiftieth anniversary of a number of milestones of the War for Independence, and writers of this period worked to establish a causal, genealogical relation between these events that not only extended national history 150 years but also constituted an American bloodline suspiciously similar to the aristocratic lineages it was presumed to unseat. Catharine Sedgwick's 1835 historical romance *The Linwoods* reiterates the by-then commonsense connection between these events, asserting, "It has been justly said, that the seeds of our revolution and future independence were sown by the Pilgrims."[12] This novel's revolutionary hero models a new American nobility: Eliot Lee's "parentage would not be deemed illustrious, according to any artificial code; but . . . he might claim what is now considered as the peculiar, the purest, the enduring, and in truth the *only* aristocracy of our own. He was a lineal descendent from one of the renowned *pilgrim fathers*, whose nobility, stamped in the principles that are regenerating mankind, will be transmitted by their sons on the Missouri and the Oregon, when the stars and garters of Europe have perished and are forgotten" (25).[13] Biological descent from the colonial settlers came to be regarded as membership in an American aristocracy, superior to the rejected aristocracies of Europe but exactly reproducing their values: endurance and purity. Although hereditary distinctions were regarded as anathema to the republican project in the preceding generation, genealogical pride reemerged in the nineteenth century, transformed into patriotism by a nationalist discourse that offered all Americans membership in a noble lineage.

For Daniel Webster, most famous as a grandiloquent senator from Massachusetts who supported the Compromise of 1850, the coincidence of the bicentennial of the Pilgrims' landing and the fiftieth-anniversary celebrations of Revolutionary War milestones provided a handy context for the construction of a genealogical national history, which he then called upon to assuage sectional division.[14] Webster's acclaimed 1820 oration in Plymouth, Massachusetts, clearly finesses the transition from republicanism to nationalism in relation to the family. This speech discredits the traditional dynastic family defined by the descent of real estate and offers in its stead a genealogical vision of the nation as a lineage that would provide all Americans with a relationship to the long dead and the unborn.

From the beginning, Webster assures his audience of their familial relationship to the Pilgrim settlers: "We have come to this Rock, to record here our homage for our Pilgrim Fathers . . . And we would leave here, also, for the generations which are rising up rapidly to fill our places, some proof that we have endeavored to transmit the great inheritance unimpaired."[15] This exemplifies prevalent antebellum rhetoric that cast Americanness as family property that each generation must safeguard and bequeath lineally. Oddly, this national familial duty of transmitting inheritance from the Pilgrims to the twentieth century frames Webster's celebration of republican property laws that break up family estates by curtailing the lineal descent of property. He declares one set of practices to be most crucial and correlative to social equality throughout American history: "A republican form of government rests not more on political constitutions, than on those laws which regulate the descent and transmission of property. Governments like ours could not have been maintained, where property was holden [*sic*] according to the principles of the feudal system; nor, on the other hand, could the feudal constitution possibly exist with us."[16] He speaks specifically to the abolition of entail and primogeniture, rehearsing early republican arguments against the accumulation of family property through lineal descent, a system that works against sociopolitical equality.[17]

Webster denounced, on one hand, societies based on ancestral distinctions and the descent of real property, while on the other, enjoining his audience to regard their Americanness as a lineally inherited family property and their relationship to other Americans as genealogical. Negotiating this contradiction, he insists that some kinds of family pride are degrading while others are elevating: "There may be, and there often is, indeed, a regard for ancestry, which nourishes only a weak pride; as there is also a care for posterity, which only disguises an habitual avarice, or hides the workings of a low and groveling vanity. But there is also a moral and philosophical respect for our ancestors, which elevates the character and improves the heart."[18] Urging each listener to feel pride in "his country's heraldry" and "genealogy," he constructs nationalism as a modern blood identity that would replace the aristocratic family.[19]

Webster traces the genealogy of the United States to the Pilgrims' break with England, which he narrates in terms of the transition from consanguineous to conjugal models of family:

> As a son, leaving the house of his father for his own, finds, by the order of nature, and the very law of his being, nearer and dearer objects around which his affections circle, while his attachment to the parental roof becomes moderated, by degrees, to a composed regard and an affectionate remembrance; so our ancestors, leaving their native land, not without some violence to the feelings of nature and affection, yet, in time, found here a new circle of engagements, interests, and affections; a feeling, which more and more encroached upon the old, till an undivided sentiment, that this was their country, occupied the heart; and patriotism, shutting out from its embraces the parent realm, became local to America.[20]

Transplanting the Enlightenment rejection of parental authority in favor of more egalitarian, chosen relations onto the historical narrative of the Pilgrims' emigration, he metaphorizes their break from England as the "natural" evolution away from one's family of origin. However, in Webster's account, the Pilgrims' children embraced the land as their own because their parents had lived and died there, so that in only one generation, American belonging became a symbolic property passed down the family line, a vertical inheritance from their fathers: "They beheld their fathers' graves around them, and while they read the memorials of their toils and labors, they rejoiced in the inheritance which they found bequeathed to them."[21] The first settlers, initially described as liberated sons seeking more modern relations, become patriarchs of the new vertical family of nationalism. The important work of this comparison is to establish that the United States does not represent a final break from the familial paradigms that had ordered old world societies; Webster understands it instead as a departure from one family and the beginning of a new one on different soil. Domestic families are not a fundamentally different kind of relation but rather links in this larger chain, the building blocks of generational lineage.

He concludes by imagining the twentieth-century Americans who would return to Plymouth 100 years in the future to "trace, through us, their descent from the Pilgrims" and once again memorialize "our common ancestors."[22] He forecasts that in 1920, "the voice of acclamation and gratitude, commencing on the Rock of Plymouth, shall be transmitted through millions of the sons of the Pilgrims, till it lose itself in the murmurs of the Pacific seas."[23] Webster foretells the settlement of the continent by people who share an identity as Americans by virtue of their shared descent from this particular New England colony, eliding not only the heterogeneity of colonial origins but also the sectional animosity of his own time.[24] His final lines invite unborn future generations to both the national family and the nuclear family, the twin structures that will replace the aristocratic family decried earlier in his remarks: "Advance, then, ye future generations! . . . We bid you welcome to this pleasant land of the fathers. . . . We greet your accession to the great inheritance which we have enjoyed. . . . We welcome you to the transcendent sweets of domestic life, to the happiness of kindred, and parents, and children."[25] Having distanced himself and the national history he celebrates from traditional forms of lineal descent associated with class stratification in which family lines are perpetuated in real property and titles, Webster offers his audience immortality through the vertical descent of national identity, a privileged lineage in which each nuclear family, charged with the reproduction of these Americans, will serve as a link.

The construction of genealogical nationalism in this period depended in part on the alteration of Americans' attitudes toward their individual ancestries. While pride or even curiosity about one's ancestors had been considered politically unacceptable in the early Republic, by the 1840s and 1850s, genealogical research was considered scholarly and patriotic rather than aristocratic.[26] Historian François Weil has observed that "the practice of genealogy was still associated with some colonists' grasping attempts to secure social standing within the British empire. In the context of post-Revolutionary America's future-oriented egalitarianism, then, genealogy had no rightful function."[27] The most important figure in transforming individual Americans' relationship to family history was Webster's contemporary, John Farmer, the "father" of American genealogy.[28] Farmer and his associates persuaded Americans that studying their lineages was crucial to understanding and recording both local and national history. "They succeeded, in short, in inventing and legitimating ideologically acceptable forms of genealogical interest."[29] Farmer's landmark work, *The Genealogical Register of the First Settlers of New England* (1829) was the first American genealogical study to move beyond a single lineage, tracing the descent of multiple families and aiming at a broader readership than the small family circle these volumes usually addressed.[30] Inspired at least in part by the popularity of bicentennial celebrations of the Pilgrims' landing, the organizing principle of Farmer's book relates numerous lineages through this historical event, contributing to the construction of a genealogical nationalism with a mythic, single beginning in New England, which remains the catchall story of American origins.[31]

Thanks to Farmer and his contemporaries, delving into one's genealogy became popular as a patriotic hobby. Family records evolved from vital information on small groups to lavishly illustrated charts of multigenerational descent, further effacing the slim distinction between domestic and dynastic family forms.[32] Commercially printed genealogical registers allowed Americans to see their families as a part of a politicized genealogical web, sometimes emblematized by nationalist iconography (Figure I.1). These broadsides connect individual families to a genealogical American history, highlighting the domestic unit's vital contribution to the continuity of the overarching national lineage.[33] Americans recorded the births and deaths in their households as part of a larger national story, positioning them not only as personal life events but also as biopolitical data. Indeed, some declarations of loyalty to the Union during the Civil War borrowed the form of the illustrated family record, making explicit the nationalistic function of this form by substituting "American allegiance" for the chart's usual record of family history and membership (Figure I.2).

Illustrated family registers evidence the success of Webster's construction of nineteenth-century domestic families as links in a national lineage

Figure I.1
Dittmore family record, undated, Library of Congress.

Figure I.2
Affirmation of Allegiance, 1862, Library of Congress.

stretching back to the "Pilgrim Parents."[34] This lithograph presents the landing at Plymouth as an ancestry shared by a husband and wife, a common inheritance that supercedes their biological parents (Figure I.3). Their children will not only unite these immediate forbears but also inherit the nation that has descended from the settlers of the Plymouth Colony. Moreover, like Webster, these texts present American culture not as a definitive break from ancestral paradigms of identity, but rather as a departure from one family in order to begin another. Genealogical arbors from this period often represent the immigrant ancestor as the trunk of a tree that takes root in the New World, dating the inception of the family to the year of his arrival and sometimes depicting in the background the ship that brought him across the Atlantic (Figure I.4).[35] These illustrations present a new patriarchal lineage that is temporally and spatially coextensive with the emergent United States. This also works to fold Colonial history into the national past through genealogy, a sort of inheritance in reverse: the English immigrant is retroactively made an American patriarch by his descendants, his life constituting part of a proto-national history by virtue of his offspring's Americanness.

These broadsides bespeak a fervent blood pride among Americans after family crests and other aristocratic trappings had supposedly met their demise in the new republic. The popularity of this practice supports anthropologist Elizabeth Povinelli's contention that once genealogy was no longer solely the purview of monarchs and nobles, it actually became "more vital and real to the political order" because it was democratized: "The polity no longer unfolded out of the (fictive) ranked affiliations of the people from the point of view of the sovereign family. Now everyone could have a little heritage of his or her own—diagrammed as a personal tree—a stake in some plot that tracked generationally."[36] This ennobling of every domestic unit granted them the status of both dynasties in miniature and links in a genealogical chain that extended shared "blood" to the boundaries of the population, a process Etienne Balibar and Immanuel Wallerstein have described as the "nationalization of the family."[37] Consanguinity was something more than a metaphor in the advent of American nationalism, a genealogical concept in which the distinction between biological relation and symbolic national belonging is blurred. Old World genealogical paradigms survived in the nineteenth-century construction of two intimately related macro families: "race" and "nation." Whiteness and Americanness became the privileged identities to which genealogical title must be proven.[38]

Frederick Douglass famously articulated the exclusion of enslaved people and their descendants from the sort of genealogical schema that these lithographs represent: "Genealogical trees do not flourish among slaves. . . . They keep no family records, with marriages, births, and deaths."[39] Even more elaborate than texts that construct the blood relation of white Americans were the genealogical narratives American science and law developed to position people of African descent, both free and enslaved, as definitive outsiders to the national, and even human, family. African Americans were shackled to the genealogical paradigm of racial

Figure I.3
Illustrated family record, 1889, Library of Congress.

Figure I.4
The Peabody Family (St. Louis, MO.: L. Gast & Brother lith., 1852). Genealogical table;
66 cm. x 41 cm. Image courtesy of the New England Historic Genealogical Society.

identity even as they were accused of the incapacity for both family feeling and its modern correlative, national consciousness. White authors expounded the absence of appropriate family relations in people of African descent to justify their exclusion from American politics. For example, writing in 1868 against the Reconstruction Acts that would enfranchise black men, Lindley Spring offers a sensational study of life in Africa. The author dwells on the African's lack of emotional connection to his or her relatives: "The mother, to suit her convenience, consult her safety or comfort, will kill her child . . . Children will sell their parents, or abandon them to starvation."[40] Importantly, patriotism is paired with familial love: "love of country is, seemingly, as great a stranger to their breasts as social tenderness and domestic affection."[41] Native Americans were saddled with a similar double bind, accused of having chaotic or arbitrary kinship systems but also constrained by genealogical paradigms excluding them from civic participation. Mark Rifkin argues that Native governance systems were devalued because of their association with kinship: "Native forms of collectivity ordered around 'kinship' signify as local, racially defined enclaves rather than fully sovereign governments."[42] The settler state yokes native people to discredited genealogical paradigms and then excludes them from citizenship by ostensibly separating "*kinship* from what gets to count as *politics*."[43] Both of these examples support Povinelli's claim that the "Liberal love" of the modern family "instantiat[es] as its opposite a particular kind of illiberal, tribal, customary, and ancestral love."[44] White Americanness emerged as a modern form of citizenship by excluding peoples constructed as genealogically determined, even while the conceptual roots of nationalism in ancestry and blood relation were disavowed.

Despite, or perhaps because of, a cultural fixation on genealogical continuity and national inheritance, the end of proud white lineages is a favorite gambit of American literature from Edgar Allan Poe's Ushers to William Faulkner's Sutpens. The anachronistic persistence of dynastic patriarchs and ancestral estates as gothic tropes hint that the ghostly palimpsest of a blood-based society still haunts the nineteenth-century United States. Even in comic works, writers like Mark Twain portray white family honor as a farce, sending up American myths of descent from the Pilgrims, the "first families of Virginia," Captain John Smith, Pocahontas, African royalty, and other threadbare genealogical lore as ludicrous aristocratic residue, insinuating that the contaminating "drop" of black blood is equally fictional.[45] Despite its context in a cult of genealogy, imaginative literature in this period retains an interest in the value of cutting blood ties, wondering what might be possible if the American promise of freedom from inherited identity were realized.

II. "FAMILY VALUES" AND ITS MALCONTENTS

Nationalism's conflation of the family with the state and the peculiar American doubletalk that denounces some blood distinctions and cherishes others gave rise to a long tradition of what we now call "family values" political rhetoric: the strength of the nation-state depends on the health of the family, a vulnerable institution that must be protected at any cost. The conception of the nation as a genealogical nexus connecting its constituent families proved to be an effective strategy not only for uniting the population in the face of political disagreement, but also for naturalizing social inequalities and quashing progressive reform. This logic can be detected as early as 1637 in John Winthrop's declaration, frequently quoted but seldom in its revealing entirety, "A family is a little commonwealth, and a commonwealth is a great family. Now as a family is not bound to entertain all comers . . . no more is a commonwealth." Winthrop was writing in defense of a legal act establishing that colonial authorities could exclude people with unorthodox religious beliefs from living in their jurisdiction. The court's order that "none should be received to inhabit within this jurisdiction but such as should be allowed by some of the magistrates" was intended to keep antinomians out of the colony.[46] Winthrop's maxim exemplifies how familial metaphors for community, transferring the family's "natural" restrictedness and primacy to civil society, have been used to justify sociopolitical exclusion.

Despite their prevalence and durability, discourses asserting family sanctity as a political goal and framing any perceived disruption of the family as an attack on the nation-state have long met with resistance from the American people. A tradition of political antifamilialism connecting eighteenth-century republicanism, nineteenth-century utopian radicalism, and contemporary queer theory sheds light on the rhetorical manipulation of familial metaphors, rails against encroaching genealogical paradigms, and refuses to accept the domestic family as a gentler alternative to traditional patriarchy. Thomas Paine's bestselling pamphlet *Common Sense* (1776), the most influential American Revolutionary text before the Declaration of Independence, offers an astute analysis of how the language of family relation is employed to quiet ideological differences and suppress social change. He deprecates attempts to stay a revolution for independence by those who insist that England is the "parent country." Paine argues, "the phrase parent or mother country hath been jesuitically adopted by the king and his parasites, with a low papistical design of gaining an unfair bias on the credulous weakness of our minds."[47] He rejects "the phrase of parent or mother country" in part because it is literally untrue that all Americans are of English descent. Immigrants from all over Europe have fled to the new world, "not from the tender embraces of the mother, but from the cruelty of the monster."[48] But even hypothetically granting, Paine continues, "that we were all of English descent, what does it amount to? Nothing. Britain, being now an open enemy, extinguishes every other name and title: And to say that reconciliation is our duty, is truly farcical."[49] Paine insists that the imperative for familial harmony has no application to politics, that the right to revolution must not be silenced by the demand for generational continuity: "Since nothing but blows will do, for God's sake, let us come to a final separation, and not leave the next generation to be cutting throats, under the violated unmeaning names of parent and child."[50]

Given the widely lamented postlapsarian state of the American family in our time, we might assume that the nineteenth century was the golden age of this institution when the sentimentalized domestic family emerged in a still predominately rural society. On the contrary, many nineteenth-century Americans considered their own time a dangerously low point in the family and were already bemoaning the deterioration of traditional values. Historian Michael Grossberg observes that this "gnawing fear" troubled many antebellum Americans, and "by the 1840s they began to speak of a 'crisis of the family' . . . By mid-century, family critics warned that divorce and desertion, male licentiousness, and women's rights threatened the very fabric of the republic."[51] In 1870, William Aikman, a Presbyterian pastor and writer from Delaware, expressed concern about living in "a time when the sacredness of the marriage relation is so much called into question, and when the bonds which hold the family together are in danger of being lightly esteemed."[52] Specifically, Aikman pinned the Civil War on the weakness of families: "Had families been all or even a part of what they ought to have been, perhaps most of the evils which afflicted us and imperiled our existence in the late Rebellion would not have had a being."[53] Clearly, blaming sociopolitical upheavals on familial weakness was already a well-established rhetorical tactic. In 1857, proslavery pundit George Fitzhugh claimed, "Abolition contemplates the total overthrow of the Family and all other existing social, moral, religious, and governmental institutions."[54] Demonstrating the slippery slope reasoning that still characterizes family values political rhetoric, he writes, "First domestic slavery, next religious institutions, then separate property, then political government, and, finally, family government and family relations, are to be swept away. This is the distinctly avowed programme of all able abolitionists and socialists."[55] For conservatives then as now, painting progressive social changes as subversive to the American family was a stock method for combating reform movements. The movement for women's suffrage, for example, was regarded as women's unnatural abandonment of home life for a "brash entrance into the public sphere" that would "destroy America by undermining society's very foundation: the family."[56]

The manipulation of anxieties about familial vulnerability and blood pollution served as a central rhetorical strategy of nineteenth-century racism, confirming Roddey Reid's observation, "'Family' has always been an alibi if not a license for visiting social others with unremitting violence."[57] For example, Tocqueville observed that because it was "impossible to anticipate a period at which the Americans of the South will mingle their blood with that of the negroes," white southerners asserted their obligation "to keep that race in bondage in order to save their own families."[58] This sentiment was largely unchanged in 1905, when Benjamin Smith wrote, "Compared with the vital matter of pure Blood, all other matter, as of tariff, of currency, of subsidies, of civil service, of labour and capital, of education, of forestry, of science and art, and even of religion, sink into insignificance."[59] Thus, he argues, "the South is entirely right in thus keeping open at all times, at all hazards, and at all sacrifices an impassable social chasm between Black and White. This she *must* do in behalf of her blood, her essence, of the stock of her Caucasian Race."[60]

Of course, nineteenth-century Americans who regarded the domestic family as an institution under siege were right.[61] As the divorce rate rose and the birthrate fell, radicals plotted to abolish the family altogether. Free Lovers Thomas and Mary Gove Nichols affirmed in 1858, "The religious conservatives, who allege that all the efforts of reformers tend to destroy marriage, are entirely correct."[62] Refusing to shy away from accusations that abolishing marriage would destroy society, they reasoned, "If marriage is false it must be destroyed; and the social system that rests upon a false-hood, must be false, as every one sees and feels society to be—false and rotten to its heart's core; rotten and corrupt. Let it be destroyed; the sooner, the better."[63] Even more to the point, Victoria Woodhull averred, "They say I have come to break up the family . . . I say amen to that with all my heart. I hope I may break up every family in the world that exists by virtue of sexual slavery."[64]

A wide range of sources provided what many Americans took to be compelling criticisms of, or alternatives to, the sentimental vision of the nuclear family.[65] Conservatives believed that the liberalization of the family toward an affective rather than hierarchical model destroyed traditional values, while feminists, Free Lovers, and socialists believed that the new sentimentality around the domestic family simply veiled its repressive workings.[66] Thousands of Americans engaged in utopian socialist projects, "united by a belief that the nuclear family posed a threat to a harmonious society."[67] This leftist antifamilialism was by no means a fringe position disconnected from real cultural and political influence. Representing only one branch of this movement, there were as many as one hundred thousand American followers of Charles Fourier seeking a new social organization.[68] Diverse communal settlements in every region of the country throughout the nineteenth century actively broke with the domestic family. John Humphrey Noyes, leader of the Oneida Perfectionists, called for the various strains of utopian radicalism with divergent philosophies to unite as one American socialist movement with the shared goal of "the extension of family union beyond the little man-and-wife circle."[69] Albert Brisbane, a prominent American Fourierist with a column in Horace Greeley's *New York Tribune*, described the social system based on the domestic family as "the fundamental defect of our societies," the cause "of poverty, of disunion, of an anti-social spirit." He contended, "The isolated household, with its single couple or family . . . is the main cause of the conflict of interests, discord, waste, poverty, antagonism, and selfishness, which exist so generally in the world around us." He charges the domestic family with encouraging social atomization, self-interest, and competition rather than cooperation and civic-mindedness.[70] Marx Edgeworth Lazarus, a mid-century anarchist from Alabama, similarly held that "marriage, with its corresponding institution, the isolated family household, is the grave of spontaneity and of individual liberty."[71] His book includes personal correspondence from others who dreamed of a way of life where people will be "no longer smothered up in the little selfish *family*."[72]

Although this radical strain of nineteenth-century thought has been subordinated in popular memory and scholarship to the liberal branches of movements like abolitionism and suffragism, its analysis of marriage and the domestic family strikingly anticipates twentieth-century feminist and queer critique. The writings of antebellum American Free Lovers provide an unacknowledged precedent to contemporary feminist arguments tracing women's oppression to the sex roles dictated by kin structures.[73] Stephen Pearl Andrews, anarchist, spiritualist, and co-founder of the Long Island commune Modern Times, wrote, "The intense concentration of all the affections upon the little circles of immediate family relations and connections, instead of being a positive virtue, as has been assumed, is in fact" to blame for the "falseness and antagonism of all the relations outside of the family. It is a secret and contraband hoarding of the affections."[74] Precisely the same argument appears in *The Anti-Social Family* (1982) by feminist sociologists Michele Barrett and Mary McIntosh: "the family embodies the principle of selfishness, exclusion and pursuit of private interest and contravenes those of altruism, community and pursuit of the public good."[75] Like their nineteenth-century predecessors, Barrett and McIntosh hold that "the family ideal makes everything else seem pale and unsatisfactory . . . The family sucks the juice out of everything around it, leaving other institutions stunted and distorted."[76] Furthermore, utopian socialists formulated a critique of marriage that will be familiar to readers of contemporary queer theory, centered in the idea that this institution oppresses not only those who enter into it but even more acutely those who do not. One Oneida Perfectionist pamphlet argues that "outsiders" to "the marriage system," namely "old maids" and bachelors, are degraded by the existence of marriage. If marriage were abolished, "their reproach would be taken away, and the genial influence of equality and restored self-respect would be greatly for their improvement."[77] Compare this to Michael Warner's assertion that marriage "is designed both to reward those inside it and to discipline those outside it: adulterers, prostitutes, divorcees, the promiscuous, single people, unwed parents, those below the age of consent—in short, all those who become, for the purposes of marriage law, queer."[78] They share the view that the cultural hegemony of marriage produces a structural position for degraded outsiders.

While the literary critiques of the family uncovered in *American Blood* are not, for the most part, characterized by the flat refusals offered by Fourierists and Free Lovers, authors of nineteenth-century fiction were unquestionably aware of movements afoot to unseat conventional domestic arrangements in the name of individual liberty. To take an obvious example, Herman Melville's *Pierre* traces the disillusionment of an American aristocrat from nationalistic ancestral pride to communitarian association with a group of "strange nondescript adventurers and artists, and indigent philosophers of all sorts . . . Teleological Theorists, and Social Reformers, and political propagandists" who subsist on Graham crackers.[79] Recounting Pierre's initial vanity in his distinguished lineage, the narrator notes, "if you tell me that this sort of thing in him showed him no sterling Democrat, and that a truly noble man should never brag of any arm but his own; . . . believe me you will pronounce Pierre a thorough-going Democrat in time; perhaps a little too Radical altogether to your fancy."[80] Melville suggests that radical utopianism may be the lifestyle most in line with republican ideals, although many Americans regard it as extremism. Indeed, when Pierre loses all claim to his patrimonial property, his grandfather's camp bedstead from the War for Independence somehow ends up at the Apostles' residence that Pierre shares with three women, intimating that his unconventional domestic circumstances constitute a Revolutionary inheritance.

Despite the acknowledged involvement of canonical American authors from Nathaniel Hawthorne to William Dean Howells in reform movements aiming to redefine family, there is surprisingly little in literary criticism to suggest that these ideologies form part of the cultural landscape that has shaped American literature. This scholarly field tends to focus on progressives who wielded the "family values" banner themselves, claiming that their seemingly threatening reform agendas would actually strengthen the American family. *American Blood* focuses instead on the dissident tactics of works that strategically embrace, in both form and content, the very phenomena that the mainstream feared—interracialism, national death, failed marriages, willful sterility, and atavism—appropriating discourses of familial decline for activist ends.

III. AMERICAN LITERATURE AGAINST THE FAMILY

With this historical context in focus, *American Blood* reconsiders the uneasy and uneven relationship between American literature and the family that some readers have considered characteristic of the tradition. As Carol Singley notes, "disrupted biological families and elective family units are a defining feature of American literature, in a way that is strikingly absent in other national literatures."[81] Although classic studies assumed that American literature was distinguished by its disinterest in the marriage plot and domestic concerns, decades of scholarly work aimed at constructing a more inclusive canon has revealed the family's central position in the nineteenth-century novel. Jane Tompkins rescued authors like Harriet Beecher Stowe from critical contempt by elucidating their expert manipulation of the culture's profamily Christian worldview in the service of abolitionism: "*Uncle Tom's Cabin* retells the culture's central religious myth—the crucifixion—in terms of the nation's political conflict—slavery—and of its most cherished social beliefs—the sanctity of motherhood and the family."[82] Following Tompkins's "cultural work" thesis, subsequent critics of nineteenth-century reform fiction have detailed how white women and African Americans staked their claims to fuller civic inclusion on the rhetoric of familial sanctity and fortification.

Having established that representations of the family are central to these devalued literary traditions, scholars focused on the national implications of these representations to emphasize their objectives beyond the domestic sphere. To mention only a few examples from the 1990s, scholars like Shirley Samuels, Amy Kaplan, and Karen Sanchez-Eppler established that literary treatments of the family, children, and domesticity must be read as political allegory and intervention, since "a powerful nation constitutes much of its political identity through the language of heterosexual

and patriarchal family relations."[83] Samuels theorized the reciprocal relationship between the family and the political ideologies and anxieties of
the early nation, arguing that "these [sentimental] novels, which frequently
show the family as a model for the nation, also demonstrate the ways it has
become an instrument of social control."[84] Recognizing that portrayals of
American home life not only reflected national anxieties but also served
nationalist agendas, some critics disparaged the sentimental novel, reversing earlier celebrations of this women-centered tradition. For example,
Elizabeth Barnes writes, "in holding up the family as a model for sociopolitical union, sentimental rhetoric conflates the boundaries between familial and social ties."[85] Barnes condemns sentimentalism for failing to firmly
separate the family from the nation: "by displacing a democratic model
that values diversity with a familial model that seeks to elide it, sentimental literature subordinates democratic politics to a politics of affinity."[86]
While this reading recognizes that the overvaluation of the family ob-
structs democratic equality, it upholds the critical supposition that American authors, especially women, esteemed the family as the ideal model for
governance and community rather than historicizing the American family
as a site of social struggle.

More recently, Cindy Weinstein has questioned this assumption, suggesting instead that sentimentalism communicates a desire to reform the
family into a consensual rather than blood-based institution. She argues
that "at precisely the moment that the affective lives of antebellum Americans seem to be coalescing around an ideal of the biological family, these
texts consistently represent its insufficiencies and the necessity of coming
up with alternatives."[87] This reading reflects the view that the novel form
supports the move away from the traditional vertical family to a companionate, elective model. While Weinstein argues that these authors seek to
"revise" the family but conserve the essential importance and stability of
the institution itself, *American Blood* examines works that are suspicious of
the expansion of the concept of family, viewing kinship as not only inadequate but dangerous in application to politics. They suggest that democratic citizenship ideally should serve as the basis for coalitions across
ascriptive differences, definitively outside of kin groups.

Overlapping with this critical tradition on American women's writing,
African American literary studies has mined the political objectives of
nineteenth-century representations of family. This scholarship has established that abolitionist literature illuminates the degradation of enslaved
families, slave-owning white families, and the "national family" as a whole
to incite pathos, sympathy, and outrage. In the postbellum years, when
white women's representations of family and domesticity were becoming

more obviously critical, African American women wrote "domestic allegories of political desire" and "romances of ideal family formation."[88] Claudia Tate explains that, having won the legal right to marry and the independence to fulfill traditional gender and kinship roles, African Americans held "the family as the basis of self-definition and social mobility."[89] Unquestionably, kinship was a tool for black survival in the face of white racism, and these studies have demonstrated the centrality of narratives of domestic family formation to racial uplift and civic self-assertion. Because African American political uses of the family differ so much from exclusionary uses of the white American family, I follow Hortense Spillers in differentiating black kinship from the hegemonic cultural formation of the American family that is conceived as definitively white and aimed at the perpetuation of white supremacy. Spillers explains that "the captive person developed, time and again, certain ethical and sentimental features that tied her and him, across the landscape to others . . . of the same and different blood in a common fabric of memory and inspiration. We might choose to call this connectedness 'family,' or 'support structure.'" But by any name, she asserts, this "is a rather different case from the moves of a dominant social order, pledged to maintain the supremacy of race."[90] Refusing to consider this state of kinlessness and unconventional gender relations "a fundamental degradation," Spillers avers the radical potential of subjects produced under this regime. She writes, "we are less interested in joining the ranks . . . than gaining the *insurgent* ground."[91] Although the African American novels examined in this project insist that "black blood is everywhere" in the white American family, they do not simply desire to be recognized as members of this exclusive institution but rather seek to dispel its mythic power.[92] A sustained critique of the white family as a racist national institution is the understudied counterpart of the African American novel's positive and politically instrumental representations of the black family. The African American authors in this study register political dissent by rejecting white kinship as the basis of American national identity, tracing the genealogy of racist national conditions, and refusing any future that would reproduce them.

The interrelated scholarly traditions that have successfully expanded the canon of American literature have also ingrained the view that a profamily ideology is the core of nineteenth-century social justice politics. On the contrary, authors who wrote against the dynamics of oppression emerge in this study as particularly keen critics of the American family. The nineteenth-century American reform novel retains traces of the republican utopian vision of print as a fundamentally public vehicle for collectivity and cultural transmission, even in opposition to the familial consciousness, context, content, and temporalities of the novel form. Although this study focuses primarily on works by white women and African Americans that analyze the role of familial politics in the most imposing social issues of the day, it aims to sensitize readers to an antifamilial impulse in American literature more broadly. Rather than reducing the nineteenth-century politics of the family to a single ideological plane, it highlights an ongoing dynamic between the domestic family, the genealogical family, the national family, racial families, and various modes of nonblood "kinship" crisscrossing American science, law, literature, and political cultures.[93]

The following chapters chart the literary representation of the American family, particularly in reform-minded fiction, in relation to legal, scientific, literary, and political discourses from antebellum abolitionism through the Reconstruction suffrage debates, the burgeoning of feminism, fin-de-siècle nativism, and the "nadir" of the post-Emancipation African American experience at the turn of the twentieth century. Chapter 1 provides an overview of republican opposition to the generational transmission of property and status in relation to Nathaniel Hawthorne's *The House of the Seven Gables* (1851). This romance illustrates a transition from the aristocratic family model rooted in real estate to the middle-class domestic family reliant on the symbolic property of racial whiteness, representing blood paradigms as a curse that haunts the nineteenth-century United States until it is disinfected, but ultimately reconstituted, by cross-class white marriage. *House* celebrates the American family's institutional capacity to preserve power in the face of modernization and serves as this study's primary example of a romance of white national family formation, a touchstone for the ideological configuration that the works featured in the following five chapters reject.

Of all the evils of slavery, Harriet Beecher Stowe singled out "its outrage upon the family" as "more notorious and undeniable than any other," and critics have long held representations of slavery's toxic effects on both black and white families to be the core strategy of abolitionist literature.[94] However, chapters 2 and 3 rethink the abolitionist novel's negotiation of the issues of heredity and kinship in response to scientific and literary discourses that grounded the oppression of African Americans in the naturalizing paradigm of family blood. Chapter 2 focuses on the reproductive ideology of antebellum nationalism, specifically the demand for generational continuity in the face of grave political unrest, arguing that William Wells Brown's *Clotel; Or, The President's Daughter* (1853) radically embraces the association of the "mulatta" with sterility and national death, linking mid-century theories of hybrid infertility to anxieties concerning the nation's crisis of political continuity on the brink of the Civil War. Specifically, through an analysis of the relationship between death, socially deviant sexualities, and citizenship, this chapter argues that *Clotel* stokes the pervasive fear of demographic crisis in antebellum American culture to call for a national rupture that would end the hereditary oppression of African Americans. This repositions the "mulatta" not as a "tragic" trope, but rather as a figure of queer negativity and a formal representation of the biopolitical tactics of the enslaved. Moreover, this chapter introduces new findings about the sources and print history of Clotel's climactic leap from the Long Bridge.

Chapter 3 turns to the American author perhaps most associated with the enshrinement of domestic kinship, arguing that Stowe's second novel, *Dred: A Tale of the Great Dismal Swamp* (1856), surprisingly deconstructs both scientific and sentimental conceptions of the family, the very locus of cultural power that she had so masterfully mobilized in *Uncle Tom's Cabin* only four years earlier. While recent readings of this work have emphasized the importance of elective kin paradigms to this genre, this chapter considers sentimentalism's relationship to the discourses of racial and national families theorized in the American School of Ethnology's *Types of Mankind* and the Supreme Court's *Dred Scott* decision. The interracial communities in this novel that scholars have insistently characterized as "non-kin families" provide an opportunity to explore the limits of alternative kinship as a basis for coalitional politics in a society defined by exclusionary political familialism.

Moving beyond the near exclusive focus on the sentimental novel in scholarship on the nineteenth-century family, *American Blood* extricates the politics of blood relation from sympathy and the web of other "private" matters with which it is habitually grouped in literary criticism. Although the second half of this study treats the postbellum decades, it resists developmental narratives of the history of the American family that underestimate the enduring significance of traditional genealogical paradigms and the stubborn resistance of this institution to change. Thus, Chapter 4 considers the emphasis on marriage in the national family metaphor during Reconstruction alongside an ongoing insistence on sectional genealogical similitude in a reading of *What Answer?* (1868), a neglected work by one of the most famous but now forgotten American women of the century, antiracist feminist Anna E. Dickinson. This work exemplifies a literature of dissent that disrupted the conventions of the "romance of reunion" to call attention to the neglected project of racial integration, insisting that universal suffrage, rather than family feeling, must be the solution to the nation's political divisions. The central interracial marriage, seemingly the symbol of a future integrated nation, comes to a tragic and precipitous end, foreclosing the idea that romance can suture ideological division. A glance at Henry James's fictionalization of Dickinson in *The Bostonians* provides clues as to how the Reconstruction culture of forgetting banished this celebrated figure from national memory.

Advancing this consideration of the nascent first-wave feminist movement, chapter 5 addresses white women's growing interest in controlling reproduction and family size, the shift in feminist thought away from the idealization of maternity, and the influence of Free Love radicalism. This chapter considers Sarah Orne Jewett's *The Country of the Pointed Firs* (1896) in light of sociological discourses decrying New England's diminished birthrate as a harbinger of national decline. Despite the nativist sympathies of first-wave feminism, the stark sterility of Jewett's vision of women's independence illuminates the conflicting demands of feminism and the reproductive imperative of white nationalism in Roosevelt's America. While chapter 1 traces the process by which race, family, and nation became ideologically fused by 1850, this chapter suggests that by the turn of the twentieth century, these elements had become nearly impossible to disentangle, constituting a fundamental impasse for certain kinds of progressive politics. Moreover, the development of Jewett's narrator into an author of New England local color fiction, a genre long associated with spinsters, infertility, and decay, initiates a comparison of literary and biological reproduction that informs the remainder of this study.

In Chapter 6, further exploration of the fin-de-siècle politics of racial devolution centers in the verbatim reproduction of the Long Bridge narrative from Brown's *Clotel* (which, as chapter 2 reveals, was already a verbatim reproduction of a prior source) in Pauline Hopkins's first serialized novel, *Hagar's Daughter* (1901). Although this appropriation itself serves as a bridge uniting antebellum and turn-of-the-century African American literature, Hopkins ultimately utilizes this duplication to indict a larger cultural failure to escape the conditions of slavery decades after Emancipation, a formal strategy of stasis and regression that I describe as textual atavism. African American writers of the nadir like Hopkins and Charles Chesnutt engage with the socioscientific discourse of black atavism to indict white savagery as the barrier to black political evolution. In these works, atavism is not the sign of biological primitivism but the nightmarish breakdown of progress and self-determination. Hopkins and Chesnutt indict the family's institutional role not simply as a metaphor for the nation but also as the mechanism for the reproduction of its unequal social relations, formulating a genealogical theory of American racism. Considering the lifespan of the Long Bridge meme in American print culture, this final chapter examines the potential of literature as an alternative medium of cultural transmission that, as Michael Warner has suggested, might serve as a mode of affiliation and continuity beyond the family. I pursue this idea further in a coda addressing the application of kinship metaphors to literary forms and traditions, exploring how the acknowledgment of antifamilialism in nineteenth-century American fiction might change our understanding of the novel form itself.

CHAPTER 1

⌘

The Transformation of American Family Property in *The House of the Seven Gables*

A certain disdain for the traditional economic, political, and social effects of the family was a pillar of republican thought. Founders of the nation-state and theorists of American identity for generations after the Revolution believed that laws governing the transmission of property not only must represent democratic values in spirit but must also function as a practical mechanism to maintain social equality. Although the new republic adopted much of English common law, the reform of inheritance laws became symbolically central to the project of defining and establishing a new democratic society. Inherited estates were denounced as the basis of aristocratic, "artificial" social hierarchies, laws of partible inheritance were vaunted for their supreme political importance, and new state constitutions instated inheritance laws that would obstruct the creation of perpetual family distinctions.[1] James Kent's *Commentaries on American Law*, the first major work to deal exclusively with United States common law, states, "Entailments are recommended in monarchical governments, as a protection to the power and influence of the landed aristocracy; but such a policy has no application to republican establishments, where wealth does not form a permanent distinction."[2] Kent proudly asserts, "Every family, stripped of artificial supports, is obliged, in this country, to repose upon the virtue of its descendants for the perpetuity of its fame."[3] His description of the old-world system for the descent of property as an "artificial" means of buttressing family status typifies the early American conviction that the new nation must eschew the transmission of privilege through bloodlines.

Of the many eighteenth-century Americans who viewed the family as a powerful conservative institution that inhibits social change by exerting control over the future, Thomas Jefferson was perhaps the most prominent. He framed his work in Virginia to abolish entails and primogeniture as key measures against the perpetuation of "unnatural distinctions," the privileges and disadvantages of birth under systems of nobility, in American society. Jefferson expressed his desire to form "a system by which every fibre would be eradicated of antient or future aristocracy; and a foundation laid for a government truly republican. The repeal of the laws of entail would prevent the accumulation and perpetuation of wealth in select families."[4] These early changes to inheritance were viewed as practical applications of republican philosophy that would enable egalitarian individualism and discourage the genealogical distinctions associated with monarchical systems.

Furthermore, the goal of weakening the power of inheritance in the United States was not only applied to material property. The framers expressed their desire to free future generations from not only the prosperity but also the wrongdoing of their forebears in Article Three of the Constitution by declaring that treason against the United States would not be punishable by "corruption of blood." It declares that "the Congress shall have power to declare the punishment of treason, but no attainder of treason shall work corruption of blood, or forfeiture except during the life of the person attainted."[5] This means that the descendants of a person convicted of treason cannot be punished by the loss of property. Article Three represents another break from rules of inherited status so that, in the United States, both guilt and wealth are ideally limited to the individual, rather than heritable through bloodlines.

For Jefferson, the crusade to curtail political applications of inheritance extended beyond the protection of individuals from the misdeeds of their ancestors to the protection of all Americans from the political decisions of previous generations. While his work to abolish entail in Virginia was designed to disrupt the positive effects of inheritance, namely the shoring up of wealth, his letters reveal a concern about the ill effects of large-scale public inheritance. For example, he believed that incurring national debts infringed upon the rights of future generations; indeed, he suggested that any constitution or governmental structure that outlived the individuals who had devised it is an inappropriate imposition. In a well-known letter to James Madison, written in Paris on September 6, 1789, Jefferson elaborates a theory of generational sovereignty centered in his belief that "the earth belongs in usufruct to the living."[6] This begins primarily as an argument against national debts, but he extends it as a political theory on the duration of governments: "no society can make a perpetual constitution, or even a perpetual law. The earth belongs always to the living generation. They may manage it . . . as they please, during their usufruct."[7] In its mildest form, this logic underlies the mechanism of constitutional amendments, allowing for a revisable rather than static instrument of governance, but Jefferson's rejection of inheritance as a natural right has more radical implications. He is wary of the possibility that despite its democratic specificity, the United States might reproduce the fundamental inherited structure of monarchical succession, curtailing the liberty and self-governance of future Americans by binding them to laws and practices to which they did not consent. Thomas Paine had denounced the hereditary succession of monarchy on the same grounds in *Common Sense*: "no one by birth could have a right to set up his own family in perpetual preference to all others for ever," and if they do, "the right of all future generations is taken away."[8]

Historian Herbert Sloan has argued convincingly for the centrality of this letter to any understanding of Jeffersonian thought: "If a single text were to be taken as the key that would unlock Jefferson in all his contradictions, surely this is it. He meant every word of it, and he meant it deeply."[9] Sloan holds that Jefferson hoped to see this theory put into practice and that we might understand his career in the 1790s as an attempt to implement it. He pays particular attention to Jefferson's odd choice of the term "usufruct" in describing the relation of the living generation to the earth and society. Sloan interprets the term as synonymous with "trust"; that is, the legal situation in which someone holds property for someone else's benefit. Indeed, he suggests that Jefferson chose the word "usufruct" simply to avoid "entail," a concept he had worked to eradicate from American paradigms of inheritance. This understanding of the term leads Sloan to conclude that "in a curious way, Jefferson ends by proposing the equivalent of a universal entail."[10]

But a very different political vision emerges if we understand Jefferson's use of this term to suggest a relation to property quite different from entailment. Usufruct is the right to possess, use, and enjoy something that one does not own. Jefferson wrote, "The earth belongs to each of these generations during its course, fully and in its own right."[11] In his view, each generation of Americans has the right to make full use of its society, even remaking it to suit their needs, with the understanding that they do not finally own it and have no right to pass down their version of it to later generations. Sloan's trust model would suggest that society is owned by unborn future generations, having been set up by ancestral forbears, for whom the living are merely preserving it. But in Jefferson's formulation, the nation does not belong to posterity; it belongs neither to the dead, nor to the unborn, but only to the living. While Jefferson treats the political system as a kind of property in his use of this legal metaphor, it is definitively not a hereditary property. He does not project the absolute ownership of society onto future generations. A man's political relevance ends with his life, and those who survive him have no duty to carry out his civic vision.

This radical vision of discontinuity expressly rejects the familial paradigm of inheritance in application to the political community, suggesting that American citizens all deserve the opportunity, which Jefferson's generation had seized, to start with a clean slate unmarked by the dead hand and theorize their own governance. Jefferson does not see the nation as a multigenerational inheritance: "one generation is to another as one independent nation to another" and between generations there is "no municipal obligation."[12] He revisited this theory in a letter to John Wayles Eppes on June 24, 1813: "We may consider each generation as a distinct nation" with no right to "bind the succeeding generation, more than the inhabitants of another country."[13] Rather than a perpetual state, Jefferson imagined a renewable republic. Nations, in Jefferson's formulation, do not survive the men who established them because only a living community can consent to unite under laws of their own creation.[14]

But could this kind of society be stable and permanent? Would each generation relive the bloody warfare of revolution and the long political work of forging a new society? Jacksonian-era commentators reflected with patriotic pride on the reform of inheritance laws in the early republic, lauding their success in rooting out aristocratic tendencies that might have compromised the American project. At the same time, however, palpable apprehension arose about the diminished power of the family and what would take its place as the stabilizer of property and society. Because republicanism seemed to weaken at every turn the connection of ancestors to descendants, diminishing the link between successive generations through shared fortune as well as misfortune, many Americans wondered what would become of the institution of the family in a society that seemed hostile to its perpetuation. Indeed, even those who lauded the political significance of inheritance reform often noted with at least some degree of anxiety its perceived social impact: while individuals may rise in America, families tend to fall. Indeed, there was a pervasive suspicion in the nineteenth century that American society was actually antagonistic to the traditional meaning of the family as an institution. Alexis de Tocqueville forecasted that American inheritance laws would result in the demise of family identity. Tocqueville explained that the older systems ensured an enduring, even metaphysical connection between a family and its ancestral home, arguing that family identity was inextricable from the physical estate and that the survival of the treasured property underwrote identification with the family: "Among nations whose right of descent is founded upon the right of primogeniture landed estates often pass from generation to generation without undergoing division, the consequence of which is that family feeling is to a certain degree incorporated with the estate. The family represents the estate, the estate the family."[15] When bloodlines are no longer tied to lasting material property, he argued, "the idea of family becomes vague, indeterminate, and uncertain . . . Thus not only does the law of partible inheritance render it difficult for families to preserve their ancestral domains entire, but it deprives them of the inclination to attempt it, and compels them in some measure to co-operate with the law in their own extinction." In this way, American law succeeds in "dispersing rapidly both families and fortunes."[16] Tocqueville ruefully conceded that the diffusion of ancestral estates, even if it lead to the extinction of families, was a necessary pre-condition for the successful exercise of American political ideals.[17]

Not everyone acceded so readily to this compromise. In light of the disconcerting possibility of the demise of the institution of the family, the very bulwark of tradition, in the name of relatively newfangled political ideals, many Americans tenaciously sought to secure property within the boundaries of the bloodline, calling the dictates of republicanism into question. As proslavery ideologue George Fitzhugh declares in *Sociology for the South*, "entails and primogeniture are as odious to us as kings were to the Romans; but their object—to keep property in our families—is as dear to us as to any people on earth." Dismissing republican theories of the ill effects of inheritance, he asserts, "Property is too old and well-tried an institution, too much interwoven with the feelings, interests, and prejudices, and affections of man, to be shaken by the speculations of philosophers." To combat the "too frequent ups and downs of American life," Fitzhugh advocates a return to primogeniture and entailment to keep estates together.[18] For this reason, among others, he holds the agrarian South, where plantations often remain in families for many generations, to be superior to the industrial North, where property is unstable.

Fitzhugh dedicates a chapter of *Sociology* to criticizing the treatment of inheritance in the Declaration of Independence and the Virginia Bill of Rights, documents written by men whose "minds were heated and blinded" by Enlightenment philosophy.[19] He derides the hypocrisy of the Virginia Bill of Rights for casting aspersion on hereditary distinctions like titles of nobility (which he describes as "harmless baubles") while "the author saw no objection to the right secured by law to hold five hundred subjects or negro slaves, and ten thousand acres of land, to the exclusion of everybody else, and to transmit them to one's children and grand-children, although an exclusive hereditary privilege far transcending any held by the nobility of Europe."[20] Just as he sought to retain the right to own and bequeath property in human chattel, Fitzhugh calls for the right to transmit one's real estate unbroken to future generations, regardless of the republican association of this practice with old-world nobility: "We need not fear the mad dog cry of aristocracy. . . . We have the *things*, exclusive hereditary privileges and aristocracy, amongst us, in their utmost intensity; let us not be frightened at the *names*." He holds that the honorable desire to provide for one's posterity is a powerful inducement to industry and suggests that Americans will admit this once they "have cooled down from the fervor of the Revolution."[21]

Although Fitzhugh is a particularly extreme example, his denunciation of Jeffersonian ideals gives voice to currents of his time that were not limited to such notorious reactionaries. My Introduction offers the example of Daniel Webster's 1820 oration at Plymouth, which boasts proudly of the founding generation's political accomplishment in reforming inheritance, but then narrates the conversion of this paradigm into a conception of the nation as property descending lineally from the Pilgrim settlers. The shift in emphasis from the vertical family line to the tandem forces of the conjugal family and the national "family" was not a clean break. Rather than unilaterally contributing to the idealization of the liberalized domestic family, the literature of this period imagines coexistent, overlapping, proliferating, contradictory paradigms of inheritance. One need only recall the novels of E.D.E.N. Southworth in which the landed aristocratic family exists in the United States alongside not only the domestic family but also Native American royalty, European nobility, Jewish maternity-by-proxy, orphans, adoption, cursed inheritance, lost inheritance, renounced inheritance, secret marriage, bigamy, and divorce.[22] Herman Melville's *Pierre* (1852) voices a famous forecast of the weakening of families under democracy but follows it immediately with a catalog of examples in support of the claim that the old aristocratic family model based in inheritance is as strong on American soil as it is in Europe. This passage begins by outlining the repercussions of republican inheritance reforms:

> With no chartered aristocracy, and no law of entail, how can any family in America imposingly perpetuate itself? Certainly that common saying among us, which declares, that be a family conspicuous as it may, a single half-century shall see it abased; that maxim undoubtedly holds true with the commonality. In our

cities families rise and burst like bubbles in a vat. For indeed the democratic element operates as a subtile acid among us; forever producing new things by corroding the old.[23]

Melville names the abolition of entail as a primary contributing factor to the abasement of families. Indeed, he indicates that an essential antagonism exists between the institution of the family and the enterprise of the United States, a place where "families rise and burst like bubbles in a vat." With this declaration that democracy corrodes old institutions, the novel's tale of the termination of a time-honored family line and estate seems to presage the fate of the American family more generally.

However, after this well-known passage describing the evanescence of American families, *Pierre* notes just the opposite tendency at work, turning attention to those American families that seem immune to the corrosive effects of democracy, maintaining themselves as hardily as their European counterparts: "if in America the vast mass of families be as the blades of grass, yet some few there are that stand as the oak; which, in stead of decaying, annually puts forth new branches."[24] He offers lengthy evidence that the United States is not actually different than England in terms of the permanence of ancestral property and the bloodlines they represent, despite official regulations: "in England an immense mass of state-masonry is brought to bear as a buttress in upholding the hereditary existence of certain houses, while with us nothing of that kind can possibly be admitted."[25] Although the state does not officially lend its weight to upholding hereditary distinctions, he notes the long and uninterrupted lineages in New England and "the old and oriental-like English planter families of Virginia and the South; the Randolphs for example, one of whose ancestors, in King James' time, married Pocahontas the Indian Princess, and in whose blood therefore an underived aboriginal royalty was flowing over two hundred years ago."[26] He mentions ancient Dutch manors in the northern states renting land to tenant farmers over generations, "which hints of a surprising eternity for a deed, and seems to make lawyer's ink unobliterable as the sea."[27] Republican posturing notwithstanding, Melville argues, Americans use the law to buttress blood and ensure its effects. "Whatever one may think of the existence of such mighty lordships in the heart of a republic, and however we may wonder at their thus surviving, like Indian mounds, the Revolutionary flood; yet survive and exist they do."[28] This comparison imagines the modern American nation-state built on top of an older civilization based on aristocratic estates, a persistent social order that coexists and entwines with the opposing norms that are supposed to have replaced it.

Nathaniel Hawthorne's *The House of the Seven Gables* (1851) voices classic American political ideals in citing the dangers of wealth, as well as wrongdoing and guilt, "entailed" on descendants. However, in its ultimate protection and restoration of the family and its material legacy, perhaps no other work so clearly captures the ultimate American ambivalence on this issue and the mechanisms by which blood paradigms powerfully reemerged at midcentury, despite their antidemocratic implications. Describing the enduring ideological commitment to the exclusive property rights of the blood family, even in a nation supposedly inhospitable to ancestral estates, Hawthorne writes: "there is no one thing which men so rarely do, whatever the provocation or inducement, as to bequeath patrimonial property away from their own blood." Even when someone detests his family members as individuals, "the strong prejudice of propinquity . . . impels the testator to send down his estate in the line marked out by custom so immemorial that it looks like nature."[29] This passage acknowledges that the preservation of property within the biological family is a social construction but powerfully appears to be natural. To this end, despite the enunciated public opposition to enduring inheritance, many Americans secured the transmission of family property through the freedom of testation in order to guarantee the wealth of their posterity and the perpetuation of their family identity. As John Orth observes, the abolition of entail and primogeniture affected only estates that were left intestate. The freedom of testation provides a loophole that reconciles the republican stance on inherited wealth with individualist prerogatives, allowing Americans to transmit estates through the bloodline as surely as they were under formal entail. Despite his contempt for the rule of the dead hand through inheritance, Jefferson was apparently not willing to go as far as Robespierre and other French revolutionaries in limiting the power of individuals to control the distribution of property upon their deaths.[30] Thus, Americans can effect the accumulation of lineal property simply by writing a will, creating precisely the inherited inequalities Jefferson had warned against. Noting these inconsistent inheritance practices, Hawthorne suggests that Americans are no less likely, for all their republican ideology, to break from the naturalized practice of keeping material property in the hands of their blood kin, thereby shoring up the power of the institution of the family to determine an individual's social status at birth.

In true republican fashion, *The House of the Seven Gables* rails against the dangers of inheritance, tracing "most of the wrong and mischief which men do" to the desire to "plant and endow a family" (185). Hawthorne's preface announces that the "moral" of this romance is that "the wrongdoing of one generation lives into the successive ones," and the author's stated aim is to convince readers "of the folly of tumbling down an avalanche of ill-gotten gold, or real estate, on the heads of an unfortunate posterity, thereby to maim and crush them" (2). Through the tale of the Pyncheons, this romance critiques the aristocratic family model, arguing that passing down property more often brings misfortune than fortune to the inheritors. It aims to show that "the weaknesses and defects, the bad passions, the mean tendencies, and the moral diseases which lead to crime are handed down from one generation to another, by a far surer process of transmission than human law has been able to establish in respect to the riches and honors which it seeks to entail upon posterity" (119). The romance's central conflict binds together a family's real estate, their "blood," and a curse. In the Pyncheon inheritance, the ancestral House of the Seven Gables and Maule's curse are inextricable, both originating in the seventeenth-century title dispute with which the novel begins. Through the exercise of the Pyncheon patriarch's political power, Matthew Maule is executed as a witch. From the scaffold, he proclaims, pointing at Pyncheon, "God will give him blood to drink!" (18). This prophesy proves true when Pyncheon is found dead with blood cascading from his mouth on the day that his ancestral manse on contested ground was to be revealed to the public.

In spite of his untimely death, Pyncheon achieves his aim of leaving "his race and future generations fixed on a stable basis, and with a stately roof to shelter them, for centuries to come" (17). This seventeenth-century estate proceeds through the generations by the old model for the intact transmission of property down the family line. Pyncheon sets into motion the kind of willful dynasty regarded as intrinsically un-American in the Revolutionary era. Moreover, his descendants experience a literal form of corruption of blood in the deadly effects of the curse. Indeed, this curse is singular in that it affects both the concrete and metaphorical forms of blood. It seemingly causes death by choking on one's own sanguineous bodily fluid, and it is also transmitted through the "bloodline" of the Pyncheons. Thus, the Pyncheons inherit their ancestor's real estate as well as his guilt, two examples of the old-world connections between generations ostensibly weakened by American law.

When the narrative resumes around 1850, the Pyncheon descendants are in a state of bad decline: "In respect to natural increase, the breed had not thriven; it appeared rather to be dying out" (24). So low have they sunk that Hepzibah has been forced to turn a portion of the first floor of the house into a store to earn her living, the ultimate blow to her aristocratic standing. Furthermore, plebian outsiders have penetrated the old realm of exclusive privilege in the person of her tenant. Holgrave is a daguerreotypist and a radical, representative of new technology, new ideas, and new socioeconomic mobility.

Most characteristic of these ideas is Holgrave's Jeffersonian abhorrence for hereditary real estate. The anti-inheritance sentiments of this "wild reformer" strikingly echo Jefferson's belief that "the earth belongs to the living, not to the dead."[31] Holgrave asks, "Shall we never, never get rid of this Past? It lies upon the Present like a giant's dead body!" (182). Holgrave extends his rejection of perpetual family property to the lifespan and transmission of political institutions and practices. Like Jefferson, he asserts that just as private estates should not be passed down whole from ancestors to descendants, neither should the public institutions of American democracy because all hereditary institutions are tyrannical. Holgrave declares, "I doubt whether even our public edifices—our capitols, state houses, courthouses, city hall, and churches—ought to be built of such permanent materials as stone or brick. It were better that they should crumble into ruin once in twenty years, or thereabouts, as a hint to the people to examine into and reform the institutions which they symbolize" (184). This closely resembles Jefferson's proposal that because "no society can make a perpetual constitution, or even a perpetual law . . . every constitution then, and every law, naturally expires at the end of 19 years."[32] Jefferson held that generational sovereignty would be required for the true exercise of democracy so that no American would be chained to his predecessors, breaking from the old-world traditions of inherited fortune and misfortune in family lines. In other words, the nation should not be perpetuated according to the aristocratic model of family property. Government by the people, according to the needs and values of their own time, would require radical noncontinuity with the ancestral past. This theory rejects the family and the deterministic power of inheritance as models for American national identity.

Hawthorne's characters insist that this social theory must dictate the policies governing the descent of private homes as well as public offices. Holgrave declares that "if each generation were allowed and expected to build its own houses, that single change, comparatively unimportant in itself, would imply almost every reform which society is now suffering for" (183–184). Even Clifford, a member of this fallen aristocracy, agrees: "What we call real-estate—the solid ground to build a house on—is the broad foundation on which nearly all the guilt of this world rests. A man will commit almost any wrong—he will heap up an immense pile of wickedness . . . only to build a great, gloomy, dark-chambered mansion, for himself to die in, and for his posterity to be miserable in" (263). The virulent criticism that these characters level at the titular piece of real estate throughout the novel represents republican antipathy for hereditary property. Clifford declares that "there is no such unwholesome atmosphere as that of an old home, rendered poisonous by one's defunct forefathers and relatives" (261). They repeatedly proclaim that the house should be destroyed. Clifford avers, "it were a relief to me, if that house be torn down, or burnt up, and so the earth be rid of it, and grass be sown abundantly over its foundation" (262). Holgrave agrees that the Pyncheon house "ought to be purified with fire—purified till only its ashes remain!" (184). These pronouncements seem to foreshadow a conventional gothic conclusion in which the ill-gotten estate is physically destroyed.

Yet, despite these ominous prophesies, the House of the Seven Gables is not "torn down, or burnt up," the fate of other hereditary estates in American literature. Unlike Poe's House of Usher or Faulkner's Sutpen's Hundred, the Pyncheon house still stands at the novel's end. Indeed, the family property is not only secure at the conclusion but has in fact multiplied, as the main characters find themselves the inheritors of not one but two imposing family houses upon the death of their cousin Jaffrey. Thus, this putatively anti-inheritance novel concludes by rewarding the main characters with even more family property and wealth.

The conversion of Holgrave from outsider to insider in the Pyncheon family and from tenant to owner of the family's estate registers this reversal in the romance's ideology. He retracts his anti-inheritance sentiments and extols the virtues of lasting building materials, claiming that a sense of generational permanence is fundamental to happiness in the present. He assures Phoebe that only "men ill at ease" have a progressive bent: "The happy man inevitably confines himself within ancient limits. I have a presentiment, that, hereafter, it will be my lot to set out trees, to make fences—perhaps, even, in due time, to build a house for another generation." The newest inheritor of the Pyncheon's hereditary wealth through his marriage to Phoebe, he declares "you find me a conservative already," attesting not only to the conservative but also to the conservatizing force of his new joint roles of family man and home owner (315).[33] In narrating the most radical character's turn to conservatism, the novel itself loses its radical character, restoring family relation as the most powerful guarantor of "the peaceful practice of society," signified by the survival and orderly transmission of property (306–307). Holgrave's sudden ideological shift mirrors the nineteenth-century abandonment of the republican stance against the antidemocratic effects of inheritance.

This conclusion allows family inheritance to be recast in a positive light, abruptly silencing all the concerns about its antidemocratic repercussions. As Gillian Brown notes, the end of the novel imagines a happy ending as the separation of property from the misdeeds of the past so that it can be safely inherited and enjoyed: "No longer liable to the past, they are no longer liable to the moral debts and physical debilities property entails. The forgiving of such debts makes heritable property secure in a double sense: securely possessed by the inheritors, and safe in its effects on them."[34] The ending portrays hereditary property laundered of its undesirable connotations. So while the novel seems to advance an anti-inheritance, republican ideology, decrying the outsize family pride that manifests in the desire to plant a dynasty, its conclusion not only secures property but ultimately shores up the power of the family as the basis of identity and society itself.

This conclusion has puzzled and disappointed critics. The abrupt conservative turn has been considered an aesthetic and ideological failure, evidence of Hawthorne's need to please the market with a happy ending.[35] I argue on the contrary that it culminates Hawthorne's account of a transformation in American conceptions of the family and its basis in hereditary estate. The product of a watershed historical moment in which racial theories grounded in the paradigm of kinship proliferated, *The House of the Seven Gables* narrates a conversion in the boundaries of family property through the resignification of "blood." Ultimately, this romance allegorizes the transition from a system of social relations based on real property to a system of symbolic estate.[36] It illustrates the rise of a new conception of the American family in the nineteenth century based on an evolving understanding of property transmitted by "blood" and its relationship to social hierarchy.[37]

Critics agree that *The House of the Seven Gables* narrates a shift in historical conceptions of kinship between "the collapse of this aristocratic dynasty and its displacement by the domestic family."[38] The seventeenth-century Pyncheons model the colonial family, which Michael Grossberg describes as "hierarchical, patriarchal, and vested with overlapping and undifferentiated internal and external obligations."[39] From the Revolution through the Jacksonian period, economic changes undermined this traditional family form. Stephanie Coontz argues that "the expansion of opportunities for investment or employment outside the inherited family property meant that for both rich and poor reliance on the extended family or the lineage decreased."[40] Anxiety about the status of the family as an institution accompanied this reorganization of traditional power arrangements. Carroll Smith-Rosenberg notes that with this transition from patriarchal to more democratic kinship structures, many Americans "feared that altered relations within the family paralleled the decline of a hierarchical world order."[41] On the contrary, although the traditional family based on inherited real estate receded, the "natural" power relations of kinship continued to provide a powerful model for a hierarchical social order organized by "race," determined by "blood."

Blood is the point of overlap between the traditional regime of power based on class and a new regime based on race. Michel Foucault describes the resignification of "blood" over the century and a half that this romance addresses: "Beginning in the second half of the nineteenth century, the thematics of blood was sometimes called on to lend its entire historical weight toward revitalizing the type of political power that was exercised through the devices of sexuality. Racism took shape at this point (racism in its modern, 'biologizing,' statist form)." The blood metaphor that had buttressed dynastic privilege reemerged as the powerful conceptual basis of "race" that continued to validate hierarchical social relations.[42] *The House of the Seven Gables* signals its engagement with the emergence of this new system governing the family by returning to "the thematics of blood" of the previous epoch and tracing its transformation in the nineteenth century, demonstrating the shift away from the form of power emblematized by the Pyncheon patriarch, a dynastic landholder with the authority to impose death on the less powerful.

In the mid-nineteenth-century United States, the concept of ancestral "blood" was resuscitated to support emergent biodeterministic conceptions of discreet human "races" so that racial identity became the most salient form of symbolic family estate. Race, conceived as a hereditary trait unavoidably transmitted through descent, determined basic social status at birth. Although the stated aim of republican politics was to weaken the power of familial inheritance to determine individual position, the conceptual invention of race kept ancestry at the forefront of American identity. As Etienne Balibar has argued, the "national family," a racialized conception of community, emerges when "lineal kinship, solidarity between generations and the economic functions of the extended family dissolve" and the previous kinship of social class is "imaginarily transferred to the threshold of nationality."[43] The emergence of both nationalism and "race" created a new kind of family property, indeed a new conception of the family itself.

The best-selling racial scientific writings of the 1840s and '50s returned to the antiaristocratic rhetoric of inheritance reform to defend American slavery on the basis that it reflected a natural inequality between the races, in opposition to the "artificial" class distinctions under systems of hereditary aristocracy. In 1853, John Van Evrie argued: "The English peasant is the work of British institutions; the negro the creation of nature. The former *artificially* degraded; the latter *naturally* inferior." He asserts that "the law of primogeniture, and the ten thousand other contrivances" produce this false distinction, whereas in the South, "the planter rules as *naturally* as the negro obeys *instinctively.*"[44] Whereas republican denunciations of hereditary monarchy like Paine's *Common Sense* scoffed at the notion that "a race of men came into the world so exalted above the rest, and distinguished like some new species," mid-nineteenth-century racial science used precisely the logic of species taxonomy to argue that differences between white men are socially constructed but the difference between white and black men is a biological, immutable blood difference.[45] Unlike the social designations of aristocrats and peasants, which were inherited by law and custom, defenders of slavery argued that the distinctions between whites and African Americans were truly "racial," immutable manifestations of ancestral difference. These texts rely on the multivalent social meaning of "blood" to theorize discreet "types," "races," or "families" of mankind, popularizing the polygenesist conception of whites as members of one kin group to which people of African descent are permanently, genealogically inferior.[46]

The reification of family blood through the concept of race secured whiteness as an inalienable family asset, assuring that this privileged identity was, as Albion Tourgee described it in the brief filed on Homer Plessy's behalf, "the most valuable sort of property" in American society. Cheryl Harris has expertly argued that "the law has established and protected an actual property interest in whiteness itself, which shares the critical characteristics of property and accords with the many and varied theoretical descriptions of property."[47] Furthermore, Eva Saks expounds the role of the concept of racial "blood" in the construction of this new property in nineteenth-century American case law. Making use of the metaphor of "blood" that had long been used to naturalize kinship relationships, American law "reifies blood as inalienable estate." "Blood" serves as a representational strategy to shore up the white family's property in its own socially privileged identity. In the 1840s and '50s, the metaphor of "blood" evolved from its traditional association with family genealogies to include a concern with the shared or divergent "blood" of racial groups. Saks explains that the concept of racial "blood allowed courts to conceive all whites as members of a family. Because the entire white family shared 'race-as-property,' blood was therefore a form of collective property." This form of "blood" unifies whites as holders of the same family estate.[48]

While medical doctors and Egyptologists convinced Americans of the existence of distinct racial bloodlines, a new theory of white civilization's ancient departure from native kinship practices based on the descent of property emerged in what would become the anthropological field of kinship studies. For Lewis Henry Morgan, a New York politician and attorney whose work inaugurated that field, white kinship structures are built on the desire to transmit real property down the bloodline.[49] Morgan's *Systems of Consanguinity and Affinity of the Human Family* theorizes that claiming a larger, nonlineal group as kin would be beneficial in primitive societies for the sake of physical protection. He reasons that for civilized peoples, this system for assuring one's safety is transferred to national membership: "the protection of the law, or of the State, would become substituted for that of kinsmen."[50] Beyond this replacement of extended kin with the social contract, Morgan singles out one powerful inducement to overthrow the primitive system: the inheritance of estates. Establishing degrees of relation that would prioritize one's immediate family over all others would serve man's desire for his property to descend to his "real" son rather than to be divided among his other "sons" that Morgan viewed as merely fictive. For "natural justice" to be served in property inheritance, the claims of kinsmen outside the direct genealogical line would have to be nullified.[51] This is another discourse that recentered the inheritance of property as a natural determinant of racial superiority and distinction.

Contemporary with the invention of race as a form of hereditary property, Hawthorne's romance narrates a reconfiguration of the family and its relationship to material and immaterial forms of inheritance. The emphasis on blood and its cultural value identifies this work as part of a contemporary debate about the relationship of white racial identity to previous models of social hierarchy based on hereditary distinctions. *The House of the Seven Gables* begins with a colonial title dispute between the property-owning Pyncheons and the working-class Maules; however, this difference is transformed in the nineteenth century through the legal convergence of these groups into one family so that the property can be shared by the descendants of both lines. The Pyncheons must break from the obsolete model of aristocratic distinction that secures both fortune and misfortune within the boundaries of their increasingly feeble bloodline to embrace a new social order that equalizes them with their neighbors but elevates them all as holders of the new collective estate of whiteness.

The decline of the historic Pyncheon family line is analogous to the demise of a land-based economy and power structure, represented not only by their ancestral abode but also by a tract in Maine described as "more extensive than many a dukedom, or even a reigning prince's territory, on European soil" (18). This unrealized inheritance of land endows the Pyncheons with an aristocratic family pride despite the fact that the deed is lost and the land has been long developed by others. Although any entitlement the Pyncheons may have had to this land lapsed long ago, "this impalpable claim" caused them "to cherish, from generation to generation, an absurd delusion of family importance, which all along characterized the Pyncheons. It caused the poorest member of the race to feel as if he inherited a kind of nobility" (19). Even in the absence of material assets, this family maintains an anachronistic confidence in the superiority of their noble "race" based on a delusional connection to their landholding past that has in reality long expired.

While the Pyncheons accede to irrational ancestral privilege, the Maules inherit the infamy of their executed forebear. Tellingly, Hawthorne's description of this abject family line takes on racial coloring. The Maules seem to be heir to the genealogical discrimination entailed on African Americans. Each successive generation receives "as their only inheritance, those feelings of repugnance and superstitious terror" that linger in the descendants of the townspeople who had wronged their ancestor. "So long as any of the race were to be found, they had been marked out from other men" (26). In the descriptions of both the privileged aristocrats and the despised underclass, Hawthorne's use of "race" exploits the slipperiness of this term and reminds us that our modern understanding of "racial" distinctions is built upon older conceptions of the "natural" distinctions between "blood" families. In 1851, "race" could clearly still be used to describe a single family line. Yet with the proliferation of scientific writings theorizing the difference between the white ruling class and black slaves by mining the paradigm of kinship and inheritance, this word was accruing its modern usage as a justification for human hierarchy.

Being "marked out" as objects of scorn and fear is not the only link between the Maules and African Americans. In Holgrave's account of the story of Alice Pyncheon, a family servant notes that Matthew Maule, the executed man's son, has a "black" look on his face. Maule responds, "no matter, darkey! . . . Do you think nobody is to look black but yourself?" (188). Compelling us to consider Maule and his descendants as somehow black like Scipio, this exchange reminds us that a forgotten form of "racial" difference exists between the feuding families. After declaring his capacity to "look" "black," Maule makes a suggestive remark about the beautiful young Alice Pyncheon. Scandalized, Scipio says, "He talk of Mistress Alice! . . . The low carpenter-man! He no business so much as to look at her a great way off!" (188).[52] Scipio remarks upon the unsuitability of a "low carpenter-man" making even the most remote sexual advance on a daughter of the aristocratic Pyncheon family. This remark, spoken in heavy dialect by the only black character in the narrative, utilizes racial difference to suggest that the idea of a Maule marrying a Pyncheon would be a transgression of boundaries believed to be the natural basis of social hierarchy.[53]

Critics have read these references to racial inequality as a representational strategy in Hawthorne's exploration of class difference. David Anthony argues that "anxieties over class struggle—exemplified here in the centuries-long feud between the Pyncheons and Holgrave's ancestors, the Maules—are displaced onto the triangulated third term of racial difference."

He points to blackness as Hawthorne's "effort to imagine a distinct difference between working-class whiteness and whiteness of the kind inhabited
by the 'idle aristocracy.'" While Anthony interprets this as a displacement,
or "a means of obscuring or effacing the realities of class division," I argue
instead that these moments in which the Maules are marked by an Africanist presence bring pointed attention to the fact that the class distinctions
between these two families were distinctions of "blood" or family line that
were once considered quite as natural and impassable as distinctions based
on race would later become.[54] It is this extreme differentiation of the
seventeenth-century families that gives meaning to the marriage of a nineteenth-century Maule to a Pyncheon. *The House of the Seven Gables* indicates
that the transformation of the American family fundamentally rested on
the development of racial difference out of the existing class hierarchy of
family bloodlines. As Shawn Michelle Smith observes, "The very aspects of
aristocratic elitism that Hawthorne denigrated as antithetical to middle-class values were later adopted and reconfigured as racial attributes by
the white middle classes themselves."[55]

The shift that ultimately allows a Maule to marry a Pyncheon is most
efficiently captured in the deceptively comic allegory that opens the story
of the nineteenth-century representatives of these families. Importantly,
the narrator remarks that the story takes place "at the instant of time when
the patrician lady is to be transformed into the plebian woman. In this republican country, amid the fluctuating waves of our social life, somebody
is always at the drowning-point" (38). Employing the traditional rhetoric
of families rising and falling in America due to republican policies, these
opening lines pinpoint a transitional moment in the transformation of an
old American family out of its aristocratic past. The description of the first
transaction in Hepzibah's shop encapsulates the collapse of the distinction
previously held between the Pyncheons and the Maules. The necessity of
her selling goods to make money represents the new economic system that
overtakes the old land-based economy, namely capitalism founded in the
traffic in black bodies.

This new system demands the consolidation of white privilege, obviating
the differences of "blood" between historically rich and poor white families.
Hepzibah's first customer is the working-class Ned Higgins, "a square and
sturdy little urchin . . . clad rather shabbily" (49). The first purchase is a gingerbread Jim Crow, a cookie representing an African American minstrel
trope.[56] With the exchange of money for this commodity, "The little school-
boy, aided by the impish figure of the Negro dancer, had wrought an irrepa-
rable ruin. The structure of ancient aristocracy had been demolished by him,
even as if his childish gripe had torn down the seven-gabled mansion" (51).

For Hepzibah, this transaction destroys her ancestral mansion and the aristocratic system that it represents. Abandoning the class distinction that marked their line in the Colonial era, the Pyncheons must regard themselves as equals with the other white townspeople from whom they had previously held themselves apart.

Importantly, the Pyncheon family's fall from the aristocratic "pedestal of imaginary rank" revolves around the sale of a gingerbread Jim Crow, a transaction that equalizes two formerly stratified whites over an emblem of black subjugation. Susan Mizruchi describes this cookie as an image attempting to "resolve collective anxieties and conflicts. . . . Via gingerbread, the complex and troubling black populace of 1851 is transformed into an eatable sweet doing an obliging 'it's jes me folks' dance."[57] Rather than exploiting the symbolic resonance of racial difference in order to clarify class difference, Hawthorne reveals the subjection of African Americans to be at the center of the modernization of the white American family that attended the emergence of market capitalism.[58]

Thus the aristocratic distinction that has separated the Pyncheons from their neighbors is abolished. Moreover, the same economic transition allows Holgrave to sever his prospects from his ancestral background. The marriage between the two lines is now acceptable, indeed necessary for the survival of both. As Balibar has argued, a racial conception of national community has been firmly established "when nothing prevents marriage with any of one's 'fellow citizens' whatever, and when, on the contrary, such a marriage seems the only one that is 'normal' or 'natural.'"[59] Or, to use Elizabeth Povinelli's formulation, "liberal love," the paradigm underlying the modern conjugal family, is what renders genealogical differences irrelevant.[60]

The withered old system of nobility, represented by the diminished Pyncheon inheritance—including the House of the Seven Gables, Maule's curse, and the Maine territory—must be abandoned. Importantly, this revelation is simultaneous with the tumbling down of the progenitor's portrait that has hung heavily over all of his descendants for the past century and a half. This enacts the reconfiguration of the American family in the Jacksonian area described by Stephanie Coontz: "the authority of the grandfather, characteristic of agrarian society, was undercut. . . . Thus in all classes the marital unit was strengthened at the expense of the lineage."[61] The deed for the land in Maine is finally proven to be worthless, but a stronger form of family property replaces it and brings the Pyncheons into the modern era, appropriately represented by a wooden country house, precisely the sort of domicile trumpeted by Andrew Jackson Downing as befitting the republican American family.[62] The narrative shows the passage in the United States from the old system of entrenched class difference to a time when people whose ancestors had held radically divergent social positions can be considered social equals, indeed part of the same family. In the end, even the insolvent Uncle Venner, a peculiar old man who does odd jobs around the neighborhood, is welcomed into the benefits of the new collective inherited property like a member of the family, as his name suggests, underscoring that class is no longer the most important determinant of social organization. Both of the characters who were formerly associated with Fourierism, Holgrave and Uncle Venner, are made beneficiaries of inheritance and their opposition is not merely silenced but replaced by familial enthusiasm. The aristocratic family and the threat of radical reform are abandoned simultaneously.[63]

Mirroring the historical shift from family identity centered on the patriarch to racial nationalism fixated on posterity, The House of the Seven Gables moves from a focus on the ancestral past to a concern with sexuality, marriage, and the future of the "race." The reproductive prospects of the new marital alliance between the Pyncheons and Maules are indicated by a sudden change in the breeding habits of the family of chickens to which the Pyncheons are plainly analogized throughout the novel. As long as they live in the yard of the House of the Seven Gables, these chickens produce an egg only often enough to keep their "race" from utterly disappearing: "It was evident that the race had degenerated, like many a noble race besides, in consequence of too strict a watchfulness to keep it pure" (89). When they are transported to the new family estate in the country, however, "the two hens had forthwith begun an indefatigable process of egg-laying, with an evident design, as a matter of duty and conscience, to continue their illustrious breed" (314). Like the Pyncheons, this race of fowl escapes the sickly insularity of the aristocratic estate and embraces a new productivity in the name of posterity. This accords with Holgrave's concluding suggestion that property should be secured for an unborn future generation and indicates the heightened concern beginning at mid-century with reproduction and the continuity of the race. The turn from the old consanguineous Pyncheon/Maule distinction to the new conjugal union of lovers (joined in the judge's house by the law, not by blood) will ensure the nation's future.

Despite the ostensibly forward-looking trajectory of this conclusion, Hawthorne treats reproduction in its true conceptual essence as the persistence and remaking of the past. This romance offers a theory of history that denies the possibility of absolute progress, or more precisely of social innovation itself. The narrator diagnoses a flaw in Holgrave's thinking in his earlier stage of radicalism: "[his] error lay in supposing that this age, more than any past or future one, is destined to see the tattered garments of Antiquity exchanged for a new suit, instead of gradually renewing them-selves by patchwork" (155). For Hawthorne, old things are not replaced but simply renewed by the superimposition of new things in small pieces.

Not coincidentally, the other major articulation of this theory is pre-sented in the midst of Clifford's radical anti-real-estate diatribe on the train:

> [A]ll human progress is in a circle; or, to use a more accurate and beautiful figure, in an ascending spiral curve. While we fancy ourselves going straight forward, and attaining, at every step, an entirely new position of affairs, we do actually return to something long ago tried and abandoned, but which we now find ethe-realized, refined, and perfected to its ideal. [223]

On an ascending spiral curve, history moves forward by turning back. Anything new is simply a repurposed version of something old and previ-ously rejected. By the end, the plot seems to be spiraling as well, repeating itself in reverse even as it moves forward. In the final scene, as the family drives away from the House of the Seven Gables in a fine carriage bound for their new estate, Ned Higgins reappears, and his initial transaction with Hepzibah plays in reverse. Instead of simply repaying the copper, which was to have stained her hand forever, she lavishes him with silver, regain-ing her aristocratic pedestal with an act of noblesse oblige.

This scene also returns to the repetitive commentary of two "laboring men," Dixey and his unnamed companion whose "wife kept a cent-shop three months, and lost five dollars on her outlay" (47). Watching their de-parture from the ancestral manse, this companion observes, "old maid Pyn-cheon has been in trade just about as long, and rides off in her carriage with a couple of hundred thousand . . . and some say twice as much." Dixey re-sponds, "pretty good business!" (319). This interaction serves to underscore that it is ultimately not "business," or participation in market capitalism, that saved this family, as Hepzibah initially hoped and feared it must be. It is the old deus ex machina of inheritance, apparently resignified by its asso-ciation with the breaking down of old genealogical divisions between (white) Americans and their equalization under new ones. Critics have re-garded in *The House of the Seven Gables* as a narrative that supports the standard historical account of the modernization of American kinship, the progressive development of domestic intimacy, and separate spheres to re-place genealogical hierarchy. But the spiraling representation of the history of the American family in this work suggests that these seemingly distinct formations worked in tandem to undo Revolutionary-era republicanism and rebrand old chauvinisms. The racialized national family was framed in opposition to previously rejected class-bound familial societies even as it relied on this earlier model for its justification and its key terms. Republicanism recognized inheritance as the root of social inequality, but nationalism overturned the radical potential of this antifamilial bent in early American political thought. Hereditary property was protected, indeed rejuvenated as the joint symbolic estates of racial and national identity supplanted ancestral real estates. Although families were feared to rise and fall in the United States with no entailed estates to represent them, "blood" returned as the family property determining status and social position.

Some critics have asserted that Hawthorne's romance elides the social change and tumult of the mid-century. Walter Benn Michaels, for example, argues that the author aims to "domesticate the social dislocation of the 1840s and 1850s in a literary form that imagines the past and present as utterly continuous, even identical, and in so doing, attempts to repress the possibility of any change at all."[64] On the contrary, *The House of the Seven Gables* narrates the pivotal transformation in conceptions of American family property that defined the passage from the seventeenth-century colonies to the nineteenth-century nation. Far from denying historical change, this romance celebrates the plasticity of power in the face of modernization, the renovation of old hierarchies under the auspices of new ideas.

CHAPTER 2

⌘

National Reproduction and *Clotel*'s Queer Mulatta

I don't want to reproduce, I want to make something entirely new.
—Jeanette Winterson, *Written on the Body* (New York: Random
House, 1994), 108

With the passing of the founding generation, republican suspicion of both personal and political inheritance gave way to ancestor worship and the embrace of inherited status. As the demands of nationalism triumphed over Revolutionary ideals, the antipatriarchal founders became objects of filial piety. At the turn of the nineteenth century, eulogies of George Washington insisted on a hereditary model of national identity that demanded ongoing generational duty and devotion: "Americans! He had no child—BUT YOU."[1] The republic hardened into a nation, a concept rooted in ancestral community, but then the nation threatened to dissolve or break in two. Antebellum Americans faced the question of how to perpetuate the United States until the end of time while very real threats to the union mounted. To preserve the society their "forefathers" had founded, they reproduced, in many ways, the hereditary political system that Jefferson had hoped to leave behind.

Abraham Lincoln's speeches provide a clear example of this ideological shift. While Jefferson valued the possibility of ongoing disruption and rebirth, holding that no necessary political relationship binds the generations, Lincoln evinces a concern that the property entrusted to him and his generation might be destroyed, that the Revolution might not have yielded a perpetual state.[2] In his first inaugural address, Lincoln seems to defend the nation-state against the Jeffersonian idea that no permanent government should be foisted upon future generations by the dead hand: "the Union of these States is perpetual. Perpetuity is implied, if not expressed, in the fundamental law of all national governments. It is safe to assert that no government proper ever had a provision in its organic law for its own termination."[3] Lincoln describes the presidency as the duty "to administer the present government as it came to his hands and to transmit it unimpaired by him to his successor."[4] He notes a succession of fifteen presidents had preserved and advanced the union but that he takes the helm at a time of "great and peculiar difficulty."[5] Like many Americans of his generation, Lincoln seems to have imagined himself as a weak link between a larger-than-life national past and an uncertain future.

According to Stuart Hall, "crises occur when the social formation can no longer be reproduced on the basis of the pre-existing system of social relations."[6] The interruption of national generational succession constitutes political crisis, and in the 1850s, the United States faced exactly this kind of crisis of national reproduction. The previous system of relationships between white and black, north and south, was no longer tenable, and it became increasingly clear after 1850 that the nation would not be reproduced according to its existing structure. Many feared that the political enterprise founded less than eighty years earlier would not be transmitted past their own generation. Historian Michael F. Holt writes, "the notion of a political crisis in the 1850s was not simply the artificial construct that a historian blessed with hindsight could impose on the period" with the knowledge that the country was on the brink of a devastating war. "Abundant evidence suggest[s] that a genuine sense of crisis troubled Americans living in that decade."[7] In his study of the antebellum generation's connection to the founders, Russ Castronovo agrees that "throughout much of the antebellum period, this continuum seemed visible and intact. . . . Yet in the context of increasing talk of disunion, unity with the past of 1776 seemed illusory."[8]

This fear of a rupture in national reproduction was described in a variety of cultural texts as the endangerment of family property, drawing on the trope of the nation-state as inheritance that must be transmitted in unbroken succession to the last human generation. Thus, nationalist discourse advanced a concept of American identity modeled on entailed hereditary real estate, an aristocratic institution that had been denounced, even legally prohibited, in the Revolutionary period. Lincoln's Lyceum address on "the perpetuation of our political institutions" indicates that by 1832 a metaphor of the nation-state as vulnerable family property had arisen to express this fear. In this speech, Lincoln describes the United States as an edifice built by national fathers and bequeathed lineally to each successive generation, whose responsibility is then to transmit it to their descendants to assure its perpetuation until the end of time. He describes his generation as "the legal inheritors of these fundamental blessings . . . they are a legacy bequeathed to us, by a once hardy, brave, and patriotic, but now lamented and departed race of ancestors." He asserts their political obligation "to transmit these . . . to the latest generation that fate shall permit the world to know. This task gratitude to our fathers, justice to ourselves, duty to posterity, and love for our species in general, all imperatively require us faithfully to perform."[9]

Evincing the characteristic antebellum anxiety about national survival after the founding generation's death, Lincoln explains that the experiential history of the Revolution used to live on in individual families but is now attenuated and forgotten: "At the close of that struggle [the Revolution], nearly every adult male had been a participator in some of its scenes. The consequence was, that of those scenes, in the form of a husband, a father, a son or brother, a *living history* was to be found in every family—But *those* histories are gone. . . . They *were* the pillars of the temple of liberty; and now, that they have crumbled away, that temple must fall, unless we, their descendants, supply their places."[10] Now that the individuals who fought the Revolution are dead, Lincoln explains, national perpetuation depends on an understanding of the state as symbolic estate entailed by them generationally on all Americans.

These political texts echo a broad concern with paternity in antebellum American literature and, more specifically, an anxious preoccupation with uncertain or severed inheritance. The suggestion that generational continuity might be endangered links the classic works of the American Renaissance to the slave narrative, the sentimental novel, and the emergent African American novel. Consider, for example, the mystery of paternity in both *The Scarlet Letter* (1850) and *Incidents in the Life of a Slave Girl* (1861). Hester Prynne and Harriet Jacobs both refuse to speak the names of the fathers of their children. In the opening scene of *The Scarlet Letter*, Hester stands with her infant under the gaze of the marketplace, defying the orders of the religious authorities and the damning outbursts from the crowd: "Speak; and give your child a father!"[11] Compare this scene to the slave woman's plight as described by Jacobs. She defies her master's demand: "Tell me whether the fellow you wanted to marry is the father of your child. If you deceive me you shall feel the fires of hell."[12] Registering the same sense of secrecy and uncertainty, Frederick Douglass notes, "it was sometimes whispered that my master was my father."[13] Other instances of this theme include the orphaned heroines of "woman's fiction," the illegitimate shadow family of Melville's Pierre Glendinning, even the narrator of *Moby-Dick*'s invitation, "Call me Ishmael."[14] Mysterious paternal identity in antebellum literature registers the culture's increasingly tenuous relationship to the founders.

Although many antebellum Americans regarded the possibility of a disrupted national lineage with anxiety, the severance of generational inheritance was the only hope for people saddled with hereditary oppression under the existing social order. While *The House of the Seven Gables* ends by affirming reproductive continuity, William Wells Brown's fictional account of Jefferson's enslaved descendants in *Clotel; or, The President's Daughter* (1853) exposes the conservative conceptual core of "reproduction": the creation of new lives serves merely to produce the past again. Attending to the queerness of the so-called tragic mulatto trope in early African American fiction combats the recent critical tendency to treat these representations as utopian figures for an integrated future American society, which tacitly relies on a eugenic solution to sociopolitical problems. Seizing upon the scientific construction of "the mulatto" as an antagonistic force against white national reproduction, Brown reimagines the tragic circumstances of Jefferson's own mixed-race offspring to call for the abrogation of inheritance and radical generational discontinuity. Antebellum African American–authored "tragic mulatta" plots are no-future narratives, foretelling, and even embracing, a crisis of reproduction in the white national family.

In "Poem of Procreation" (1856), Walt Whitman details a eugenic fantasy in which his semen produces an improved stock of future American citizens: "I pour the stuff to start sons and daughters fit for these States." He continues:

> In you I wrap a thousand onward years,
> On you I graft the grafts of the best-beloved of me and America,
> The drops I distil upon you shall grow fierce and athletic girls, new
>   artists, musicians, and singers,
> The babes I beget upon you are to beget babes in their turn,
> I shall demand perfect men and women out of my love-spendings,
> I shall expect them to interpenetrate with others, as I and you
>   interpenetrate now.[15]

This ode to a sex act that sets into motion a thousand years of future Americans exemplifies reproductive national futurism, the celebration of cycles of "birth, life, death, immortality" that are specifically American. National identity assumes a genealogical conception of history that relies on the linear succession of generations. As Lauren Berlant notes, "the generational form of the family has provided a logic of the national future."[16] The structure of the family serves as the conceptual model for the nation's reproduction as an intact political entity over time, and sexual reproduction is the physical mechanism of national history. National time imagined through the family naturalizes linear history and the cohesion of white Americans of the past, present, and future.

Because national reproduction relies on the family as the site for the managed biological production of the population, the sexual reproduction of American citizens must reflect and also uphold the system of existing social relations. Berlant notes, "when the modal form of the citizen is called into question, when it is no longer a straight, white, reproductively inclined heterosexual, but rather might be anything, any jumble of things, the logic of the national future comes into crisis."[17] First appearing as a racial category on the United States census in 1850, "the mulatto" was the "jumbled" identity of the potential citizen threatening the national future, attesting to generations of illegitimate white paternity of America's slave labor force and posing a constant physical objection to the model of two racially discrete family lineages upon which American law and science insisted.[18] The mulatto was taken as biological proof that the nation was not being perpetuated according to the existing social conditions, the fearful symbol of a crisis of national reproduction.

For this reason, reproduction was policed in the United States by a number of discourses that trumpeted the grave dangers of interracial sex. The desire to track the population of "mulattoes" via the census likely grew in response to theories of interracialism that were a cornerstone of polygenesis, the racial scientific conception of human "races" as distinct species with separate origins popularized by the group of scientists known as the American School of Ethnology. These scientists defined a species as a permanent organic group that can only successfully reproduce within itself, despite the ever more obvious fact of "interracial" mixing in the United States. To account for this seeming contradiction, the polygenesists declared the mulatto a moribund "hybrid" with compromised longevity and reproductive capacity whose family line could not survive beyond a couple of generations. Josiah Nott popularized the theory of hybrid infertility in his article "The Mulatto a Hybrid—probable extermination of the two races if the whites and blacks are allowed to intermarry" (1843), first published in the *American Journal of the Medical Sciences* and then reprinted in the *Boston Medical and Surgical Journal*.[19] In *Types of Mankind* (1854), the best-selling compendium of polygenesist thought, Nott reprinted his argument, beginning with the following list of propositions:

1. That *mulattoes* are the shortest-lived of any class of the human race.
2. That *mulattoes* are intermediate in intelligence between the blacks and the whites.
3. That they are less capable of undergoing fatigue and hardship than either the blacks or the whites.
4. That the *mulatto-women* are peculiarly delicate, and subject to a variety of chronic diseases. That they are bad breeders, bad nurses, liable to abortions, and that their children generally die young.
5. That, when *mulattoes* intermarry, they are less prolific than when crossed on the parent stocks.[20]

The "mulatto" was constructed as a sickly, unnatural hybrid with a short lifespan and compromised fertility. Following this idea to its extreme endgame, Nott cast the prohibition against interracial sex as imperative to the survival of mankind since humanity "might possibly become exterminated by a thorough amalgamation of all the various types of mankind now existing upon earth."[21] With this threat of "extermination," racial science plainly linked interracial sex to the end of reproduction and the extinction of humankind. The first edition of *Types of Mankind* sold out immediately, and the text ran through ten printings by 1871.[22] Thus Nott's writings gained a wide audience, influencing a variety of Americans interested in questions of racial difference and its relationship to political destiny. For decades, other contributors to the large body of polygenesist literature echoed the theory of hybrid infertility and its apocalyptic implications in the United States. For example, John Van Evrie argued, "the mingling of these distinct species inevitably leads to social decay and national suicide."[23] According to Werner Sollors, "the belief that mulattoes were 'feeble' or unable to procreate among themselves, or that their children would be impaired in fertility, had so much political, scientistic, and general intellectual support that it may be called the 'dominant opinion' of the period."[24]

Sollors connects this widespread belief in "mulatto" infertility to the broader cultural fear of generational discontinuity. He suggests that the theory of reproductive barrenness in mixed-race individuals was actually a hyperbolic representation of the fear of "losing" one's child and their future offspring across the color line: "The purists' own unwillingness to accept the mixed after-generations as theirs is seen as the 'loss' of the children, and the projection of this self-constructed loss upon the descendants of mixed marriages is the cultural belief—widespread in nineteenth- and early-twentieth-century America—that 'mixed bloods,' 'mulattoes,' and 'half-breeds' were sterile."[25] Sollors' formulation of the hybrid infertility theory as a magnified fear of the end of a homogenous family line might be extended to explain the prominence of fears of interracialism in the context of the antebellum crisis of national reproduction. The figure of the mulatto, the very word signifying reproductive sterility, so threatened the national necessity for racially homogeneous generational continuity that it became associated with the apocalyptic end of reproduction itself. The national crisis of reproduction was projected onto this figure's supposedly impaired reproductive capacity.

The condition of generational severance or "natal alienation," according to Orlando Patterson, defines the status of the enslaved. Slaves held no legitimate link to either their ancestors or offspring and therefore had no recognized family identity. "Not only was the slave denied all claims on, and obligations to, his parents and living blood relations but, by extension, all such claims and obligations on his far more remote ancestors and descendants. He was truly a genealogical isolate." Because of this erasure of ancestry, enslaved people were not allowed to "anchor the living present in any conscious community of memory," which is precisely the imagined temporality that enables national identification.[26] Patterson notes that this "loss of ties of birth in both ascending and descending generations . . . also has the important nuance of a loss of native status, of deracination."[27] The removal of enslaved people from the generational structure was an institutional mechanism for the annihilation of black culture that rendered the slave definitively outside of American political genealogy. The hybrid infertility theory might be understood as the fear that black kinlessness might compromise white family lines. Just as fear mounted that the nation itself would not be reproduced in an identical and continuous future generation, the "mulatto" was recognized as a troublesome potential American, representing the disordering of generational temporality and the attendant threat that the nation would not be reproduced according to pre-existing conditions.

This scientific association of blood mixing with the end of reproductive futurity constructs interracial sex as queer, a troublesome form of sexuality antagonistic to the white American family. Although the homo/heterosexual binary as we know it had not yet emerged in the 1850s, this representation of unreproductive sexuality reveals the cultural logic that would soon produce it. As Aliyyah Abdur-Rahman notes, "slavery had the effect of corrupting and contorting the most basic familial relationships. Not only did the institution deny slaves basic claims to familial, spousal, and hereditary bonds, insidiously it also assaulted their sexuality, robbing them of the basic rights of bodily autonomy and sexual choice." She continues, "this violating, soul-shattering feature of slavery and its cumulative generational effects on black identity formation even after slavery's formal abolition is 'queer.'"[28] Because of the destruction of kinship under slavery and thus the enforced illegitimacy of black sexuality, "racial blackness" came to be associated with "an entire range of sexual perversities."[29]

My understanding of the mid-century "mulatta" as a queer trope relies on Lee Edelman's theorization of queerness as a challenge to the "presupposition that the body politic must survive," a force that calls into question "the absolute value of reproductive futurism."[30] In the antebellum period, the sterile sexual practices that seemed to threaten the perpetuation of life itself were not homosexual but interracial, exemplified in Nott's widely influential warning about the probable extinction of mankind due to reproductive blood mixing, constructing "the mulatto" as the representative of taboo and fatally sterile sex practices. Similarly, Sharon Holland has observed the figural association of African Americans with queer negativity, arguing that "what makes a subject queer is his/her relationship to death."[31] Queerness must also be understood as the subject's relationship to reproduction and the family, which in turn conditions the subject's relation to the nation. Science, demography, and the law, among other discourses, worked to fold the "mulatto" into the taxonomic system of racial identities to contain its disturbing anti-identitarian oppositionality to the paradigms of race and nation. Understanding the mid-century "mulatto" as a queer figure allows for the recognition of African American resistance to oppressive familial discourses.

Although critical accounts tend to highlight the indestructibility of recognizable family forms, especially the sanctified relationship between mother and child, despite the perversions of slavery, examples of black resistance to the reproductive imperatives of the slave system are equally compelling. Take, for example, the story of Margaret Garner. Garner escaped slavery in 1856 by crossing the frozen Ohio River with her partner Robert, their four children, and a party of other fugitives. When Archibald Gaines, the man who legally owned them, arrived in Cincinnati to remand them to slavery, Garner murdered her two-year-old daughter, Mary, and wounded the other children with the intent of killing all of them and committing suicide. During her sensational trial, feminist abolitionist Lucy Stone famously argued that Garner had murdered her child to save her from being raped by white men, which she suggested had been Garner's experience and a degradation to which all enslaved women are exposed, an inheritance that Garner refused to transmit.

The courts returned her to slavery, and Gaines sent her to his brother's plantation in Arkansas on a steamboat along with her infant daughter, Priscilla, who had survived Garner's attempt to bludgeon her with a shovel. In the night, the boat collided with another vessel, and the cabin caught fire. Newspaper coverage of this event dramatizes conflicting accounts of Garner's role in Priscilla's death, but sources agree that she displayed "no other feeling than joy at the loss of her child."[32] One account says Garner and the child were thrown into the water by the impact. A fellow passenger, the steamer's African American cook, jumped in and saved Garner, who "displayed frantic joy when told that her child was drowned," and reiterated her intention of killing herself before reaching Arkansas. According to another report, "as soon as she had an opportunity, she threw her child into the river, and jumped after it."[33] Garner's tactics deny any intrinsic value in reproduction, inheritance, and mere survival; her refusal to reproduce the population of slavery and transmit its conditions to future generations overrides any desire for genealogical perpetuation. She renounced both the immediate conditions of enslavement and the passive hope of a better future for her descendants. Especially in light of white culture's fearful preoccupation with the threat of familial decline, Garner's relentless destruction of her own lineage embodies an oppositional negativity.

Like the historical Margaret Garner, Brown's suicidal character Clotel figures "the fate that cuts the thread of futurity," demanding that "the future stops here."[34] In the 1850s, interracial reproduction itself signified the disruption of generational continuity, and this kind of disruption constitutes a "queer" position vis-à-vis linear temporality. *Clotel* stokes the pervasive fear of biopolitical crisis in antebellum American culture to call for an immediate end to the reproduction of hereditary oppression for African Americans. Brown conveys this challenge not only in content but through form, especially repetition, nonlinear narrative, generic impurity, and a "tragic" teleology that denies happy endings and foregrounds death.[35]

The early African American novel provides a sustained analysis of racial paternity and its national and narrative consequences. Most of the early works in this tradition take interracialism as their central subject, highlighting mixed-race characters to meditate on the myriad relationships between black Americans and the white family. Sterling Brown's deprecations of the "tragic mulatto" trope inspired critics to read this figure with suspicion, exposing white and African American authors alike to accusations of racial conservatism. As his famous nomination of this trope suggests, Brown's distaste for the literary treatment of interracial characters rests on their tragic endings. He disparaged the typical trajectory of the mulatta as follows: "the whole desire of her life is to find a white lover, and then go down, accompanied by slow music, to a tragic end. Her fate is so severe that in some works disclosure of 'the single drop of midnight' in her veins makes her commit suicide."[36] Brown's reading entrenched the idea that the mulatta's conventional tragic death perpetuated racist notions about blood mixing.

Recent studies of the mulatta trope have called for a reconsideration of this figure, highlighting its progressive aspects and diminishing its characteristically tragic endings. These readings follow Hazel Carby's interpretation of the mulatta heroine as "a narrative device of mediation" with "two primary functions." First, this character is "a vehicle for an exploration of the relationship between the races and, at the same time, an expression of the relationship between the races."[37] This scholarly turn recuperates the trope as a strategy of resistance, not conciliation, arguing against Brown's damning interpretation of this figure and his influence on later critics. Teresa Zackodnik argues that "the mulatta figure was used by African American women to rhetorically transgress and contest a color line that attempted to police and secure racial identities as they were interimplicated with class, gender, and sexuality."[38] Eve Allegra Raimon emphasizes the gendered aspects of the figure and asserts that the mulatta "can be viewed as quintessentially American. . . . Hugely popular and politically influential at mid-century, the trope operates as a vehicle for exploring the complexities surrounding the interrelated identifications of race and national allegiance."[39] Cassandra Jackson also reads the mulatto as a figure for the exploration of mutually constitutive racial and national identities, "a lens through which to magnify and investigate this relationship between race and nationhood." She calls for a reconsideration of the figure to correct Brown's legacy and recognize the "incendiary potential" of the mulatta as a challenge to "prevailing ideologies of race."[40]

These readings represent the current critical consensus that the African American–authored mulatta heroine is not a tragic figure but a progressive model of hybridity employed for the exploration of gender, race, and nationalism. Moreover, critics now largely agree that these novels optimistically imagine an interracial future for the nation. For example, Robert Reid-Pharr argues that, for William Wells Brown, "the mulatto . . . was fully prepared, culturally and biologically, for the great march toward the American tomorrow."[41] Similarly, on the diversity of nineteenth-century authors of the mulatta trope, Raimon declares that "for all their positional differences, they share a political sensibility and a literary vision that are forward looking—even utopian, for some—in their emphasis on contemplating the viability of an interracial republic."[42] Though these studies dispute earlier understandings of the tragic mulatta, so called for her infamously unhappy endings, none center in an analysis of this essential problem, the mulatta heroine's failure to thrive.

Far from soft-pedaling the extent to which interracialism is associated with tragic death in the mid-nineteenth century novel, I wish to emphasize the apocalyptic bent of this literature as its most subversive aspect. *Clotel* does not imagine a happy integrated future; in fact, it does not imagine an American future at all. Rather than restoring the history of interracial relations central to American life in order to suggest a future integrated nation, these novels radically insist on a break in generational reproduction that threatens the very existence of a future nation.

A glance at three of the earliest African American novels reveals interesting consistencies of not only subject matter but also narrative structure. The multigenerational scope of these "tragic mulatto/a" narratives highlights the reproduction of oppression, revealing repetition rather than progress in the succession of generations and representing the white family as dangerous to African Americans. The concern with generational repetition is signaled in part by the depiction of children as doubles of their parents, propelled toward the repetition of past tragedies. Notably, in Frank J. Webb's *The Garies and their Friends* (1857), the children's names exactly repeat those of their parents, Clarence and Emily Garie, a too-exact reproduction turning generational continuity into regressive repetition. This pattern also governs the end of Harriet Wilson's *Our Nig* (1859), as Frado also becomes a double of her mother, "poor Mag Smith," with whom the novel opens. William Wells Brown's revisions of his original novel in 1864, *Clotelle: A Tale of the Southern States*, and 1867, *Clotelle, or, The Colored Heroine*, also present a character that repeats the previous generation. In this later work, as Reid-Pharr explains, "Clotel's daughter, Mary, acts as her mother's double. She takes a slightly altered version of her mother's name" and "reproduces many of the narrative devices that Brown deploys in the earlier novel."[43] Though scholarship aiming to mitigate the negativity of the "tragic mulatta" has read this trope as an acknowledgement of an already integrated past and the bright hope of a harmonious future, these texts actually reveal the terrible, inescapable persistence of the past, in which the most desired outcome is historical rupture and the refusal of the available future. These works remind us that although reproduction seems to be future oriented, it is really about repeating the past—literally producing again rather than anew. These novels portray generational inheritance as a curse, with children doomed to repeat their parents' tragedies.

Wilson's *Our Nig* depicts the white family as sadistic, the very agent of racist violence. When she is abandoned by her white mother, Frado suffers various forms of torture at the hands of Mrs. Bellmont in the house where she works as a domestic. Frado is described as "a permanent member of the family," conveying her horrible entrapment within the realm of this racist structure, reversing the sense of safety and acceptance traditionally associated with family membership.[44] It also designates white family real estate, the "two-story white house" of the subtitle, as the space of black oppression and enslavement by another name.[45] Similarly, *The Garies and Their Friends* associates white kinship with tragedy and depicts the rejection of whiteness and the embrace of the black family as the only hope for survival. Light and comic opening scenes of the domestic tranquility of an interracial family (formerly a plantation master, his enslaved mistress, and their children) living in Philadelphia leave the reader unprepared for the graphic violence to follow. Among other horrors at the midpoint of the novel, Mr. Garie is shot in the head at point-blank range, and Mrs. Garie is found dead the next morning in an outdoor hiding place, clutching a dead newborn that she birthed prematurely during a mob attack on her home.[46] We are given a final view of these central characters as corpses in their ransacked house with curtains covering their faces, their friends and family faced with the difficulty of burying them together, since the Philadelphia cemeteries are racially segregated.

Their children present two divergent models of interracial life. Their son passes as white, nearly marrying a white woman until his African ancestry is revealed. He grows increasingly ill until his early death and is soon followed in deterioration and death by his heartbroken white beloved. Interestingly, in the period leading up to his racial exposure, Clarence seems to suffer from the same sanguineous disorder that plagues Hawthorne's Pyncheons: a "gurgling noise was heard in his throat," and when his mixed-race heritage is revealed to the white family of his betrothed, he falls to the floor "with a slight stream of blood spurting from his mouth."[47] For Clarence, his very blood is an inherited curse. Because he is committed to living in a white cultural milieu that demands absolute ancestral purity to safeguard its homogenous reproductive perpetuation, this diseased and moribund mixed-race character ultimately dies because he cannot marry his white lover. His sister, on the other hand, relinquishes her white heritage and chooses blackness, which is presented as the only hope for security and happiness in this novel and also in *Clotel*.[48]

While *The Garies and Their Friends* most obviously addresses "mixed" racial inheritance, the plot centers on racist attempts to secure real estate against the threat of black property ownership. A white mob attacks a specific list of street numbers, the homes of property-owning black families, including the Garies and Mr. Walters, a black millionaire who owns one hundred brick houses. A plot twist reveals that George Stevens, the man responsible for his death, is Clarence Garie's cousin. Although the previous patriarch of the Garie family had renounced Stevens' mother and barred her line from inheriting his property, this episode emphasizes that individual white people cannot act against white property interests by routing inheritance away from the white family line. This ostensibly disinherited white cousin becomes the heir to the Garie estate, while the orphaned Garie children have no legal claim. Any white familial relation, however remote, overrides direct relationships across the color line as well as the legal power of testation in order to deflect black incursions into white property.

These African American novels, all focused on interracial experience, depict tragedy and rupture of all kinds, including the disruption of narrative conventions, abandonments, break-ups, bodily dismemberments, and suicides. To mention only a few additional examples of bodily breakages that lend these texts a pervading air of physical doom, Clotel and Frado are both forced to cut off all of their hair; Mrs. Belmont threatens to cut out Frado's tongue and skin her; in the 1867 version of Brown's novel, Clotelle's husband is decapitated; in *The Garies*, a white mob chops off Mr. Ellis's fingers with a hatchet as he dangles from a roof by one hand. These affronts to the integrity of the body provide ample reason to accept the classic nomination of these narratives as "tragic." In contrast to the progressive generational logic of national continuity, the multigenerational scope of these novels hinges on a nonlinear structure of repetition, circularity, and disjuncture. Associating death and trauma with generational continuity, these novels envision escape from the repetition of interracial inheritance as the only viable future, privileging rupture instead of continuity.

William Wells Brown's *Clotel* makes use of a multigenerational scope to consider the role of the family in the reproduction of oppression. In this novel, the white family that denies and represses its interracial members is clearly analogous to the American national family, as its patriarch is the founding father Thomas Jefferson. Brown's novel offers a fictional account of Jefferson's enslaved mistress, his two enslaved daughters, and three enslaved granddaughters, tracing in particular the journey of the title character Clotel through the slave system to her eventual suicide in the nation's capital. Through Clotel's radical refusal of existing conditions and the available future, Brown capitalizes on the interracial figure's queer relationship to white genealogy to presage the consequences of slavery on the national family. Rather than simply claiming an American legacy for the founding fathers' unacknowledged descendants, this novel poses the more radical possibility of the termination of that national lineage.

Surprisingly, the novel's opening paragraph adopts the alarmist tone of antimiscegenation discourse. The first sentence announces that "with the growing population of slaves in the Southern States of America, there is a fearful increase of half whites, most of whose fathers are slaveowners, and their mothers slaves." Citing a politician readily associated with plans for "Negro removal" for the sake of preserving the nation's white racial blood, he continues, "the late Henry Clay, some years since, predicted that the abolition of Negro slavery would be brought about by the amalgamation of the races."[49] Brown encourages readers to feel "fearful" that racial inter-mixture is bringing on the end of existing social conditions. This novel strategically voices the antebellum refrain about the degeneration and de-mise of the social order: "Our nation is losing its character. The loss of a firm national character, or the degradation of a nation's honour, is the in-evitable prelude to her destruction" (178). Stoking the paranoia that the nation's population was becoming increasingly interracial, even to the point that a race-based political and economic system would become im-possible, *Clotel* begins with a hint of the apocalyptic forecast that the novel as a whole will offer.

We begin with Thomas Jefferson and his enslaved mistress, Currer, and their two daughters, Clotel and Althesa. When Jefferson dies, Currer is sold down the river. Clotel and Althesa both reproduce their parents' situ-ation and end up the mistresses of their white owners. Both relationships end tragically; because their marriages are illegitimate, these women do not enjoy the privileges of "wives," no matter their partners' good inten-tions. Brown explains the root of this depraved condition: "the marriage relation, the oldest and most sacred institution given to man by his Cre-ator, is unknown and unrecognized in the slave laws of the United States" (82). These early remarks on the corruption of the marriage institution lay the foundation for the novel's exposé of national unsustainability and the perversion of kinship relationships. For the protection of the false purity of the white family, African Americans must be violently excluded from the benefits associated with that privileged realm. Althesa dies of yellow fever, and her daughters, who had no previous knowledge of their black ancestry, are sold as slaves. The oldest, Ellen, commits suicide when she realizes that she has been purchased to serve as a sex slave. The other, Jane, is bought for the same purpose, and after a failed attempt to escape, she dies of a broken heart.

Building from this apparent distress over the rampant blood mixing in the southern states, Brown keeps the focus of nearly every scene on reproduction.

Among the articles for sale at the opening slave auction, he prominently describes "women with children at the breast, and some of them very prolific in their generating qualities, affording a rare opportunity to anyone who wishes to raise a strong and healthy lot of servants for their own use" (85). This description not only calls attention to the economic importance of sexual reproduction under slavery, and to the exploitation of black women's generative capacities, but also subtly indicates that slave owners deliberately impregnated enslaved women themselves, reproducing and expanding their labor force and property with their own offspring, highlighting the centrality of sexual reproduction to the slave economy.

This thematic interest in reproduction, normally associated with continuity, is paired instead with a formal strategy of disruption. Crafting a pastiche of discourses, the novel contains a series of mininarratives, offering a cycle of repetitions and closures, even from the first page. Critics have observed that as a result of this "proto-postmodern" form, "the title character's story is constantly interrupted" so that "fragmentation, and oddly disruptive juxtapositions . . . characterize Brown's narrative method."[50] Some readers have found fault with the unusual assertiveness of endings in *Clotel*. Robert Reid-Pharr argues that "Brown's novel comes to an awkward and screeching halt. . . . It is this awkward closure that marks the first real failure in Brown's literature."[51] I see these abrupt closures as an important aspect of the novel's insistence on discontinuity and another formal demonstration of the novel's tragic temporality.

This formal emphasis on dead ends might be usefully compared to nineteenth-century family tree lithographs, which provide a visual model of the negative forces that thwart the progress and expansion of families and therefore of a broader American genealogy (Figures. 2.1 and 2.2). These graphic arbors represent both early deaths and also unmarried or nonreproductive individuals as stumps or branches that break off precipitously.[52] These charts show how people who do not contribute to reproductive futurity "fall of the genealogical grid," to borrow a phrase from Elizabeth Povinelli.[53] *Clotel* is a text of stumps, full of false starts and narrative impasses that refuse the teleological imperatives of the family that underlie the novel form. Brown's queer mulatta threatens to cut short the genealogical grid of national history.

Not unlike Melville's *Moby-Dick*, this novel's central plot is interspersed with set pieces and meditations that stop the linear action. These interruptions include anecdotes repeated from Brown's autobiography, long excerpts from political writings, and most frequently, snippets from a variety of newspapers providing a collage of atrocities that were circulated heavily in abolitionist circles. This strategy is an important aspect of the novel's insistence on discontinuity, a queer formal articulation of the novel's tragic

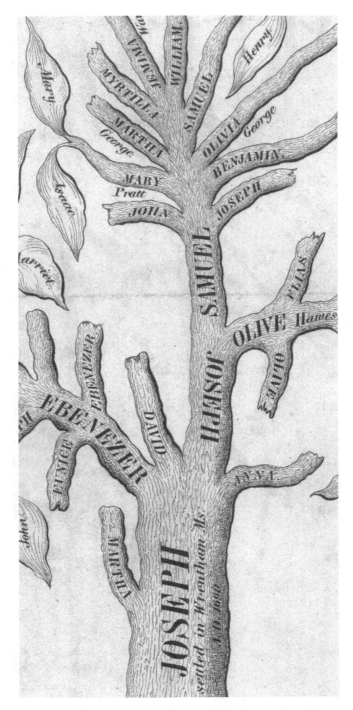

Figure 2.1
Detail from Cowell family tree (undated). 36 cm. x 27 cm. Image courtesy of the New England Historic Genealogical Society.

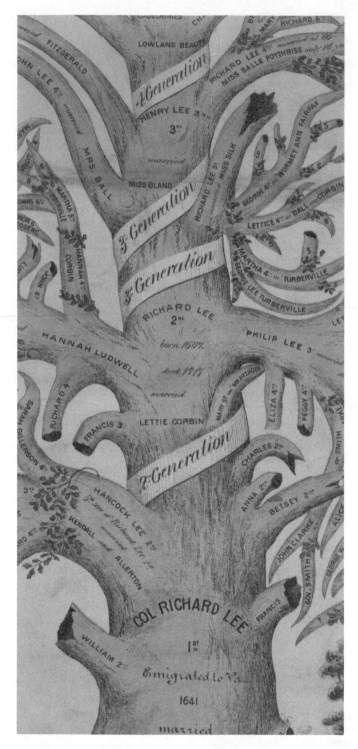

Figure 2.2
Detail from Lee family tree, Library of Congress (1886).

temporality. *Clotel* exemplifies what Judith Roof has described as a "counterreproductive perverse" narrative, that is, "a narrative about narrative dissolution, a narrative that continually short-circuits, that both frustrates and winks at the looming demagogue of reproduction."[54] Thus, *Clotel's* disruptive form expresses its perverse message of disrupted reproduction and attendant teleological catastrophe for racial nationalism.[55] This "tragic," abortive temporality underlies African American uses of the mulatto as a trope of discontinuity, subversive to a national imaginary centered in the reproduction of the white American family.

Clotel details the endings of not one but six "tragic mulattas," but the title character's demise serves as the centerpiece of Brown's work. In an act of biopolitical subterfuge, Clotel refuses to continue in her role in the reproduction of existing conditions, to live as a slave and give birth to slaves. The chapter in which she commits suicide is titled "Death Is Freedom," indicating that her suicide subverts the slave system. Clotel breaks free from a slave prison in Washington, D.C., and runs for the Long Bridge across the Potomac. Seeing the other side, she imagines herself hiding in the expanse of forest just as night falls, "and already did her heart begin to beat high with the hope of success." However, "God by his Providence . . . had determined that an appalling tragedy should be enacted that night, within plain sight of the President's house and the capital of the Union, which should be an evidence wherever it should be known, of the unconquerable love of liberty the heart may inherit" (205). The assertion that Clotel's heart has inherited an "unconquerable love of liberty," underscores her biological and ideological connection to the founding fathers and positions her suicide as a revolutionary act. But Brown does not merely want to claim the relatedness of African Americans to national history. Instead, he uses this connection to indicate the death not only of this enslaved woman but of a national legacy and the promise of its future.

In this definitively national setting, surrounded by the iconic architecture of American government, this rejected descendent of the white American family chooses death over the life available to her. Her pursuers call to men on the other side of the bridge, who block Clotel's passage to freedom. Seeing that she must choose either capture and continued enslavement or death, she throws herself into the river below and drowns. Registering the tragic irony of the death of the daughter of a founding father within sight of the White House and the Capitol, the narrator adds, "they boast that America is the 'cradle of liberty;' if it is, I fear they have rocked the child to death" (207). This image of a dead child in America's cradle, accompanying the story of a dead child of Jefferson, conveys the novel's message that the nation's insistence on the reproduction of an exclusive white lineage has in reality guaranteed the reproduction of inequality and tragedy. Utilizing the language of American political metaphor that turns to the Child as the emblem of the national future, Brown declares that there is no child and therefore no future to inherit the political edifice of the United States.

This thwarted escape abandons the triumphant donnée of the slave narrative for a far more negative representation of the obstructed, even impassable, route from slavery to freedom.[56] This character herself is a kind of bridge between a white national past and an integrated future, and this scene graphically emblematizes the seeming impossibility of this connection. Note that even if she had made it across, she would have hidden in the woods outside of George Washington's estate in Virginia, a plantation in a slave state, indicating the historical reality that after the Fugitive Slave Act there was no longer any place in the United States that could signify freedom. With this multiplication of national symbols, Brown marks the home of the founding fathers as the space of danger for their mixed-race descendants.

Surprisingly, although it has become perhaps the most emblematic scene in early African American literature, Brown did not author this account of a leap from the Long Bridge. The same story in the same words was published by New York Congressman Seth M. Gates in the *New York Evangelist* on September 8, 1842, and reprinted multiple times in the eleven years before *Clotel* was published.[57] Brown acts not as the unitary and original author but as the curator of a variety of abolitionist materials with which his audience was possibly already familiar. He samples and remixes them into a form that resembles a scrapbook connected by a narrative that is itself a mixture of the imaginative, the autobiographical, and borrowed cultural materials from both print and oral traditions. Critics have noted that Brown's formal strategy achieves a denaturalizing effect that matches his thematic focus on hybridity. That is, blurring the distinction between fiction and nonfiction, originality and reprinting, bolsters Brown's account of nation and race as constructions or cultural fictions.[58] Reprinting Gates's account where one might expect to find an original climax for this plot, Brown emphasizes the impurity of all origins. The antebellum culture of reprinting allowed opportunities to move beyond the unitary author to craft collective, public documents that cut across our contemporary expectations for appropriate forms of literary heritage and homage.[59] This verbatim reproduction of an account of slavery's atrocities formally underscores the repetition and recurrence of these atrocities. Brown's use of the Long Bridge meme is perhaps the most dramatic instance of his formal emphasis on repetition, reproduction uncoupled from progress and associated instead with stasis and death.

Brown concludes his account of Clotel's suicide with another reproduction, reprinting of the poem "The Escape" by Sarah J. Clarke, which
was published in *The Liberator* in 1844.[60] The final stanza culminates
Brown's account of the mixed-race subject's relationship to white American
heritage:

> That bond woman's corse—let Potomac's proud wave
> Go bear it along *by our Washington's grave,*
> And heave it high up on that hallowed strand,
> *To tell of the freedom he won for our land.*
> A weak woman's corse, by freemen chased down;
> Hurrah for our country! Hurrah!
> To freedom she leaped, through drowning and death—
> Hurrah for our country! Hurrah![61]

This stanza bitterly mimics a nationalistic anthem and proposes Clotel's corpse as a fitting monument to the legacy of the Revolutionary generation, implying not only that this proud national heritage is dead but
also that it demands the murder of others. Washington's grave, a literal
"sepulcher of the fathers," as Emerson might have described it, becomes
the double gravesite of the founders and their dead interracial offspring,
a particularly resonant image in light of the filial anxiety of the 1850s and
the related controversy throughout this decade over the condition of
Washington's gravesite at Mount Vernon.[62] This image captures the fate
that white Americans of this generation feared, the death of the white
bloodline imagined to underlie national identity and the final burial of
the republican principles for which the national union was supposed to
stand.

Clotel's daughter, Mary, survives as the only representative of the fictionalized Jefferson-Hemings line. Tellingly, the novel's only happy ending
is reserved for the character who severs both the cycle of tragic interracial
romances and also her ties to the United States. Mary is eventually removed from the tragic interracial cycle after being purchased by a kindly
European. "I had an only sister," he explains, "who died three years ago." He
continues: "you are so much like her that had I not known of her death, I
would most certainly have taken you for her." He adds that the love "which
I had for my sister is transferred to you" (223). Brown signifies here on the
sentimental trope of the family as the basis of extended sympathy. The important difference in this repetition is that Devenant is a Frenchman,
which subverts the familial paradigm of national, as well as racial, identification through resemblance. He conveniently dies once Mary is safely out

of the United States. She reunites with her black lover, George, and the two marry and remain in France, due to the Fugitive Slave Act. The novel's concession to the marriage plot ending that traditionally guarantees reproductive futurity imagines a future only outside of the United States. Despite the now-popular critical reading of the mixed-race figure as an optimistic representation of national integration, African American–authored "tragic mulatta" narratives are not typically invested in securing an inclusive United States but are concerned instead with the more pressing goal of black survival, whether or not it is connected to American national destiny. Brown associates the web of unacknowledged interracialism in the United States only with death and tragedy, so that severing all ties to the repressive structure of the white American family represents the only hope for escape and survival, as the overseas black marriage at the novel's conclusion signifies.

Returning briefly to the conclusion of *The Garies and Their Friends*, Emily, the only surviving Garie, also finds a happy ending by marrying a black man and leaving her white inheritance behind. The final words of the novel explain that she and her husband "took a voyage to Europe for the health of the latter, and returned after a two years' tour to settle permanently in his native city. They were unremitting in their attention to father and mother Ellis, who lived to good old age, surrounded by their children, and grandchildren."[63] This passage informs us that the couple chooses to live in the United States, though they have the means to travel to Europe, forecasting a happy future on American soil, signified by the reference to the couple's posterity. The mention of the aging Ellises in the final scene brings attention back to the dead Garies, the set of grandparents that did not live to "good old age." This is a pointedly imperfect picture of familial continuity in which all of Emily's relatives have died traumatically and prematurely as a consequence of their interracial status. Moreover, father Ellis has been submerged in a nervous reverie since his mutilation at the hands of a white mob on the night the Garies were murdered. He is mentally stuck in the past, "gazing about the room and muttering to himself," living mentally through the traumatic events again and again so that intermittently throughout every day he believes the white mob is still chasing him.[64] This qualified physical survival serves only to signify the persistence, indeed the repetition, of that horrific past in a therefore compromised future. Though this novel is slightly more optimistic than many other interracial family romances in that it imagines the survival of blackness in the United States, this survival requires a definitive break from the past, a cutting of all ties with tragic interracialism, the rejection of the very "hybridity" that these novels have been said to celebrate. The early African American novel characteristically places its hope in black futurity, not national perpetuation, but demonstrates an awareness that this survival will be marked by the persistent echo of the horrors of a tragic past, another kind of unwanted inheritance.

Clotel closes with a direct appeal for the abolition of slavery. With the novel's final words, Brown calls on British readers to inspire Americans, who he reminds us are in some sense their "descendants," to mirror their antislavery sentiment: "let the voice of the whole British nation be heard across the Atlantic, and throughout the length and breadth of the land of the Pilgrim Fathers, beseeching their descendents, as they value the common salvation, which knows no distinction between the bond and the free, to proclaim the Year of Jubilee" (227). This ending calls attention to the generational rupture between abolitionist England and the slave-holding United States, even as it manipulates the power of this metaphor of continuity, calling on familial connection for the transmission of abolitionist values.

Brown's reference to the "Pilgrim Fathers" recalls his previous mention of these prenational patriarchs in an American origin story that mimics polygenesist racial theory. Brown imagines the beginning of chattel slavery as the dark double of the Mayflower landing glorified by Daniel Webster and others in this period:

> [T]he May-flower brought the seed-wheat of states and empire.... This ship had the embryo elements of all that is useful, great, and grand in Northern institutions.... On the same day, in 1620, a low rakish ship hastening from the tropics, solitary and alone, to the New World ... it is the first cargo of slaves on their way to Jamestown, Virginia. Behold the May-flower anchored at Plymoth Rock, the slave-ship in James River. Each a parent, one of the prosperous, labour-honouring, law-sustaining institutions of the North; the other the mother of slavery, idleness, lynch-law ... and the peculiar institutions of the South. These ships are the representation of good and evil in the New World, even to our day. When shall one of those parallel lines come to an end? (180–181)[65]

In addition to his novel's overwriting of the mythology surrounding the founding fathers, Brown rejects the exclusionary genealogical nationalism that established the pilgrim settlers of Plymouth as the unitary origin of all Americans. Most importantly, this passage insists that either the inheritance of slavery must end or the lineage of the Pilgrims and the founding fathers will terminate. Indeed, the novel indicates in multiple ways that slavery has already abrogated this line.

At a time when many Northerners hoped to suture national union at any cost, *Clotel* argues that the perpetuation of existing social relations can reproduce only oppression for African Americans. Despite popular appeals to white sectional fraternity to stay the impending Civil War, *Clotel* forecasts what history eventually bore out, that it was indeed necessary for the nation to reach a crisis point, a violent break in continuity, in order for slavery to be abolished. The queer mulatta trope embraces the association of interracialism with social death and "the undoing of identity" to insist "that the future stops here."[66] Defiantly representing death as preferable to the perpetuation of a national history inextricable from the evils of slavery, Brown strategically adopts the interracial figure as a symbol of American reproduction in crisis.

CHAPTER 3

✧

"The Character of a Family"
in Stowe's *Dred*

On the Limits of Alternative Kinship

Once again one is caught, without a way out: it is simply that the means have been found
to render the family transcendent.
> —Gilles Deleuze and Felix Guattari, *Anti-Oedipus*
> (London: Continuum, 2004), 102

Herman Melville's *Pierre; Or, The Ambiguities* is far darker and more daring than *The House of the Seven Gables* in imagining the fall of an aristocratic American lineage, in part because it refuses both the domestic family and radical antifamilial reform associations as viable replacements. In *Pierre*, multiple models of family come into conflict, and all of them prove unsatisfactory. The title character feels called to assume fraternal responsibility for his newly discovered half-sister Isabel, but he is unwilling to besmirch his father's public image and destroy his mother's regard for her late husband by openly acknowledging this illegitimate offspring. His confrontation with these contradictory familial obligations, along with the realization that his mother's love relies on his doing her bidding, reveals to him the emptiness and dishonesty of "the conventional life."[1] This is the dawning of an antifamilial sensibility in one who had always been "a worshipper of all heir-looms."[2] Cast out from his patrimonial estate, he goes to the Apostles, a radical commune, ultimately living with three women and married to none.

But his "fictitious alliance" with Isabel, though it has the legal status of a "web of air," proves to have the practical effect of "a wall of iron."[3] Pierre soon discovers that freely chosen relations, even those with no official standing, are just as binding and insatiably demanding as the blood family. His new system of elective kin comes to resemble his rejected blood family in terms of its relational ambiguity and multiplicity. Long before Isabel's emergence in the plot, his is already an incestuous world where everyone is multiply related: his mother is also his "sister"; she and his male cousin are both figured as his romantic partners; even his horse is also his "cousin." At the Apostles, his half-sister is also his "wife," his former fiancée is his "cousin," and all mankind are his siblings. Cindy Weinstein has noted that in *Pierre*, Melville critiques not only the traditional family but antebellum radicals who worked to reform it: "reformers desirous of challenging conventional domestic relations ended up replicating them."[4] Rather than embracing this universal kinship as a more liberal replacement for the aristocratic blood family, Pierre becomes just as disillusioned with this new arrangement, leaving him misanthropic and homicidal. In the end, biological relatives and fictive kin alike die tragically. The proud arbor of his "double revolutionary descent" is reduced to a blasted stump, but the radical alternative fares no better. In other words, *Pierre* suggests that changing the organizing principle of family from blood to consent ultimately does not change the character of kin relations. Furthermore, expanding kinship to embrace all of humanity entails a host of unintended negative consequences. Namely, it makes family ubiquitous, destroying the distinction between incest and exogamy.[5]

Multiple aspects of the eighteenth-century changes in family norms that became ideologically tied to the nation's founding raised the specter of incest. First, a republic in which traditional distinctions of blood were devalued struck early Americans as a breeding ground for incest. Elizabeth Dill synopsizes the relationship between republican socioeconomic leveling and incest in her reading of *Pierre* alongside William Hill Brown's *The Power of Sympathy*: "one cannot mark differences in ways that organize and stratify others and still sustain the equality of democracy, but without those means, one cannot be sure his wife is not also his sister."[6] The eighteenth-century novel exhibits concern that de-emphasizing the traditional distinctions of ancestral lineage might result in the violation of fundamental taboos. Furthermore, Brian Connolly suggests that the incest narratives of the early republic bespeak anxiety about the new atomization of the domestic family: "a private sphere fully severed from public, civil society can only be monstrous."[7] Indeed, Michel Foucault's historical account of this isolated private sphere of domestic intimacy suggests that this emergent family form renders all sexuality incestuous. He argues that "since the eighteenth century the family has become an obligatory locus of affects, feelings, love; that sexuality has its privileged point of development in the family; that for this reason sexuality is 'incestuous' from the start."[8]

Finally, grounding national identity in the conceit of consanguinity made the United States a place where *non*incestuous sexual relations were impossible. This is why the illustrated family record discussed in the Introduction (Figure I.2) visually hints that the couple is related before marriage in their common descent from the Pilgrims. The Plymouth settlers appear at the top center of the genealogical grid as ancestors that unite the nuclear unit's two sets of grandparents, constructing a familial nationalism that merges symbolic inheritance with blood descent. Along these lines, Elizabeth Barnes argues that incest is the endgame of constructing civil society as a family: "the conflation of familial and social ties results in an eroticization of familial feeling of which incest is the 'natural' result. What this suggests is the cultural cost of setting up the family as a model for politics."[9] The strange thing, and possibly the thing that Melville aims to critique, is that by the middle of the nineteenth century, American novels no longer regarded this scenario as a cause for anxiety or terror; on the contrary, they celebrated it.[10]

Susan Warner's *Wide, Wide World* (1850) and E.D.E.N. Southworth's *Ishmael; Or, In the Depths* (1863–1864), both bestselling smash hits, are cases in point.[11] For Warner's protagonist, Ellen Montgomery, her "brother" John Humphreys ("It doesn't make a bit of difference that we were not born so!"[12]) is the obvious choice for a future companionate husband. Aligning herself with her adoptive brother rather than her "father" (who is really her uncle) is clearly presented as the choice of American republicanism over old-world systems including monarchy, aristocracy, and the consanguineous family. In *Ishmael*, too, the most suitable marriage partner for the exaggeratedly republican protagonist is his adoptive sibling, Bee, who calls him "dearest brother" throughout the scene in which they become engaged. The Middletons, her parents, effectively adopted Ishmael Worth from childhood and regard him as their son. Emily VanDette views the intimate opposite-sex sibling relationships of the antebellum period as a result of the emergent conjugal paradigm: "Since a chief characteristics of the nuclear family ideal is that emotional fulfillment should be contained within the immediate family, the ideology encouraged intense closeness between siblings."[13] Brother-sister relationships were understood frankly as practice for marriage, which helps to explain Pierre's discomfiting declaration, "He who is sisterless, is as a bachelor before his time. For much that goes to make up the deliciousness of a wife, already lies in the sister."[14]

The overlapping relationship between siblings and spouses in the ante-bellum novel might be understood to reinforce the idea that the national family replaced the social distinctions of unique bloodlines so that all white Americans are related. Indeed, representations of adoptive sibling love in these novels are fueled with patriotic fervor. Both Ellen and Ish-mael have a near religious devotion to the founding fathers and hold forth on the merits of American sociopolitical systems. Nationalist iconography abounds; Ishmael's surrogate family is headed by a Supreme Court Justice and housed in a mansion formerly belonging to George Washington, for example.[15] With true Republican aversion to inherited status, Ishmael ref-uses to assume his legitimate surname or his patrimonial inheritance despite a warm reunion with his biological father. Instead, the illegitimate child previously called "nobody's son" ends up the "son" or "brother" of nearly everyone he meets.[16]

Thus antebellum sentimental novels depict a world full of potential family members, where anyone might become kin by adoption or revela-tion, where family distinctions are not fixed by bloodlines but can be cho-sen and possibly extended to all of society. Nina Baym's classic study of "woman's fiction" established that this genre hinges on the idealization of elective kin systems in opposition to the family of origin. Her sample of over one hundred novels by forty-eight women writers from 1820 to 1870 reveals a common plot "about a young woman who has lost the emotional and financial support of her legal guardians—indeed who is often subject to their abuse and neglect—but who nevertheless goes on to win her own way in the world," which generally means "domestic comfort, a social net-work and a companionable husband." Recent critical work has reaffirmed that a core project of this genre was to reimagine the family outside the strict confines of consanguinity.[17] Most prominently, Weinstein has ar-gued that the tradition so firmly associated with the sanctification of the family actually depicts the family as a disordered institution in need of restructuring. She observes that "at precisely the moment that the affec-tive lives of antebellum Americans seem to be coalescing around an ideal of the biological family, these texts consistently represent its insuffi-ciencies and the necessity of coming up with alternatives." While this experimentation with nonblood "kinship" might be understood as a chal-lenge to the hegemony of the family as an institution, Weinstein insists that this literature expresses "a desire to reform the family rather than dispense with it altogether."[18] She finds in these works a call for consen-sual, volitional models of relation rather than the traditional ties of blood. Barnes concurs that the domestic novel displays a desire to reconfigure the boundaries of the family to diminish the importance of blood and elevate the importance of shared values, "reconceiving the family in terms of volitional attachment."[19]

This view of the sentimental novel aligns with the standard historical account of the shift in family forms from consanguinity to conjugality, or patriarchal authority to intimacy and consent. Moreover, the sentimental convention of alternative kinship might be understood to reinforce the ideology of the national family. If, as Weinstein suggests, sentimentalism simply transplants the idealized bonds of the family onto nonblood "kin" relations, then this literature might be understood as working to contain dissatisfaction with the domestic family in this period, reinscribing desires for unprecedented affinities back into the web of kinship, as well as serving the nationalist project of convincing the population they were held together by natural ties. While the emphasis on freely chosen ties seems to advertise the modern family's eclipse of vertical consanguinity, it ultimately insists on a new form of endogamous marriage, creating a tightly controlled genealogy resistant to branching. While the discourse of alternative kinship professes that blood is obsolete, it also insists that all of ones associates must be turned into relatives, consolidating the family and expanding it through recruitment and conversion. If it insists that the family can be "revised" infinitely so that all relations, public and private, blood based and contractual, friends, colleagues, and collaborators can be recast as merely other kinds of kin, the sentimental novel is a means through which the family was rendered transcendent.

On the other hand, it may be that critical readings of the nonfamilial affiliations that abound in the nineteenth-century novel silence the radical implications of their challenges to the institution of the family. Critics tend to read nonfamilial coalitions as merely alternative forms of kinship, but at what point might it be more useful to assert their difference from kinship? Rather than prizing more liberal definitions of kinship, it is possible that some of these works deemphasize the family to shed light on other forms of affiliation based on civic equality rather than essential similitude. What turns freely chosen relations outside of genealogy or marriage into kinship? Are we able to imagine political community without the family as its nucleus?

For a number of critics, Harriet Beecher Stowe's *Uncle Tom's Cabin; or, Life among the Lowly* (1852) has represented an important exception to the sentimental novel's preference for elective kinship networks. Moreover, as perhaps the most significant work in this genre, it has provided primary evidence for the critical commonplace that abolitionist fiction centrally relied on the sanctification of the domestic family. Stowe's focus on the family has long been understood as the cornerstone of her novel's cultural work, and despite myriad objections to the chauvinisms that this entails, recent readings maintain that her insistence on the blood family serves as a necessary refutation of the slave system's perverse paternalism and enforcement of black kinlessness. In particular, critics have understood her rejection of nonblood kinship as a refutation of proslavery ideologues like George Fitzhugh who defended slavery as an extension of the patriarchal family in which white men naturally protect and provide for dependent women, children, and servants. For example, Arthur Riss argues that *Uncle Tom's Cabin* vaunts the blood family in order to denounce the nonkin "plantation family" as fraudulent.[20] Weinstein also concludes that Stowe's "critique of slavery absolutely demands a withdrawal from the sentimental novels' experimentation with alternative kinds of family. For Stowe, the only available model for a family that is not based on the affective ties of consanguinity is the family (or non-family) produced by slavery."[21] Thus, Riss and Weinstein agree that, for Stowe, the sovereignty of the blood family must be established and protected in order to combat proslavery rhetoric that constructed slavery as a benevolent alternative kin structure.

Unfortunately, Stowe's insistence on biological kinship in this novel results in a rigid alignment of race with nation. Although its aim is to defend the family, white and black, from the perverting forces of slavery, this novel's insistence on the naturalness of blood ultimately serves the ideology of white familial nationalism. Denounced by generations of readers, the "resettlement" of the black characters in Africa at the end of *Uncle Tom's Cabin* provides the logical conclusion for a novel that so vehemently asserts the sanctity of blood families. Because *Uncle Tom's Cabin* conflates race, nation, and biological kinship, it suggests that Africa is the proper place for all black people, their only site of true political belonging. As Elizabeth Dillon observes, "The black family can and should only exist, according to Stowe, in a black nation such as that of Liberia."[22] This correlation leads Riss to assert that for Stowe, "national solidarity is simply the extension of loving one's [racial] family, the familial bond modulating seamlessly into national citizenship."[23] Thus *Uncle Tom's Cabin* shared the polygenic nationalism of mainstream antebellum culture, which posited distinct racial bloodlines with attendant political destinies. Stowe's promotion of the blood family has been credited with the novel's sentimental success at swaying hearts and minds for the antislavery cause, but the endgame of this strategy must be racial segregation and political inequality.

Almost immediately after the publication of *Uncle Tom's Cabin*, however, Stowe expressed regret about having written these black characters out of the United States at the novel's end. Robert Levine notes that as early as

March 1853, she stated in a letter to the American and Foreign Anti-Slavery Society "that if she were to write 'Uncle Tom' again, she would not send George Harris to Liberia."[24] By 1856, when the rhetoric of family had been used exhaustively to argue both sides of the slavery question and the supposedly familial population of white Americans had come to violence in Kansas and on the floor of the Senate, Stowe appears to have realized that kinship is a false, inadequate, and even dangerous way to imagine national belonging. The metaphor of family that had traditionally scaffolded the American political imaginary had revealed its racist underpinnings to an extent that Stowe faced the question of the usefulness of that metaphor in her writing. Stowe's second novel represents a dramatic shift in its deconstruction of the family, the very locus of sentimental power that she had so masterfully mobilized in *Uncle Tom's Cabin* only four years earlier. While Riss argues that Stowe's aim is to "persuade her readers that slavery and the family are essentially antagonistic institutions," her second novel, *Dred: A Tale of the Great Dismal Swamp* (1856), suggests on the contrary that *both* of these institutions are antagonistic to the exercise of democratic citizenship.[25] *Dred* maintains a belief in biogenetic particularity but divorces racial identity from kinship and citizenship, both of which it represents as performative rather than essential. Stowe elevates cooperative nonkin coalitions as the social form that can support a nonidentitarian democracy, rejecting both the biological and conjugal family along with the Southern "plantation family" as despotic and unsuitable models for political community. *Dred* rejects the race/family/nation matrix that privileges shared blood as the basis of political organization and calls instead for the intentional exercise of republican principles by both black and white Americans. Although her reliance on racial biodeterminism curtails the radical potential of her political antifamilialism, *Dred* reveals new possibilities for reading challenges to the blood family as a call for a new coalitional politics, not the expansion of kinship. Cataloguing the insufficiencies of the blood family, marriage, and models of alternative kinship as appropriate models for a multiracial democracy, *Dred* suggests the value of moving beyond familial metaphors in political thinking.

Although Fitzhugh's model of patriarchal interracial kinship provided a powerful rhetorical defense of slavery, discourses that modernized the paradigm of consanguinity in the mid-1850s had a far deeper and more lasting impact on American science and law, tying the blood family to the national family through a new understanding of race. The suggestion that humans developed from separate points of origin had been blasphemous in the eighteenth century, but the smash success of Nott and Gliddon's polygenesist tome *Types of Mankind* (1854) ensured that the belief in distinct human "races" with different "blood" became a mainstream view in the 1850s.[26] The authors did not intend for their work simply to advance scientific inquiry; they offer the theories outlined in their book for application to the "practical question" of "our inherited Institution of Negro Slavery." Indeed, their introduction brags that John C. Calhoun, prominent proslavery statesman, had consulted their ethnographical research to support his political work.[27] They argue that certain races are naturally suited to certain governments, specifically that only white people are capable of self-government. On the other hand, "dark-skinned races, history attests, are only fit for military governments. It is the unique rule genial to their physical nature."[28] The American School granted scientific credibility to the existing idea that the American political system was the racial heritage of Anglo-Saxons for which people of African descent were biologically unfit.[29] Furthermore, they insist that these blood-based political orientations precluded the possibility of integrated societies: "Nations and races, like individuals, have each an especial destiny: some are born to rule, and others to be ruled. And such has ever been the history of mankind. No two distinctly-marked races can dwell together on equal terms."[30]

Before the decade was over, the legal analog of this scientific theory, declaring that no one descended from the peoples of Africa, whether free or enslaved, could ever be a United States citizen, officially established American national identity as ancestrally determined. Chief Justice Roger B. Taney's decision in the case *Dred Scott v. Sanford* elaborates a political theory resonant with polygenesis, extending the idea of separate bloodlines into the legal definition of American citizenship. In an extreme departure from the Jeffersonian ideal of generational sovereignty, Taney narrates the formation of the United States as a kind of family trust put into motion by the founding fathers for themselves and their blood descendants that excludes nonfamily members. The nation, he explains, "was formed by them, and for them and their posterity, but for no one else."[31] His narrative insists that the social relations at the moment of the nation's foundation must be reproduced and inherited by all subsequent generations, arguing that if slaves were not then considered citizens then the founders did not intend any of their posterity forever to be included under that term: "neither the class of persons who had been imported as slaves, nor their descendants, whether they had become free or not, were then acknowledged as a part of the people, nor intended to be included in the general words used in that memorable instrument."[32] Taney describes two lines of political descent, one black and one white. National membership depended, in other words, not on a citizen/slave binary but on bloodlines so that despite any black person's putative "free" condition, his hereditary connection to Africans determined his true political identity as noncitizen.

To underscore their relatedness and their shared descent from the founding fathers, Taney refers to white American citizens as "the political family," calling on the standard metaphor for the nation's cohesion through shared blood. Russ Castronovo explains that Taney grounds his argument in the idea that "blacks, in contrast, descended from a different political family . . . and share no political blood with United States citizens."[33] Rogers Smith agrees that Taney's argument hinges on the assumption that "blacks were outside the family." His use of familial imagery was central to this decision "to define civic statuses in terms of 'natural' ascribed status, and it was rhetorically shrewd. Most white men could be expected to be repelled by the idea that black men were family members."[34] The *Dred Scott* case was one of numerous instances in which the proposition of African American civil rights was rejected with horror as the interracializing of the national family. Taney's decision was openly embraced as a political application of polygenesist theories of racial identity. Dr. John Van Evrie wrote a preface to a pamphlet edition of the decision, applauding it as "in accord with the natural relation of the races."[35] This 1859 pamphlet circulated the text of Taney's decision along with an introduction by Van Evrie and an appendix on the "Natural History of the Prognathous Race of Mankind" by Dr. S.A. Cartwright, guaranteeing that readers received the *Dred Scott* decision and its racial scientific justification in one convenient volume.

Scientific and legal culture at midcentury espoused a unified vision of white familial nationalism, theorizing an American identity transmitted exclusively through white "blood."[36] Perhaps for this reason, scholars sensitive to a shift in Stowe's familial politics have mistaken *Dred*'s more inclusive political vision for a lessened commitment to biological race. For example, Susan Ryan argues that "by the end of the novel the salience of blood, in terms of both familial and racial kinship, has faded."[37] On the contrary, although *Dred* questions and even parodies the importance of "blood" kinship as it pertains to the "naturalness" of traditional family structure and its extension into the political realm, it affirms the idea of distinct racial bloods. Though the novel locates racial difference in the "blood," it challenges the related idea that political communities must be blood-related groups structured like families. It balances a pronounced strain of genealogical determinism with a desire to dethrone the family as the indisputable site of belonging in order to advance a nonkin model of political community.

Indeed, Stowe's conception of race as hereditary "character" not only persists but is amplified in *Dred*. The novel takes for granted that ancestral racial inheritance determines identity, even down to minute personality traits. Stowe's catalogue of natural black traits include the love of bright colors, "in which the instinctive taste of the dark races leads them to delight," and also magic: "The African race are said by mesmerists to possess, in the fullest degree, that peculiar temperament which fits them for the evolution of mesmeric phenomena."[38] Furthermore, the narrator notes that "the African race have large ideality and veneration" and that "approbativeness is a stronger principle with the African race than almost any other; they like to be thought well of" (306, 307). While black blood transmits a love of colorful adornment, sorcery, and a tendency to respect and please others, according to Stowe, white blood holds intelligence, honesty, and courage. Clearly, although Stowe attempts to credit people of African descent with certain positive attributes, her schema of inherited racial traits departs little from received racist notions of inherent biological difference.

The novel introduces nearly every character with an explication of his or her genealogy and inherited traits. Harry promises to be a noble character because "the Gordon family transmitted in their descent all the traditions, feelings, and habits, which were the growth of the aristocratic caste from which they sprung" (37). Typical of the scientific interest in blood mixing, we are told that Harry "was the son of his master, and inherited much of the temper and constitution of his father, tempered by the soft and genial temperament of the beautiful Eboe mulatress who was his mother" (38). Harry's wife, Lisette, "was a delicate, airy little creature, formed by a mixture of the African and French blood, producing one of those fanciful, exotic combinations . . . From both parent races she was endowed with a sensuous being exquisitely quick and fine" (52). Milly's parents, we are told, "were prisoners taken in African wars; and she was a fine specimen of one of those warlike and splendid races, of whom, as they have seldom been reduced to slavery, there are but few and rare specimens among the slaves of the south" (50). This novel attests to the power of the newly respectable concept of biological race, even over the people most committed to the goal of emancipation.

Although *Dred* upholds and circulates ideologies of racial blood, it ultimately rejects the family as the natural basis of society and government. In particular, this novel debunks the conception of the United States as a white family and advocates the democratic ideal that black and white citizens can unite to achieve common goals. It deconstructs prevailing antebellum discourses of political familialism used to justify the continued enslavement of African Americans. A description of the militant title character's genealogy explains, "The Mandingos are one of the finest African tribes, distinguished for intelligence, beauty of form, and an indomitable pride and energy of nature . . . They resent a government of brute force, and under such are always fractious and dangerous" (113). In this sense, Stowe creatively rewrites *Types of Mankind* to argue that whites are not the only race unfitted for servitude.[39]

Moreover, the novel draws a parallel between the slave revolt led by Denmark Vesey and the War for Independence fought by the founding fathers. He is catalyzed to revolt once he "has heard, amid shouts, on the Fourth of July, that his masters held the truth to be self-evident, that all men were born equal, and had an inalienable right to life, liberty, and the pursuit of happiness; and that all governments derive their just power from the consent of the governed" (204). If Vesey observed another black man bowing to a white person, "he would rebuke him, and observe, 'that all men were born equal.'" (205) Contrary to Greg Crane's assertion that Stowe views American Revolutionary theory "as the heritage of the white race, not a set of universal truths," *Dred* portrays Vesey, a black revolutionary, as an American patriot, granting him all the traits and values that ideally accrue to the descendants of the founding fathers.[40] In this spirit, Harry declares that the story of Vesey's insurrection "is just what George Washington's would have been, if [he] had failed" (435). This aligns black freedom with the natural right to self-government that the founding fathers asserted in waging a war for independence, constructing an American nationalism grounded in republican values, an ideological rather than biological legacy separate that can be inherited across racial lines.

This parallel calls to mind an image from *Uncle Tom's Cabin*, and one need only compare the two to see the dramatic change in Stowe's thinking regarding the political possibilities for black people in America. Over the fireplace in Tom's cabin hangs "a portrait of General Washington, drawn and colored in a manner which would certainly have astonished the hero, if ever he had happened to meet with its like."[41] As Riss explains, "Tom's Washington is black."[42] Riss argues that the slave's "attraction to Washington depends as much on Washington's physical appearance as upon his connotation . . . it is not sufficient for Tom merely to worship what this Founding Father represents. If Washington is to be Tom's hero, he must be black like Tom." For Riss, the portrait "exemplifies Stowe's belief that racial homogeneity can provide the only secure foundation for either a familial or a political community." Riss argues that Washington's whiteness "prevent[s] him from serving as the symbolic national Father of black slaves."[43] On the contrary, *Dred* establishes that Washington can serve as the symbolic father of anyone devoted to republican ideals. *Dred* rejects the pervasive theory of separate political lineages, so that in this novel, slaves need not imagine that Washington was black to follow his example. Unlike Taney's impending decision in the *Dred Scott* case, Stowe asserts that the philosophical, not the biological, legacy of the founding fathers should form the basis of American citizenship. For Stowe, race is essential, but political character is defined by ideology, not ontology.

Dred begins as a plantation romance about Southern belle Nina Gordon and her two brothers: Tom, the despotic white heir to the estate, and Harry, the enslaved manager of the estate and the unacknowledged mixed-race son of the Gordon patriarch. Edward Clayton is introduced as one of Nina's several love interests. He reforms her spiritually and politically, and they pledge themselves to emancipation. While the drama of the Gordons and the title character's insurrectionary plot form the core of *Dred*'s action, the novel's comic subplot contains Stowe's most interesting exploration of the relationship between genealogical identity and the social functions of kinship. An ethos of familial performativity emerges through Tiff, who, "though crooked and black, never seemed to cherish the slightest doubt that the whole force of the Peyton blood coursed through his veins, and that the Peyton honor was entrusted to his keeping" (90). The parody of Tiff's unwavering belief in the salience of blood lines, though he serves as the representative of a family to which he has no biological connection, cements the novel's critique of genealogical determinism. Jeffory Clymer notes, "Tiff has dismissed the whole idea of blood as a method of familial demarcation. This may simply be Tiff's tragic false consciousness. Yet Tiff's insertion of himself into the family also has the potential to destabilize the rigid racial biology, built on its fetish of supposed white blood vs. black blood, which supported the entire southern system of economic distribution according to strict genealogy."[44] Through Tiff, Stowe insists that family roles can be enacted by anyone, irrespective of blood relation or "racial" heritage. Tiff's indefatigable insistence on the steadfast influence of the long-obsolete Peytons mirrors the antebellum political tendency to grant an irrational importance to genealogy in determining individual status, the novel's primary target of critique. He shows that "blood" is more powerful than "real" blood; that is, fantasies about family identity (in this case, the honor and superiority of the FFVs) trump actual biological relatedness. Family is a fiction, a conviction, a tradition, not a blood-bound immutable fact.

Known for his mastery of "feminine accomplishments," Tiff emblematizes the performativity of both gender and kinship (91). He wears a red flannel shawl "arranged much as an old woman would have arranged it" and, instead of breeches, two aprons tied around his waist, making a skirt

(82, 332). Moreover, when his mistress dies, Tiff becomes her children's "new mother," demonstrating the performative as opposed to essential nature of both femininity and maternity (397). Tiff even takes on the maternal role of transmitting white femininity. The remarkable passage in which Tiff exposes the performative nature of identity while expounding its essential relation to biology provides the best example of his function in the novel. Tiff outlines the behaviors necessary to the performance of upper-class white womanhood. "You mustn't star, like por white chil'en, and say, 'what?' but you must say 'I beg pardon, sir,' or, 'I beg pardon, ma'am . . . Old Tiff knows what good talk is . . . but he don't want de trouble to talk dat ar way, 'cause he's a nigger" (228). Apparently, Tiff is perfectly capable of using the speech of the white upper class and even demonstrates this by offering some key examples of proper conversation, denaturalizing them with his own ability to reproduce them. Fanny learns to be a white upper-class lady from a gender-bending black man.

Elizabeth Dillon has identified instances of "radically open sociality" in *Uncle Tom's Cabin* in which the mother-child pair is not restricted by biology, race, or even gender.[45] Notably, this utopian possibility becomes available only when the biological tie is broken: "Once the 'natural' mother-child bond is ruptured, unnatural, reconstructed versions of this bond are allowed to circulate."[46] In *Dred*, Tiff's maternal relation to "his children" exemplifies this model of "cross-racial transgendered mothering" (231). Elizabeth Duquette agrees, "Stowe divorces maternity from biology, stressing that this is an ethics, not a mere fact of nature."[47] This is one of many examples in *Dred* through which Stowe theorizes kinship as "a form of *doing*," to borrow a phrase from Judith Butler, rather than a form of being.[48] Butler defines kinship as the performance of practices "that emerge to address fundamental forms of human dependency, which may include birth, child-rearing, relations of emotional dependency and support, generational ties, illness, dying, and death."[49] Tiff's relationship to his white children perfectly captures this sense that kinship is a set of praxes that bear no exclusive relationship to the family as such.

Still, Stowe (and Butler) may be vulnerable to the charge of idealizing kinship despite concerted efforts to dislodge it from the blood family. Some would argue that the paradigm of kinship, no matter how it is delimited, unavoidably produces otherness. For example, Christopher Peterson argues, "In the most literal sense, the term kin denotes an erasure of difference: *you are my kin* means we are the same, we are of the same kind."[50] For similar reasons, readers have found fault with sentimentalism's construction of sympathetic identification because it insists that others must be like oneself to be worthy of concern. For example, Barnes disparages *Uncle*

Tom's Cabin for relying on "an affinitive politics wherein sympathy is made contingent upon similarity: that is, upon one's ability to perceive others as related to oneself."[51] Attentive to how the overvaluation of the family disables the prospect of multiracial democracy with a politics of similitude, Barnes argues that "by displacing a democratic model that values diversity with a familial model that seeks to elide it, sentimental literature subordinates democratic politics to a politics of affinity."[52]

Oddly enough, Stowe's racial essentialism may hedge this critique. In *Dred*, race is essential, but kinship and community are performed across differences that Stowe presents as inherent and immutable. She firmly establishes Tiff as ontologically distinct from the children, dwelling excessively on his jet blackness and exaggerating for comic effect his difference from the white family line with which he so identifies. Although Tiff seems to think it is only natural that he should assume the care of these youngsters, Stowe never allows the reader to forget that it appears outlandish. This subplot establishes that the mother-child bond, the most hallowed and naturalized familial relation, can be performed effectively across social differences and in the utter absence of "natural" ties or female "instincts." In *Dred*, Stowe distances herself from the familial metaphor of national belonging to theorize civic responsibilities between people who are radically unrelated.

Whereas in *Uncle Tom's Cabin*, the family enabled freedom, in *Dred*, entanglement in the family is viewed as another form of slavery. Even beyond the blood family, *Dred* is surprisingly suspicious of marriage and the domestic family. Understandably, the enslaved characters resist marriage because they hope to avoid the added sorrows that it would bring to their condition, such as Harry's resolve "never to marry, and lay the foundation of a family, until such time as he should be able to have the command of his own destiny, and that of his household" (39). Similarly, Milly declares, "True as de Lord's in heaven I won't never be married in dis world" (175)! However, it is not only enslaved people who view marriage in a negative light. We are told, for example, that despite "beaux, suitors, lovers in abundance," Anne Clayton "did not wish to marry—was happy enough without" (27–28). Sue Cripps declares, "O, what a fool I was for being married! O, dear! Girls little know what marriage is!" (83). She implores her daughter, "Fanny, don't you ever marry!" (86). After Sue's death, Tiff remarks of her, "she was so misfortunate as to get married, as gals will, sometimes" (101).

Most strikingly, the novel opens with Nina engaged to three suitors without the intention of being "caught" by any of them. Nina explains, "I think it's a very serious thing, this being married. It's dreadful! I don't want to be a woman grown" (79). Despite her growing attachment to Edward

Clayton, she reports, "He and I are very good friends, that's all. I'm not going to have any engagements *anywhere*" (118). In fact, though they are the novel's central couple, Nina declares to Clayton: "I cannot be bound to anybody. I want to be free . . . there's a feeling of dread, and responsibility, and constraint, about it; and, though I think I should be very lonesome now without you, and though I like to get your letters, yet it seems to me that I cannot be engaged,—that is a most dreadful feeling to me" (131). Clayton responds, "My dear friend . . . There's no occasion for our being engaged. . . . You shall say what you please, do what you please, write when you please, and not write when you please, and have as many or as few letters as you like. There can be no true love without liberty" (131). Friendship stands as the most valuable form of relation in this novel because it does not inhibit individual liberty or republican civic-mindedness. Though she breaks off her other engagements, she agrees to continue her relationship with Clayton only with the understanding that they are not engaged. The novel's ultimate rejection of marriage is Nina's death, which destroys the narrative possibility of the marriage plot ending that it seems to set up from the first pages. *Dred* rejects marriage because it transforms an elective affinity into a binding and proprietary familial relation, displaying an awareness of what Peterson describes as "the chiasmatic relation that obtains between kinship and slavery."[53] He explains, "To claim my kin as *mine* is to invoke an ideology of possession and ownership that is not finally opposed to slavery. . . . While kinship and slavery are not fully identical, they are nonetheless implicated in corresponding forms of corporeal possession and subjection."[54] We see this possessive familialism at work in Nina's blood family as well, specifically in Aunt Nesbit's relation to "her husband and children, whom she loved because they were *hers*, and for no other reason" (42). Also, Harry is described as Nina's "slave-brother," this compound moniker expressing this doubly binding relation (339). In *Dred*, Stowe proffers friendships, coalitions, and assemblages, rather than marriage or adoptive kinship, as the social forms most suitable to republican abolitionism.

The depiction of the Gordon estate debunks Fitzhugh's construction of the southern plantation as an alternative kin structure that provides protection for women, children, and slaves. First, it dispenses with the blood family as a model of natural safety and affection. Tom Gordon, Nina's white brother and the novel's violent, drunk villain, objects to his enslaved half-brother Harry's position as the financial manager of the plantation and Nina's trusted advisor, insisting that he is rightfully "the natural guardian" of his sister (140). Nina reports that her white brother makes her feel "perfectly dreadful," "worried," "anxious," "helpless," and "ashamed"

(137). This sibling pair not only establishes that love does not naturally accrue to blood relationships, it goes even further to present the claims of the family as distressing and despotic. Moreover, considering the rhetoric of sectional fraternalism in this period, this depiction of a tyrannical and dangerous brother suggests that family relation is not sufficient grounds for political unity. Tom represents the unreliability of genealogy as an indicator of worth. His dissimilarity from his noble siblings, who find common ground with fellow activists to whom they are not related, combined with the fact that he does not "care a cuss for the civil authorities," diminishes biological inheritance and puts forward shared political mission as the center of legitimate community (479). Ultimately, inherited character is not failsafe; civic participation surpasses it as a measure of personal worth.

Clayton's court case, which seeks justice for Milly, who has been attacked by the man for whom she has been working, stages most dramatically Stowe's argument against the "alternative" kinship structure of slave society. Clayton originally approaches the case from a position that seems borrowed from Fitzhugh, arguing that slavery is a protective, familial institution in which slaves with no legal rights are taken care of by their owners. He argues that the legal rights and responsibilities of "the parent, the guardian, and the master" must be the same in laws concerning slaves. Only the law's basis in familial protection, he asserts, validates the institution of slavery: "No consideration can justify us in holding this people in slavery an hour, unless we make this slavery a guardian relation" (303). The judge, Clayton's own father, corrects his erroneous faith in the law's rhetoric of paternal responsibility. He rules that the legal position of the slave owner bears no similarity to the familial role of a parent, that the power of the master is absolute and not designed for the protection of the slave. Although the relation of master and slave has been likened to "the other domestic relations: and arguments drawn from the well-established principles, that confer and restrain the authority of the parent over the child. . . . The court does not recognize their application. There is no likeness between the cases" (443). Once his father rends the veil of familial metaphor and exposes the cruelty of the law, Clayton leaves his profession as well as the United States. Abandoning his earlier notion of family as the natural base of responsible politics, Clayton establishes an interracial community based on shared political sentiment and his ethical, as opposed to familial, responsibility to formerly enslaved people.

At the end of the novel, the enslaved characters also flee the South, detach from exclusive kin relations, and remix into hybrid domestic/political assemblages. Underscoring *Dred*'s attention to the performativity of kinship, the African American characters escape to freedom by pretending to be a family: "Harry, Lisette, Tiff, and his two children, assumed the character of a family, of whom Harry took the part of father, Lisette the nurse, and Tiff the manservant" (539). Utilizing a ubiquitous and naturalized rubric of social legibility, these characters travel uninterrogated by the white passengers on their ship north. Performing ersatz family roles, or assuming the "character of a family," allows them to pass into freedom, after which point they create new civic-domestic networks indifferent to official family relation. In lieu of the convention of reuniting blood families separated by slavery, Stowe offers a multipronged conclusion depicting interracial coalitions, her vision of what lies beyond the family and the white nationalism it supports.

Harry, Lisette, and their children make a home in the Canadian community where Clayton lives with his sister. This interracial township resembles a utopian socialist collective in the sense that they share living space, civic projects, and political commitments irrespective of the privatizing forces of the domestic family. Unlike the Apostles in *Pierre*, these communal relations do not fall prey to normative heterofamilial paradigms. VanDette presents the Clayton siblings as an exemplar of the intense brother-sister relationships esteemed in antebellum culture. She claims that they "enjoy their monogamous, marriage-like relationship" after Nina's death so that "the couple that lives 'happily ever after' at the end of this novel, then, is not a traditional pair of newly weds, but a sibling couple."[55] However, when Livy Ray, a school friend of Nina's, comes to live with the Claytons, we are assured that a "most intimate friendship exists between the three" (544). Despite this flirtation with a new partner for Clayton, the conclusion diffuses heterosexual marriage (as well as the sentimental conventions of incestuous marriage and adoptive kinship) into a more group-oriented affinity, once again elevating friendship and denying special significance to relationships that guarantee the reproductive futurity of the social order, the traditional maneuver of the marriage plot.

Although this group prefers to leave the United States behind, *Dred's* African American characters are not banished from the nation as they are at the end of *Uncle Tom's Cabin*. In another interracial community, Milly and her grandson share a tenement dwelling with Tiff and "his children" in New York. "She, finding employment as a pastry-cook in a confectioner's establishment, was able to provide a very comfortable support, while Tiff presided in the housekeeping department" (543). Although this passage emphasizes the flexibility of their nonkin group by flipping gender roles, the structural positions of the domestic family remain relatively intact; Milly takes up wage labor while Tiff keeps house.[56] Their relation to one another is defined by a shared history, shared goals, and a shared household, not a legal marriage that would make their domestic unit a conjugal family.

Despite Stowe's dramatic rethinking of the relation between kinship, nationalism, and narrative development, scholars describe the communities depicted at the novel's end as alternative familial models for an ideal American citizenry: "Stowe's portrayal of these households asserts the possibility—even the desirability—of establishing interracial (though technically non-kin) families within the borders of the United States."[57] Van-Dette agrees: "Stowe is careful not to undermine the nuclear family; rather, she expands the possibilities of familial bonds."[58] Furthermore, Ryan holds that these so-called families "anatomize the future of the nation . . . the hope of a single, reformed nation."[59] By establishing nonblood communities in both the northeastern United States and southern Canada, however, *Dred*'s conclusion takes emphasis away from the nation-state, and its inherent suggestion of a racially homogenous blood-related population, as the preeminent form of political organization. Whereas *Uncle Tom's Cabin* glorifies nationality and dichotomizes the United States with Africa, *Dred* vaunts classical republicanism but mutes the importance of national particularity for black as well as white people. Despite Stowe's focus on the American Revolution as a treasured example of political conviction turned to action, the United States is ultimately inessential to the novel's principles of coalitional politics and interracial community. Stowe's final vision of belonging is anti-identitarian: neither exclusively black nor white, not bounded by national territory, gender fluid, and not defined by heterosexual pairing.

Moreover, critical designations of these communities as families— albeit "alternative," "non-biological" or "(non-kin) interracial families"— demonstrate the enduring power of the familial metaphor as a signifier of legitimate community.[60] These readings shore up the power of the family as the only imaginable form of relation and restore the novel to the very paradigm that it critiques. If "family" can describe relationships by contract, affinity, shared ideology, and civic cooperation as well as by blood, then this institution becomes all-encompassing, effectively dispensing with the possibility of political alliances outside of familial bonds, which are the very essence of democratic politics. Reifying nonfamilial relations as alternative kinship dulls our ability to imagine significant connections definitively beyond the family, lulls us into overlooking the disciplinary work that this simile accomplishes, and provides a false solution to the problematic exclusivity of blood relation.

Tiff and Milly's enactment of an only slightly revised "alternative" to the domestic family anticipates Butler's view that non-normative kinship must initially "assume a recognizable family form" to be socially legible as kinship.[61] However, she maintains that these alternate arrangements have the power to erode the hegemony of the conventional family (the very form through which they become visible) because they "call into question the distinguishability of kinship from community" or "call for a different conception of friendship. These constitute a 'breakdown' of traditional kinship."[62] For Stowe, too, the easily recognizable positions of the domestic family serve as a kind of on/off switch that activates our awareness that these characters inhabit interdependency differently. This is not simply an alternative family that replaces the rejected blood-based and nuclear units but then becomes comparably rigid; Milly and Tiff perform these roles to meet the economic requirements of survival outside the slave system, and this instrumental coalition can disband or change shape to meet the needs of the members.[63] Sociologist Kath Weston observes that longevity seems to be the most significant criterion in Western culture for defining kinship; a relationship is eligible for this designation only if it promises to last forever. Family relationships are generally regarded as more "real" than all other attachments because they are presumed to be long-lasting or permanent, rendering more temporary, contingent, and voluntary relationships meaningless and superficial.[64]

While critics have stressed the affective basis of nonblood relations in the sentimental novel, the assemblages at the end of *Dred* more closely resemble practical networks of the kind theorized by Pierre Bourdieu. Granting the significance of relationships outside of genealogy, Bourdieu notes that there are still limits on who can function as kin, even if that limit is not the bloodline: "One cannot call on absolutely *anyone* for *any* occasion, nor can one offer one's services to *anyone* for *any* purpose." He argues that people work to maintain "a privileged network of practical relationships," a selection of both genealogical and nongenealogical relationships "that can be mobilized for the ordinary needs of existence."[65] For Bourdieu, the limits of kinship are not biological or emotional but rather practical, meaning that the network changes as needs change.

What, then, is the value of retaining the language of kin, which is etymologically based in race, ancestry, blood relation, and essential sameness, when progressive politics can only be diminished by the analogy? In a network defined by practical roles rather than identities in which no difference is observed between genealogical and nongenealogical relationships—in which Clayton's sister, his potential romantic partner, and a formerly enslaved family are all his "friends"—the distinction between kin, nonkin, and elective kin has begun to break down. Rather than prizing a more liberal definition of family, *Dred* suggests that deemphasizing kin distinctions that grant primacy to those deemed to be the same allows other forms of relation that maintain a civic character to flourish.

Ultimately, the experimentation with kinship that Weinstein has observed in the sentimental novel might simply be understood to reflect the modernization of the institution of the family, the move away from traditional blood hierarchies in preference of the conjugal domestic unit and forms of affiliation grounded in consent and intimacy.[66] However, with this shift in the family form, blood-based racial and national identities took the place of the old distinctions based on ancestral lineage. Thus we might understand the cultural work of these novels to be simultaneously installing the familial discourse of nationalism and curtailing dissatisfaction with the increasingly atomized domestic unit by suggesting that anyone (white) might be considered honorary kin, that an institution readers might regard as limited and exclusive is actually malleable and capacious. Along these lines, Carol Singley recently argued that in sentimental adoption plots, "The middle-class adoptive family . . . recapitulates the nation's sense of itself as capable of extending its boundaries and absorbing new ideas and individuals."[67] The interracial coalitions at *Dred's* conclusion, however, cannot be reduced to the conventions of white adoption and substitute kin. Whereas existing critical models of alternative kinship assume that the family is an indestructible social form that will pop back into shape with new members when necessary in order to retain its fundamental meaning and perform its irreplaceable functions, performative or practical affiliation in *Dred* portrays varying levels of human interdependence as instrumental, bearing no necessary relationship to disciplinary, exclusionary blood paradigms, even symbolic ones. Stowe calls readers to regard citizenship as a public performance explicitly designed to govern our relationship to people to whom we are not related. Although the race/family/nation ideology of *Uncle Tom's Cabin* has come to dominate critical understandings of Stowe's abolitionist project, *Dred* calls for a departure from familialism in political thinking, a public unbound by blood.

CHAPTER 4

✃

Resisting Reunion

Anna Dickinson and the Reconstruction Politics of Friendship

In the wake of the Civil War that killed two percent of the population, an exhausted but nominally salvaged United States faced a number of questions, including how to transform military enmity back into national solidarity and how, or whether, to integrate African Americans and reintegrate former Confederates into full citizenship. Many Americans hoped that the sacrifices of the war had won the nation another chance to realize republican ideals, viewing Reconstruction as the opportunity for a second and improved founding. However, the demand for sectional unity ultimately fueled an intensified ethnic nationalism that trumpeted the shared Americanness of whites in the North and South so that the goal of African American advancement was supplanted by the project of sectional reunification.[1]

Although familial metaphors had not succeeded in averting the war, they resumed a central role in the postwar project of white reunion. Gregory Jackson argues that familial rhetoric was used in the Reconstruction era "to diffuse partisan passions by transfiguring them through a sacred idiom held apart from the crass or corrupting world of business and politics. As an affect-saturated institution . . . family evoked our deepest feelings, constituting an emotional zone beyond the rational ken of the political."[2] Similarly, Nina Silber explains, "removed as it supposedly was from the world of crass public interest, the family could apparently nurture and regenerate the type of emotional bonds that would truly and completely heal the national rift. Northerners and Southerners, once joined like a family, would rebuild a domestic union, which would provide the truest and most sincere basis for national harmony."[3] In this way, the naturalizing language of kinship once against served to override ideological division, establishing pure white ancestry as a unifying structure above and beyond the mere political. If the nation's white population was a family, their deep relatedness would stitch them back together even after the worst imaginable rift so that they could realize a shared destiny as one American people.

A number of critics have established that the familial idiom of nationalism shifted in the postbellum years from an emphasis on consanguinity to marriage. Silber notes that "the family metaphor rested less on images of brotherly cooperation or paternal legacies and more on images of marital bliss." This new iteration of the national family metaphor was useful since "a marriage of North and South would be freed from the burdens of a familial past; reunion, in this context, was seen as a new familial entity for the present and the future."[4] Kathleen Diffley observes that in the Congressional debates over the Reconstruction Amendments, deployments of national family discourse "shifted precipitously" toward the "language of gender relations rather than the generational relations that had recently characterized the 'national family.'"[5] In these accounts, the period of Congressional Reconstruction was shaped by the paradigm of heterosexual romance, particularly the institution of marriage, as lawmakers labored to construct a model of affiliation that was both permanent and contractual to imagine recently warring factions as one political entity.

American literature was instrumental in the circulation of these romance narratives of sectional reconciliation that painted over ideological conflict in the service of white cohesion. Popular literature abounded with "romances of reunion," marriage plots between Union soldiers and Southern belles, displacing the political content of the war and recasting the recent combatants as lovers. David Blight argues that in Reconstruction culture, due in part to the vogue for the romance of reunion, "real politics fell by the way, displaced in a flood of marriage metaphors that transformed them into romance."[6] This genre became a mainstay in American culture, offering the vision of social harmony for which many readers longed in the postwar years: "So powerful and compelling was the image of intersectional romance that it would be constantly repeated, refurbished, fictionalized, and dramatized for many years to come."[7] This literature abetted the growing sense that the war was not about slavery or even opposing conceptions of the American political enterprise, but rather a lovers' quarrel that could be resolved with love and commitment.

Among the most celebrated romance-of-reunion writers was John De-Forest, a Union veteran. His most successful work in this vein was *Miss*

Ravenel's Conversion from Succession to Loyalty (1867). This novel usefully displays many of this genre's distinguishing characteristics, including the conventional gender formula that casts the South's feisty resistance but ultimate acquiescence as womanly, the complement to Northern manliness and triumph. As the title indicates, the plot concerns the "conversion" of a Southern woman, typically a diehard Confederate hostile to the Union, its projects, and its representatives. It details her transformation and eventual marriage to a Northern man despite much resistance and many obstacles. In the romance of reunion, intersectional couples make lasting bonds despite what first appear to be irreconcilable differences.

Even writers committed to African American advancement were not exempt from romanticizing white sectional marriage at the expense of racial reform. Albion Tourgée's *Bricks without Straw* (1880) dramatizes how this genre drowns out racial politics with white marriage. The novel begins with a burgeoning critique of the role of normative family structures in the oppression of African Americans. Tourgée charts the transition from the exclusion of enslaved people from marriage and family to the red tape of registering their relationships after the war, including the practice of saddling freedmen and their descendants with the family names of their former owners. Moreover, a friendship between two African American men, Nimbus and Eliab, serves as the central relationship, a bond described as more powerful than family relation and more effective than marriage as a basis for black advancement. But the plot soon shifts to the love story of Mollie Ainslee, a white Northern teacher, and Hesden Le Moyne, a veteran of the Confederate army and heir to an ancestral plantation. Much like Melville's Pierre Glendinning, Hesden experiences a political awakening when his mother threatens to disinherit him if he chooses a wife who would constitute a departure from her aristocratic Southern lineage: "Then he heard his mother's reproaches, and saw that even her love was not proof against a mere change of political sentiment on his part. The scales fell from his eyes, and from the kindly gentle Southern man of knightly instincts and gallant achievements was born—the 'pestiferous Radical.'"[8] Being disabused of his blind filial piety to learn that even a mother's love is contingent on ideological conformity allows him to take a stand against inherited prejudices.

Ultimately, however, the novel recuperates and bolsters the marital and genealogical paradigms that it first seems to interrogate. Molly turns out to be the rightful inheritor of the Le Moyne plantation, her ancestor (Red Jim) having been swindled by his (Black Jim). The couple eventually marries, and the estate becomes their shared property, the nominal color difference and dispute between their forbears obviated along with their sectional difference. As in *The House of the Seven Gables*, hereditary adversaries barred from marriage by an "impassable chasm" of social difference become the rightful joint inheritors of family property.[9] Clearly, although marriage served as the central familial metaphor for a reconstituted national community based on contract and chosen commitment, the paradigm of shared ancestral blood remained powerfully in play. The romance of reunion plot echoes earlier historical romances in its use of the marriage plot to affirm that "blood" distinctions between white Americans of any background have become obsolete.

Constance Fenimore Woolson's "Old Gardiston" (1876) also relies on this conjugal affirmation of Northerners and Southerners as members of the same race and nation through the overthrow of defunct genealogical paradigms, returning to the trope of the decaying ancestral manse. In this story, the South is associated with an archaic, feudal entrenchment in genealogy and ancestral property.[10] Gardis, a fiery Southern belle, keeps up haughty appearances to the Union soldiers who are camped on her grounds, even though the war has completely impoverished her. Her only living relative is cousin Copeland, who barely notices the war or a yellow fever outbreak because he is so absorbed in genealogical research of their remote forebears, such as the "first wife of one of the second cousins of our respected grandfather."[11] Although Gardis initially swears never to marry a Northerner out of loyalty to "her country," Captain David Newell ultimately makes her accept that they share a "common country."[12] Furthermore, affirmations of their anatomical sameness replace the previous emphasis on Gardis's cultural particularity. "You do not, can not, understand the hearts of Southern women," she tells Newell. He responds, "the hearts of Southern women are much like those of other women."[13] Newell also presumably overcomes his initial belief that the complexions of Southern women have a regionally specific creamy color. Interestingly, "Old Gardiston," the ancestral manse, willfully burns itself down at the conclusion of the story. Assuming the ability to speak, the house exposits victoriously that it will never be owned by anyone outside the family, nor be refurbished by the contractor who has purchased it from Gardis, suggesting that genealogical paradigms are beyond recuperation.[14] Gardis can no longer rely on the way of life represented by ancestral real estate, and she has no choice but to move to the North as a wife. This story suggests that Southerners must overcome not only their allegiance to the defunct Confederate States of America but also their aristocratic pride in their noble family lines. But of course, even this narrative of stark conversion from a society based on ancestral verticality to conjugal intimacy is nevertheless marked by the persistence and renovation of blood-based identities. Conjugal love can replace ancestral distinctions and military enmity but only for those who share the modern genealogical properties of race and nation.

Despite the pervasiveness of this genealogical-conjugal Reconstruction rhetoric, historians observe that it met a modicum of resistance. Silber notes that "in this atmosphere of historical amnesia, only a few lone voices called out in protest."[15] She explains, "not surprisingly, some of the staunchest opponents of the early reunion sentiment were former abolitionists, especially those who continued to work for, or feel strongly about, racial reform."[16] These dissenters asserted the need to remember slavery as the real cause of the Civil War. They feared that the nation was quickly losing sight of the goal of black freedom out of a desire to forget the painful conflict. Blight argues that "a small but important group of dissenters, some of them veterans and some from the postwar generation, could not escape the reality of their experience and refused to allow the nation to do so."[17] Blight's account of this literature of dissent is distinctly male-dominated, with particular focus on Grant, Tourgée, and Bierce, privileging narratives that highlight the bloody realities of the war. He posits a conflict between the popular national marriage plot and an emerging ethos of aestheticism: "against this thick growth of the romance of reunion, literary *realism* tried to get traction."[18] Duquette notes a handful of Reconstruction-era writers who theorized models of reunification not centered in marital idiom but also their subordination in an overwhelmingly familial cultural paradigm: "there were options available to writers interested in depicting national reconciliation besides the nuclear family; that authors, including De Forest and Phelps, chose to rely primarily on romantic heterosexual love speaks volumes about Americans' symbolic investment in a particular model of family as the repository of national legitimacy and personal morality."[19]

While Silber highlights former abolitionists who combated the culture of reconciliation in their public speeches and political writings, and Blight focuses on the writings of a handful of men who wrote unsparing accounts of the war and its aftermath, there are also salient examples of literary reactions against the romance of reunion on its own terms that question the efficacy of romantic love and marriage as metaphors for national healing after the war.[20] Offering a reconsideration of the social functions of the literary marriage plot in the Reconstruction era, this chapter turns to an activist novel by one of the most famous American women of this period, Anna E. Dickinson's *What Answer?* (1868). Although Dickinson has been the subject of two biographies, Giraud Chester's *Embattled Maiden* (1951) and J. Matthew Gallman's *America's Joan of Arc* (2006), she is otherwise strangely omitted from histories of the Civil War and Reconstruction period in which she was an influential national celebrity. From a Philadelphia

Quaker family, Dickinson rose to national prominence as an abolitionist orator over several months in 1863. Her ascent was so meteoric that by January 1864, at the age of twenty-one, the entire government assembled on Capitol Hill to hear the speech in which she endorsed Abraham Lincoln's renomination. After the war, she was the most celebrated of the Lyceum speakers. She retained her polemical style, demanding racial justice and women's advancement. In the seventies, she pursued a career as an actress, but the press was increasingly cruel to her as the century wore on. She made headlines again when she was committed to an asylum in 1891 and then sued those responsible for her internment. She died in obscurity in 1932.

Where it is remembered at all, her only novel, *What Answer?*, is known as a clichéd, tragic interracial love story. Unfortunately, most readers of her time as well as our own witheringly contend that Dickinson "was a lecturer and not a novelist."[21] On the contrary, this work is significant not only as a document of the Congressional Reconstruction period but also an intervention into the familial paradigm of American political culture more broadly. Dickinson's critically overlooked work disrupts the conventions of the romance of reunion to call attention to the neglected project of racial integration, insisting on democratic proceduralism, rather than family feeling, as the solution to the nation's political problems. Dickinson does not simply substitute an interracial marriage for the intersectional romance of reunion but rather rejects the facile premise that marriage guarantees social harmony. Moreover, this novel calls attention to the interlacing of genealogical paradigms of race and nation with the conjugal vision of sectional marriage.

The depiction of an interracial romance in *What Answer?* is certainly nothing new if viewed as a contribution to the tradition of "tragic mulatto/a" narratives, many written by abolitionists. However, when located in its proper historical context, it becomes clear that this novel is not particularly interested in the prohibition against interracial sex itself but rather in the relationship of this taboo to both sectional reunion and the fight for universal suffrage. In the 1860s, white intersectional marriage rhetoric was paired with a heightened anxiety about interracial marriage in the wake of Emancipation. Throughout the nation's history, the possibility of an integrated American citizenship has been met with white fears about "social equality" and the interracializing of the population's biological stock. Nancy Cott's study of the national politics of marriage points to both the symbolic and biopolitical roles of this institution: "no modern nation-state can ignore marriage forms, because of their direct impact on reproducing and composing the population. The laws of marriage must play a large part in forming 'the people.' They sculpt the body politic."[22] Furthermore, the debates over black enfranchisement in the 1860s openly considered inter-racial marriage an undesirable potential outcome of the extension of suffrage. Cott explains that "white southerners saw not only political but sexual empowerment in African American men's votes. . . . Civil rights meant freedom of marital choice as well as potential admission to the ballot." Illustrating this connection, she notes that President Andrew Johnson cited the vulnerability of antimiscegenation laws when he vetoed the Civil Rights Act.[23]

Laws governing marriage are aimed at controlling the population rather than romance or sex for its own sake, and *What Answer?* is concerned with the larger rhetorical and biological functions of marriage in relation to citizenship rights and national identity. Specifically, Dickinson debunks the white national remarriage plot, subordinating the role of romance and familial structures in the remaking of national identity to focus attention on the receding goal of a functional and racially integrated democracy.[24] Insisting that ideological battles still raged after Appomattox and rejecting reconciliation with "traitors" to the founding ideal of equality, this novel constructs the Fifteenth Amendment as the final battle of the Civil War.

What Answer? begins much like a romance of reunion. On the streets of New York, we are introduced to William Surrey, the son and heir of a Northern industrial fortune. He soon falls in love with a mesmerizing girl named Francesca Ercildoune who delivers a surprisingly rancorous abolitionist speech at a boarding school graduation. Despite his overwhelming infatuation, Surrey is bothered by one glaring incompatibility. He is patriotic while she is bitterly anti-American. At the beginning of their acquaintance, another character informs Surrey, "Francesca don't like America; she's forever saying something witty and sharp about our 'democratic institutions,' as she calls them; and, if you had looked this morning, you'd have seen that she didn't sing The Star-Spangled Banner with the rest of us . . . she wouldn't sing that, she said,—no, not for anything; and though we all begged, she refused."[25] When Surrey questions her about this, she plainly responds, "I do not love America" (85).

Significantly, Surrey thinks they are having this disagreement because of sectional difference. When she tells him that her late mother was English and that her father is a Virginia gentleman, he thinks, "Southern—Virginia—gentleman. No wonder she has no love to spend on country or flag; no wonder we couldn't agree." This sets up the possibility of an inter-sectional romance and this fiery Southern lady's "conversion," to use the terms DeForest had popularized the year before, from succession to loyalty by her Northern lover. However, thinking back to her impassioned aboli-tionist speech, Surrey corrects this misapprehension: "And yet it can't be that . . . remembering that terrible denunciation of the 'peculiar institu-tion' of Virginia and of the South, he found himself puzzled the more" (88).

This mystery is later resolved when Surrey finally learns that Francesca's father is a Virginian of mixed racial heritage. He married a white English-woman and settled in Philadelphia but never escaped racist discrimination. Before her racial background is revealed to Surrey, however, they have a misunderstanding about Abe Franklin, a black man who works for his father. Franklin's white coworkers banded together and demanded his dismissal from the company, and Francesca mistakenly thinks that Surrey supported them. On the contrary, Surrey detests the racism of Northern industry, but before he and Francesca have the chance to reconcile, war is declared and he joins the fight for the Union cause.

Much of the novel is devoted to representing dramatic wartime scenes and the conversion, not of Southern belles, but of racist Northern soldiers moved by the noble contributions of African Americans to the war effort. The main character in this strain of the plot is Jim Given, one of the workers in Surrey's company responsible for Abe Franklin's ouster. Before his con-version, Jim's speech abounds with racist slurs, fulfilling the stereotype of the working-class Union soldier who hates Confederates and African Ameri-cans with equal vehemence. However, having met Francesca in New York, he excludes her from these pronouncements because of her white appear-ance. Comparing her to a group of "folk" African Americans characters they encounter, he dares his interlocutor to say that she "belongs to the same family,—own kith and kin,—you ca-a-n't do it" (220). He continues: "when I hear anybody mixing her up with these onry, good-for-nothing niggers, it's more than I can stand" (221). He upholds the idea of separate racial families, using the naturalizing paradigm of kinship to justify his tolerance for the beautiful, wealthy, and effectively white Francesca by denying her relation to the African Americans that repel him.

Over the course of the war, Jim witnesses numerous acts of bravery and service to the Union by black soldiers and also black civilians who aid the Union army. He is converted from his racist biases to recognize African Americans as his brothers in arms. Indeed, after the heroic self-sacrifice of a black soldier saves Jim's life, he declares that he will fight "the first man that says a nigger ain't as good as a white man, and a damn'd sight better'n those graybacks" (233). His language here indicates an important strategy used throughout the novel of elevating African Americans over white Southerners. Rejecting the culture of reconciliation, Dickinson remains hostile to the South, pointedly stoking old sectional prejudices.

Noting Jim's enthusiasm for the black soldiers, an officer in the camp observes sarcastically, "the niggers have plenty of advocates here." Jim replies, "we love our friends, and we hate our enemies, and it's the dark-complected fellows that are the first down this way" (234). Evacuating the politicized, racial meaning from the variation in appearance between black and white soldiers, Jim discontinues his use of the term "niggers" and switches simply to "dark-complected fellows," once again reminding readers that African Americans were the Union's "friends" while Southerners were their very real "enemies." This novel asserts the shared American-ness of Northern whites and African Americans while persistently calling Southerners "graybacks," "enemies," "rebels," and "traitors." In this way, Dickinson constructs Southerners as irreconcilably other, even resorting to the language of racial difference when describing the soi-disant F.F.V.s as a distinct "race" characterized by "superciliousness" and other negative qualities (137).

While other Northern white women writers asserted their own participation in the Civil War by plotting the wounds and losses of battle onto the home front, Dickinson prioritizes the representation of masculine combat and bodily sacrifice as the true wartime experience.[26] Her novel particularly emphasizes the loss of limbs to signify the shared suffering and bravery of black and white Union soldiers. Francesca's brother, Robert, for example, carries the flag in the midst of a frenzied battle, holding it high even when his other arm is shattered by a bullet. Surrey also loses an arm, and while he is away on medical leave, he finds himself on a streetcar in Philadelphia with a black soldier missing a leg. A dirty, drunk passenger loudly insists upon his ejection from this "whites only" car. A woman speaks up against this man and when he responds with an insult, Surrey knocks him out with his remaining arm. The woman is revealed as Francesca and the lovers see each other for the first time in two years.

Just before this reunion, Surrey's meddling aunt discovers Francesca's racial background. She demands that Francesca reject his romantic attention in order to salvage Surrey's position in his family and society at large: "His father would disinherit him . . . his family disown him, his friends abandon him, society close its doors upon him. . . . Do you flatter yourself by the supposition that you can be father, mother, relatives, friends, society, wealth, position, honor, career,—all,—to him" (179–180)? Despite these threats, Surrey announces his intention to marry Francesca. His family disowns and shuns him, and they are married against the wishes of the community. His parents, "putting her on the one side, placing themselves on the other, said, 'Choose,—this wife, or those who have loved you for a lifetime. Cleave to her, and your father disowns you, your mother renounces, your home shuts its doors upon you, never to open" (207). They assure him that "no judgment of indifferent strangers shall be more severe than ours" (207). In the romance of reunion, the family supersedes political divisions and guarantees the peaceful cohesion and continuity of the social order. Dickinson, on the other hand, depicts the family as a conservative and disciplinary institution, committed to the preservation and reproduction of existing social relations. Their enunciated strategy in trying to control their son's marriage plans is to make use of the psychological and emotional hold of the domestic family and punish him with harsher treatment than even "indifferent strangers" would offer. Love and commitment do nothing to sway the Surreys' opinion of their son's marriage, and the relationship itself does not result in social harmony. In *What Answer?*, marriage signifies fracture rather than accord.

Meanwhile, even with the consummation of this marriage plot, the novel's focus remains on the soldiers at the front. A newspaper carrying an alarmist account of this high-society interracial marriage reaches the Union troops. In response to a fellow soldier's disgust, Jim jumps to Francesca and Surrey's defense: "'twas the slaveholders and their friends that made a race of half-breeds all over the country; but, slavery or no slavery, they showed nature hadn't put any barriers between them,—and it seems to me an enough sight decenter and more respectable plan to marry fair and square than to sell your own children and the mother that bore them" (216). Touting the decency of an interracial marriage as opposed to the widespread exploitation of unofficial interracial relationships, he continues: "'tain't the living together that troubles squeamish stomachs; it's the marrying" (216). Jim declares that interracial sex is an accepted part of American life, but interracial marriage is disturbing because it violates the legal sanctions that uphold a racialized population when there are in fact no "natural barriers" between people.

The soldiers then engage in a debate about what mixture of white "blood" constitutes white identity. Jim declares, "I call anybody that's got any mixture at all, and that knows anything, and keeps a clean face,—and ain't a rebel, nor yet a Copperhead,—I call him, if it's a him, and her, if it's a she, one of us" (218).[27] This formulation suggests once again that Southerners and their sympathizers do not share the racial identity with Northerners that was widely considered the basis of sectional reunion. Furthermore, it is significant that this construction of an "us" that rejects rebels and Copperheads, despite their whiteness, heartily includes those with any "mixture" of racial background, as well as women. This is an anti-identitarian vision of community based on common political goals, excluding traitors to the Union but welcoming all who would participate, an articulation of Dickinson's goal of race-blind, gender-blind universal suffrage.

However, Dickinson's vision of a new American "us" excludes the foreign-born, especially the Irish, in addition to rebels and Copperheads. These groups figure menacingly in her account of the New York City draft riots, which are described as a "new Reign of Terror . . . an effort on the part of Northern rebels to help Southern ones . . . traitors to the Government and the flag of their country" (272). The hordes who carry out the violence are pointedly described as "not of native growth, nor American born," but "the worst classes of Irish emigrants, infuriated by artful appeals, and maddened by the atrocious whiskey of thousands of grog-shops" (272). Dickinson elevates her patriotic, native-born, wealthy black characters in contrast to lawless, drunken immigrants. Indeed, the Northern white racists who set into motion the three pivotal events that drive the plot are all marked as Irish: the workers that demand Abe Franklin's ouster in the first chapter, the drunk man on the streetcar who demands the ejection of the legless black soldier, and finally this murderous, anti-Union throng.

Surrey, in his Union uniform, is caught in the riot while visiting his old friend Abe Franklin. Franklin is sadistically lynched, and Surrey and Francesca are gunned down near the Surrey family home. As they die, she mumbles to him the line from "The Battle Hymn of the Republic" that they had taken as a vow when he announced his plans to reenlist in the army: "Let us die to make men free" (282). Thus, their deaths in the riot are depicted not as a random incident but rather martyrdom for the Union cause. Dickinson's frightening depiction of the riot is a spectacle of failed democracy. The mob's rejection of the rule of law serves as a dramatic counterpoint to the novel's two privileged civic acts, military service and voting. Dickinson repeatedly asserts that there are traitorous rebels in the North as well as the South, and these two die in their ongoing battle against these forces.

After their quarrel and long separation, theirs is ultimately a failed reunion despite their legal marriage. They sacrifice everything to be together, but the extreme racist climate does not allow them to survive. The couple quarrels during the Civil War, underscoring the analogy between their romantic relationship and national politics. However, their reunion is brief and tragic, indicating the inadequacy of marriage as a model for Reconstruction. This rejection of the culture of familialism that would shore up an unequal model for political relations must be understood not as a failure to imagine a successful interracial romance but rather as a protest strategy that privileges public rather than private modes of integration. Dickinson asserts that the true story of Reconstruction is not the happy reunion of North and South but the failed union of black and white.

The narrative goes on for three chapters, covering two years, after the demise of this interracial marriage, decentering it as the novel's primary subject matter. After the romantic model of integration fails, two other pairs are solemnized as representatives of Dickinson's hope for the postwar future: first, a white northern working-class couple, the converted soldier Jim and his sweetheart Sallie, both transformed by their contact with African Americans; and then an interracial friendship between Francesca's brother, Robert Ercildoune, and Tom Russell, two soldiers who served together and vow to continue the fight until the goal of unfettered black citizenship rights is won. Gregory Jackson has written of the romance of reunion that "this genre's emphasis on the sacrifice and suffering of virtuous citizens of all classes and ranks obscured national and domestic divisions of gender and race."[28] In its tactical revision of this genre, *What Answer?* reinforces the political divisions between the North and South and minimizes divisions based on ascriptive identities like race, class, and gender within Northern society.

The wedding of the white working-class couple, Jim and Sallie, marks the completion of the "conversion" of their racial sentiments. This intrasectional marriage underscores again the transformative power of the war experience for average Northerners, not Southerners. This is a commitment to a rejuvenated North faithful to its wartime goals of social and political equality, in opposition to the romance of reunion's pledge of compromise with the Southern adversary in the name of national continuity.

The pair that ends the novel and encapsulates Dickinson's ultimate hope for the American future is Robert Ercildoune and Tom Russell. "These two young men, unlike as they were in most particulars, were drawn together by an irresistible attraction. They had that common bond, always felt and recognized by those who possess it, of the gentle blood,—tastes and instincts in common, and a fine, chivalrous sentiment which each felt and thoroughly appreciated in the other." Although this description seems at first to racialize class, that is, to assert that Robert and Tom are equals because they come from the same upper-class background, sharing tastes and even "blood," this passage ultimately stresses that their shared past as soldiers "bound them together as with chains of steel" (309). This homosocial rather than heterosexual couple distills the novel's aim of building a basis for integrated citizenship on the shared military sacrifices of black and white soldiers. Once again, Dickinson advances friendship, not family, as the interpersonal relationship most analogous to the coalitional democracy she imagines.

When Robert avoids the polls on election day, Tom scoffs: "a fellow that'll get his arm blown off for a flag, but won't take the trouble to drop a scrap of paper for it . . . it's a ballot in place of a bayonet, and all for the same cause" (310–311). Signaling the novel's key transition from wartime fighting to postwar suffrage, this exchange equates voting with military service so that the use of the ballot should be open to anyone who used the bayonet for the Union's cause. When the two are met by a racist throng barring the black man from the polls, Robert asks, "1860 or 1865?—is the war ended?"[29] This is the question to which the novel's title demands a response. Tom answers, "No, my friend! So you and I will continue in the service" (311). Diverging radically from the cultural imperative for reconciliation, this novel declares that the war is not over. Tom's vow to secure his friend's right to vote is framed as the necessary continuation of their military service together. Whites and blacks loyal to republican values and the rule of law must continue to fight against "rebel" sentiments in the North and South.

This insistence that the Reconstruction period would decide the true outcome of the war was a powerful rhetorical strategy among the few who saw the postwar battle to secure black citizenship rights as the continuation of the Union's fundamental aims. In an 1866 essay, Frederick Douglass declared that the decisions of lawmakers in this period, namely the handling of the proposed amendments, would determine "whether the tremendous war so heroically fought and so victoriously ended shall pass into history a miserable failure, barren of permanent results . . . or whether, on the other hand, we shall, as the rightful reward of victory over treason, have a solid nation, entirely delivered from all contradictions and social antagonisms, based upon loyalty, liberty, and equality."[30] Displaying the same logic that Dickinson utilizes in *What Answer?*, Douglass analogizes the instrumentality of black soldiers in the war effort to the importance of African American rights to a successful Reconstruction: "in conquering Rebel armies as in reconstructing the rebellious States, the right of the negro is the true solution of our national troubles."[31] On this ground, Douglass calls for the protection of the franchise for African Americans, elevating their deserving patriotism in opposition to former Confederates "who do not even conceal their deadly hate of the country that conquered them."[32]

Similarly rejecting the nation's desire to forget the racial goals of the Civil War, *What Answer?* insists that the ideological battle has not been won and must continue. Rather than the social suturing that the romance of reunion offers, this novel focuses instead on instances of violent racist resistance to political change, including the chaos of a young couple killed in an urban riot and two friends violently turned away from the polls. Gallman observes, "Dickinson is clearly illustrating the evils of racism within northern society, but also appears to be questioning the power of a single individual to change such a society."[33] This novel insists that love between individuals is nothing compared to the need for large-scale social change. It holds that the conversion of private feelings is only important insofar as it serves the conversion of public policy.

The novel's final passages appeal to readers to take up the same pledge of continued service to the Union cause until the real war is won: "How and when will it be closed? A question . . . to which America must respond." The final paragraph marshals the enormous cultural power of the Civil War dead to demand that their sacrifice be honored by political action to ensure that the goals of the war are not lost: "From their crowded graves come voices of thrilling and persistent pathos, whispering, 'Finish the work that has fallen from our nerveless hands. Let no weight of tyranny, nor taint of oppression, nor stain of wrong, cumber the soil nor darken the land we died to save'" (312). Three years after the end of the combat, the novel ends by insisting that Americans vow to "finish the work" of the fallen soldiers by protecting black freedom. Historian Drew Gilpin Faust details the profound importance of the Civil War dead in Reconstruction culture. She argues that "sacrifice and its memorialization" was the basis of North/South reconciliation.[34] In opposition to this logic, *What Answer?* ignores the Southern dead because they did not sacrifice to save the Union, focusing instead on black and white Northern soldiers. Aggressively naming the cause of the war even as this became increasingly unpopular, this novel proclaims that "slavery buried these men, black and white, together,— black and white in a common grave. Let Liberty see to it, then, that black and white be raised together in a life better than the old" (246).

What Answer? not only resists sectional reconciliation but also rejects marriage as a symbol of political harmony, putting Dickinson's feminist skepticism of this institution to work for the cause of black male suffrage. The central interracial marriage, seemingly the symbol of a future integrated nation, comes to a tragic and precipitous end, foreclosing the idea that romance can suture social wounds. In its place, Dickinson focuses on the bonds between loyal Northerners across the boundaries of race, class, and gender. A rare example of postbellum fiction overtly hostile to the culture of reconciliation, the novel repeatedly reminds readers that southerners and Copperheads were villainous traitors. For Dickinson, interracial friendship between Union soldiers and respect for democratic procedure, not romantic love between the sections, ultimately epitomizes the ideal American democracy.

Although I argue that the novel pointedly subordinates the role of love relationships in its political vision for Reconstruction, critical responses to

What Answer? in Dickinson's time as well as our own have focused almost exclusively on its depiction of an interracial marriage. One of its first reviewers bitterly announced: "To break down the barriers of prejudice and bring the two races into loving communion at the fireside and the altar; to forget distinctions of color in matrimonial alliances and bring about an era of 'fashionable marriages' between *white bridegrooms* and *sable brides* and *vice versa*—is the express object of Miss Dickinson."[35] Interestingly, even aside from the many who were disgusted by the idea of interracial marriage, debate over the meaning of the novel's central romantic relationship divided its first readers along the lines of the schism between African American and women's rights advocates that defined reform culture of this period. Elizabeth Cady Stanton gave the novel a harsh review, finding its racial thematics hackneyed and ineffectual. Theodore Tilton defended the novel, "pointing out that interracial marriage could be viewed as an affirmation of women's rights," particularly since Southern men had for so long carried on exploitative relationships with black women with no legal ties. Stanton responded by pointing out "that with her marriage Francesca had—regardless of race—essentially abandoned most of her civil and economic rights because she was a woman."[36]

This exchange between Tilton and Stanton was a small battle in a larger struggle between two progressive groups. *What Answer?* was written in support of the Fifteenth Amendment and published during the time of most intense debate on this bill, the ultimate bone of contention between former abolitionist colleagues who split into factions prioritizing either black male or white women's suffrage. Eric Foner offers the traditional evaluation of this rift, arguing that because Stanton and the women's suffragists "reject[ed] the idea that the Constitution should prohibit racial discrimination in voting while countenancing disclusions based on sex, they opposed ratification, thus dealing a final blow to the old abolitionist-feminist alliance."[37] Historians of American feminism date this division to around 1867, the first anniversary meeting of the Equal Rights Association, when Stanton spoke out fervently against black suffrage.[38] Recounting the Fifteenth Amendment in her autobiography, Susan B. Anthony writes, "what words can express her [the white woman's] humiliation when, at the close of this long conflict, the government which she had served so faithfully held her unworthy of a voice in its councils, while it recognized as the political superiors of all the noble women of the nation the Negro men just emerged from slavery, and not only totally illiterate, but also densely ignorant of every public question?"[39]

As a devoted antiracist activist who had also been associated with women's rights throughout her career, Dickinson had to navigate carefully between the sides of this standoff. In her speeches on the Lyceum circuit after the war, Dickinson's aim shifted from abolition to universal suffrage. She proclaimed: "[give] to every intelligent and respectable person, black and white, man and woman, a ballot and freedom of government, and you will see that this country will stand stronger. . . . Let us, then, that justice may be done by the American people, introduce into Congress and pass a bill, of not more than ten lines in length, which shall assert that suffrage in the United States shall be impartial and universal wherever its flag floats and liberty has a name."[40] She imagines a universal suffrage amendment that would enfranchise white women and all African Americans, part of which would soon be realized in the Fifteenth Amendment.

Indeed, some believe that Dickinson had a significant personal role in the drafting and approval of the Fifteenth Amendment. Chester asserts that in September 1866 at the National Loyalists' Convention in Philadelphia, Theodore Tilton, Frederick Douglass, and Anna Dickinson "formulated the idea of a fifteenth amendment to the Constitution to prohibit disenfranchisement of any person on account of race, sex, color, or previous condition of servitude. Not long thereafter the proposal was accepted in slightly modified form by the Republican party and a forty-six word amendment was added to the Constitution of the United States. The word 'sex' was omitted, however, despite the vigorous protests of the women's rights advocates."[41] Gallman offers a different version of this story, asserting that the Southern Republicans actually introduced the bill but that it would have been tabled if Tilton, Dickinson, and Douglass had not taken to the stage and swayed the North and the border states with oratory and recriminations. Either way, Dickinson's friends considered her central to the victory. Frederick Douglass wrote, "To dear Anna Dickinson and brave Theodore Tilton belongs the credit of forcing that amendment upon the attention of the nation at the right moment and in the right way to make it successful." Stanton and Anthony agreed that "to Anna Dickinson belongs the honor of suggesting the 15th Amendment."[42]

To this pair of women's suffragists, it was a dubious honor indeed. Stanton and Anthony often cited Dickinson as a shining example of women's political accomplishments, but her support of black male suffrage galled them. In 1866, when the American Equal Rights Association officially split from the American Anti-Slavery Society, Dickinson chose to attend the women's meeting but would not speak. She evaded Anthony's persistent requests for her official backing, demurring, "I don't like to take up any work till I feel called to it. My personal interest is perhaps stronger in that of which thee writes me than in any other, but my hands are full just now."[43] Despite her "personal interest" in the enfranchisement of women, she stuck to the cause of antiracist activism and did not make an appearance on the platform for women's suffrage until February 1869, the same month that the Fifteenth Amendment passed the House and the Senate, ensuring ratification.

As a Northern white woman reformer who remained firmly on the side of black suffrage in this schism, Dickinson proves an exception to the traditional binaries that structure scholarly accounts of this period. Her novel similarly diverges from the conventions usually ascribed to Civil War writing by Northern white women. While best-selling novels like Louisa May Alcott's *Little Women* and Elizabeth Stuart Phelps's *The Gates Ajar*, both published in the same year as *What Answer?*, focus on the sacrifices and suffering of the women the Union soldiers left behind, Dickinson enshrines military combat as the definitive wartime experience that must be remembered. Noting the link between *What Answer?*'s decidedly masculine subject matter and the author's single-minded prioritization of black suffrage, Gallman writes, "surprisingly, Dickinson explicitly omitted any reference to women who were home-front volunteers, sanitary commission workers, nurses at the front, or facing the loss of loved ones on the battlefield. For an author who had deep commitments to both women and African Americans (both men and women), Dickinson had opted to push one agenda over the other in her first work of fiction."[44] *What Answer?* offers many accounts of black men's bravery and militaristic patriotism to indicate that they deserve citizenship rights in the postwar era but contains no evidence of white women's participation in the war effort that might warrant similar consideration. While her contemporaries focused on white women's home front sacrifices, Dickinson's novel features only one white female character, Sallie, a domestic worker for the Ercildoune family.

In this way, *What Answer?* disrupts critical expectations for the gendered representation of the Civil War. Timothy Morris described war novels like *The Red Badge of Courage* as "disengaged" because of their single focus on combat and the battlefront. He argues that "engaged" stories "deliberately seek to complicate combat experiences with experiences in other arenas, and at times even present battle itself as marginal to the real essence of the war, which they see as social, familial, and marital." He claims that "disengaged war stories are nearly always by men; engaged stories are preeminently women's stories."[45] On the contrary, Dickinson's novel rejects popular representations of the war that cast it into the realm of the social, familial, or marital in order to call attention back to physical sacrifices for the sake of black liberation. The fact that she privileges this subject matter distinguishes her from the female reformers and authors who shape the critical conception of this period.

However, although Dickinson seemingly ignores women's suffrage in this novel, *What Answer?* is by no means bereft of a feminist consciousness. Her public critiques of marriage, in addition to her own personal choice of work over marriage and motherhood, clearly aligned her with the first-wave feminist movement.[46] Chester notes, "Anna spoke for the right of women to enter the professions, to participate in government, to live full, well-rounded lives free from domination of father or husband."[47] Similarly, Gallman observes, "Dickinson would often speak out against the institution of marriage."[48] However, rather than seeing the political aims of women at odds with those of African Americans, she held to a universal vision of suffrage that would embrace both groups. For this reason, even though she was obviously an energetic supporter of the Fifteenth Amendment, she interrupted an American Anti-Slavery Society meeting in 1867 "demanding to know how the Society could support the vote for black men while ignoring the political future of black women."[49]

Although her novel does not explicitly reflect on the political future of black women, it is worth considering, as Tilton and Stanton did, the gender politics of Dickinson's representation of her mixed-race heroine, Francesca Ercildoune. From the beginning, Francesca is characterized not only by her magnetic beauty but also by her intense ideological commitments and her facility with language. Indeed, the descriptions of Francesca's powerful gifts as a speaker recall no one so much as Anna Dickinson herself. This transracial identification calls to mind Karen Sánchez-Eppler's critique of antebellum feminists' rhetorical appropriation of the bodies of enslaved people to symbolize their own oppression under male domination. These representations emphasize "their shared position as bodies to be bought, owned, and designated as grounds of resistance," obliterating "the particularity of black and female experience, making their distinct exploitations appear as one. The difficulty of preventing moments of identification from becoming acts of appropriation constitutes an essential dilemma of feminist-abolitionist rhetoric."[50] In Dickinson's speeches, there is some hint of this language that conflates marriage and slavery, such as when she declared "it is not respect to train a young girl for the matrimonial market, and strike her down to the highest bidder."[51] However, the character of Francesca is not a slave but a wealthy and cultured free woman of color. Moreover, this novel diverges from the tradition of "tragic mulatta" narratives written by both African American and white authors because its depiction of a racist society does not depend on depictions of sexual violence or exploitation against this woman. Characterized by her autonomy and integrity, Francesca is the novel's moral center, aiming her contempt and vituperation at the dismal racial situation of the United States as well as any character contributing to it. She displays the characteristics, including education and political acumen, that Stanton and Anthony claimed made white women more fit for suffrage than black men. Far from using Francesca as a symbol through which to express her own longing for political empowerment as a white woman, Dickinson's heroine is her appeal for universal suffrage that would give all white and black men and women a political voice.

The depiction of this character as well as the politics of marriage in the novel more generally come into relief when compared to another work from the early Reconstruction period, Lydia Maria Child's A Romance of the Republic (1867). In her biography of the author, Carolyn Karcher positions this novel as a reaction against the racial amnesia of Reconstruction culture: "Written against the backdrop of the betrayal Johnson was engineering of all the promises the war had seemingly endorsed—genuine emancipation for African Americans; recognition of the indispensable role they had played as soldiers, spies, and auxilaries; and their incorporation as equal citizens into a truly reconstructed Union—A Romance of the Republic insistently rehearses the history that its white audience was so rapidly forgetting."[52] This novel, however, imagines interracial marriage and reproduction as the symbol of a harmonious integrated political community, adapting the problematic premise of the romance of reunion but simply substituting the interracial for the intersectional. While this novel is exceptional in its positive portrayal of interracial marriage, it still relies on a kind of eugenic logic that offers the biological solution of "blood mixing" to the political problem of racial division.

Moreover, critics have objected to Child's representation of women of color in this novel as vapid, flowery victims to all kinds of patriarchal authority. Interestingly, Karcher argues that A Romance of the Republic fails because of the plot's reliance on marriage while the author was all too aware of its inherent inequality: "as bitter experience had repeatedly taught Child, marriage in the nineteenth century was not an egalitarian institution; hence, it could not provide the model she sought for an equal partnership between the races."[53] The trap of appropriation described by Sánchez-Eppler compromises the political efficacy of this novel. For Child, "patriarchy and slavery are synonymous" and the novel "unmistakably equates the two institutions."[54] Her awareness that marriage was an inherently unequal and even oppressive institution undermined her attempt to execute a narrative that shared the fundamental assumption of the romance of reunion: "Writing within the patriarchal literary conventions that a marriage plot necessarily imposed—even a marriage plot that overturned the bans against interracial unions—Child found it impossible to envision a truly egalitarian, multicultural society."[55]

Dickinson's refusal to model egalitarian social relations on marriage illustrates the radical significance of literary representations of the breakdown of familial structures in the second half of the nineteenth century. A web of national, racial, and gender politics coalesced around marriage as both a metaphor and an institution in the Reconstruction period, and Dickinson's rejection of the culture of familialism that would shore up this unequal model for political relations must be understood not as a failure to imagine a successful interracial romance but rather as a protest strategy that privileges large-scale public rather than individual or private modes of inclusion.

Despite Dickinson's efforts to shift attention away from personal relations toward public issues, her contemporaries scrutinized her private life in relation to her critical stance on marriage. In the decade after the Civil War, newspapers all over the country regularly ran false reports of her engagement to various politicians, newspapermen, and other public figures, although she never actually married. Gallman's biography makes it clear that she had scores of admirers, male and female, with whom she had passionate, if ambiguous, relationships over the years, but she never made a legal arrangement with anyone. The mill of rumors in the press about her purported engagements was paired with a growing hostility toward her for not marrying. She responded a number of times to misogynist accusations tied up with her status as a single woman. One newspaper reported, "Anna Dickinson, in reply to the remark that people call her a 'man hater,' demurely says that it 'depends upon the man.' But Anna herself will never depend upon a man—which is lucky for the man."[56] In 1872, another remarked that "people have come to regard her as a privileged scold. And now that she has become quite too old for spanking, we suppose we shall have to bear with her until she ceases to think herself too young for marrying."[57] The newspapers that had been fascinated with the beautiful and youthful activist a decade before had no tolerance for a woman of thirty who remained unmarried, politically active, and would "never depend upon a man." The Reconstruction culture of forgetting and conciliation wanted her and her reform agenda to be silenced with marriage.

The growing disrespect with which the newspapers treated her was perhaps even directly caused by her refusal to marry; many assumed that her rejection of the editor Whitelaw Reid's proposal was at least partially responsible for her subsequent bad press. Indeed, the most canonical literary revision of the romance of reunion draws upon this situation as a model in its depiction of the crossroads in American reform culture in the Reconstruction period, as well as the penetrating intrusions of the press.

Dickinson's divided allegiance between Reid and Susan B. Anthony seems to be the basis of Basil Ransom's competition with Olive Chancellor over the inexplicably magnetic young orator Verena Tarrant in Henry James's *The Bostonians*. Although there are many fascinating correlations between this novel and Dickinson's life, James was likely unaware of the intimate nature of Anthony's relationship with Dickinson or of the fact that she actually did ask the younger woman to promise never to marry, as Olive does in his novel. More significant is James's use of a Dickinsonian figure to explore how the voice of social reform is silenced in an unhappy union with a former Confederate.[58]

Despite his unflattering depiction of feminists in particular and reformers in general, James's representation of the Reconstruction web of political compromise and romantic entanglements in which Dickinson was embroiled sheds light on the relationship between Civil War memory and the attenuation of activist aims. After all, the pivotal scene in which Verena decides to keep a secret from Olive, the shift that leads to her eventual abandonment of reform for marriage to Basil, takes place at Harvard's Memorial Hall. In this scene, as Ann Brigham notes, "union-making at the national scale intersects with the making of a heterosexual union."[59] Confronting the memorials to the Union dead, Basil "forgot, now, the whole question of sides and parties; the simple emotion of the old fighting-time came back to him, and the monument around him seemed an embodiment of that memory; it arched over friends as well as enemies, the victims of defeat as well as the sons of triumph."[60] His awareness that the war had meaningful "sides" is supplanted by "simple emotion." The process of memorialization effaces the distinction between "friends" and "enemies" that Dickinson stresses in *What Answer?*, even though the Confederate dead are pointedly excluded from Memorial Hall. Brigham observes, "Basil's response to the monument explicitly conveys the replacement of a contested ideological commitment with the memory of an allegiance to fighting and sacrifice." Similarly, "Verena and Basil begin the scene as ideologically opposed; their political differences shape their encounters. By the end of the scene, the language of ideology has been reduced to one of personal allegiance."[61] A cascade of conciliation sentiment results in the realignment of allegiances, and the romance of reunion is realized at the end of *The Bostonians*, although with every indication that it will be unhappy.

However, the historical Dickinson was never swayed by indiscriminate sentimentality for the sacrifices of North and South alike, nor did she allow her personal story to end in the marriage plots into which the press persistently tried to write her. Her own unhappy ending remains obscure. Her life was intertwined with a veritable who's who of the nineteenth-century

American political and cultural scene, including Abraham Lincoln, Frederick Douglass, Mark Twain, Charles Sumner, Harriet Beecher Stowe, William Lloyd Garrison, and many other statesmen, journalists, reformers, and authors. In 1876, one New York newspaper called her "the most talked-about woman in America," yet she died "without heirs, without fame, without friends . . . forgotten by public and history."[62] Her biographers blame alcoholism, a number of scandalous legal battles, and health and psychological problems. I want to suggest that by the end of the century, her unremitting radicalism guaranteed her a place in history's dustbin with all the other unpleasant reminders that the war had been about real conflict, violence, and division. Her rejection of marriage (personally and also as a political metaphor) and her refusal to abandon her mid-century reform tactics resulted not only in a sharp decline in popularity but her erasure from history. Given her undeniable importance, her absence from contemporary consciousness suggests that she was part of the Civil War that had to be forgotten in the name of sectional conciliation.

This trajectory is clear in the disparity between the public responses to two seemingly similar speeches that she made against reconciliation with the South during the war and then after the end of official Reconstruction. On January 16, 1864, barely twenty-one, she spoke on Capitol Hill to the President, the Congress, the Cabinet, and the Supreme Court to great acclaim. She declared, "Let no man prate of compromise!" Insisting that the war must continue, she stoked sectional animosity: "there is not an arm of compromise in all the North long enough to stretch over the sea of blood and the mound of fallen Northern soldiers to shake hands with their murderers on the other side!"[63] This hugely popular speech established her reputation as the young lady who had rallied flagging enthusiasm for the Union cause and told Lincoln how to win the war.

In 1888, she returned briefly to the stage for the Republican Party, which the press called "a case of resurrection." The spirit of compromise that she had railed against had become the dominant political climate, and Dickinson publicly addressed the manipulative prevalence of romantic rhetoric in this culture of reconciliation: "The fashion of the day has been, and is, to talk of the love feast that is spread between old foes, till at last we of the North and they of the South are doing what our forefathers did thirty years ago—grasping hands across the prostrate body of the Negro."[64] Artfully revising Horace Greeley's celebrated image of the North and South grasping hands across the bloody chasm of the war, Dickinson asserts instead that the culture of reconciliation has enabled whites in the North and South to come together over the violent suppression of African Americans. "Young men just voting," she continued, "remember it is your father that lies buried on a Southern field." Again, she called attention to the Civil War dead but not in the hope for sectional reconciliation. Instead, she wanted a new generation to regard the South as a violent military enemy, underscoring familial relation within the North as opposed to between sections. Anachronistically, Dickinson clung to the old abolitionist vow of "no union with slaveholders" two decades after the end of the war. By this time, however, wartime rhetoric had fallen out of favor, and the press eviscerated her. Even the Republicans concluded that Dickinson's return to their platform "did us more harm than good" and wished that she would not "wave the bloody shirt quite so vigorously."[65] Sectional politics, especially her continued insistence on the war's racial and ideological content, had become indigestible in a culture steeped in saccharine white reunion rhetoric.

Despite this increasingly unfavorable response, her contemporaries took for granted that Dickinson was guaranteed a place in history among the most important Americans of her time. Announcing her appearance on the Republican stage in 1888, one Boston newspaper remarked that her return "recalled most vividly one memorable feature of the days during and immediately following the civil war." The author continues with a forecast of how Dickinson's role in the war years would be remembered:

> No complete history of that period can ever be written without taking into account the career of this remarkable woman. Her name will find a place among the names of statesmen, orators and warriors who unitedly led the common people who saved the Union. There was a time when it seemed to Lincoln himself and to his most devoted supporters that no other voice was so potent in kindling patriot fires in breasts burdened with discouragement as was the voice of the brilliant, magnetic and loyal girl who went everywhere, throughout the North, speaking to listening thousands.[66]

Of course, histories of the Civil War and Reconstruction have paid no significant attention to Anna Dickinson. Her name is not remembered among the leaders who saved the Union, or even among this period's familiar pantheon of activists, despite her astounding prominence in politics and in the culture at large. This omission has abetted both the historical enshrinement of the male leadership of the abolitionist movement and also the blanket allegation of American feminism's alliance with white supremacy, which I reevaluate here and in the following chapter.[67] Scholars have been wedded to a reading of this period that silences an important voice of reform, carrying on the culture of forgetfulness that Dickinson critiqued.

CHAPTER 5

cᴏᏙᴏ

"Why I Hate Children"

The Willful Sterility of The Country of the Pointed Firs

Woman has never attempted one advanced step which has not been blocked by these two words—wifehood and motherhood.
> —Ida Harper, "Small vs. Large Families" *The Independent* (Boston, MA),
> December 26, 1901: 3056.

Although Anna Dickinson and her contemporaries lost the fight for a Fifteenth Amendment providing universal suffrage, women made significant sociopolitical inroads in the postbellum era, and American feminism grew into a full-fledged movement. With the emergence of the "New Woman," who had access to higher education and career prospects outside of marriage and motherhood, female roles seemed on the verge of complete redefinition. But just as the rhetoric of white family endangerment was used to hinder programs for African American civil rights both before and after the Civil War, white women's advancement met with reactionary cries of alarm about the negative consequences of sexual equality for the family, the race, and the nation. Specifically, many commentators blamed women's activities in traditionally male public realms for a declining white birthrate that would soon lead to the demographic ascendancy of people of color and recent immigrants. The willful childlessness of "female reformers" became a favorite scapegoat for antifeminist attacks during a period of pronatalist politics that flowered into the eugenics movements of the early twentieth century.

For foes of women's education, *Sex in Education; Or, A Fair Chance for Girls* (1873) by Dr. Edward H. Clarke, an overseer of Harvard University and a physician at its medical school, offered scientific evidence that women's academic pursuits were unnatural and dangerous. This runaway bestseller argued that higher education not only made women unwilling to marry but also interfered with menstruation and caused a variety of reproductive diseases. Clarke recounts instances of women he has attended who "graduated school or college excellent scholars, but with undeveloped ovaries. Later they married, and were sterile."[1] Women's rights advocates sprang into action to disprove Clarke's influential argument, publishing four book-length rebuttals within the first year.[2] Unfortunately, these debates about the reproductive consequences of women's education succeeded in reorienting the conversation away from civic inequality back to women's biological and social responsibilities to the family.[3]

The idea that upper-class white women in the northeast were either refusing the traditional duties of childbearing or unfitting themselves for the task by pursuing public advancement became an issue of widespread political discussion. Theodore Roosevelt assailed the falling white birthrate throughout the 1880s and '90s as well as during his presidency. He declared that "unquestionably, no community that is actually diminishing in numbers is in a healthy condition . . . no race has any chance to win a great place unless it consists of good breeders as well as of good fighters."[4] Roosevelt expressed his sympathy for people who are childless "from no fault of their own" but avowed that "the man or woman who deliberately forego these blessings, whether from viciousness, coldness, shallow-heartedness, self-indulgence, or mere failure to appreciate aright the difference between the all-important and the unimportant,—why, such a creature merits contempt as hearty as any visited upon the soldier who runs away in battle."[5] For Roosevelt, only adherence to the gendered roles of reproductive femininity and militaristic masculinity would safeguard the perpetuation of the white race and the national future. The decline of the white birthrate over the course of the late nineteenth century induced panic that "willfully sterile" white Americans would be outnumbered and overpowered by racial minorities. Coined by Edward A. Ross, the term "race suicide" came to describe the ultimate fear underlying this apocalyptic mix of antifeminist and anti-immigration ideologies. After Roosevelt used the term in print in 1903, it became a household phrase, circulating widely in the press and even appearing in the title of a 1904 silent film, *The Strenuous Life; Or, Anti-Race Suicide*, which depicts a white middle-class man coming home from work to find his wife giving birth to multiple babies, a comic representation of Roosevelt's national reproductive imperative.[6]

Paranoia that white women's increased freedom was depressing the white birth rate had been brewing for decades, especially in and around Boston. In 1867, one commentator decried the deliberate suppression of white births as a problem stemming from the region's women's rights agitation: "The anti-offspring practice has been carried in New England and wherever New England ideas prevail. These female reformers see that if they are to act the part of men in the world, they must not be burdened with the care of young children."[7] By the time the "race suicide" panic peaked in the early twentieth century, New England was well established as the locus of the problem in the minds of nativists and antifeminists, and its documented decline was regularly cited as a signal of an impending national crisis. In 1882, Nathan Allen, a New England doctor, revisited the 1860 census to argue that the foreign-born population of the region had long been producing more children than the native-born population.[8] In 1907, Ross reported that "the native married women of Massachusetts bear only seven-elevenths as many children as women coming in from Germany, seven-thirteenths as many as those from Ireland." He blamed this state of affairs in part on "the emancipation of women."[9] Taking stock of earlier studies in 1917, sociologist Warren S. Thompson noted that "most of the evidence of race suicide comes from investigations made in New England." Scholars of the region, he reported, "have borne almost universal testimony to the effect that the families of the older native people are smaller than those of the newer immigrant peoples."[10] In a 1930 article, Joseph J. Spengler, a professor of economics, confirmed that "the native stock of New England was dying out in the latter half of the nineteenth and in the early part of the twentieth century" because "the fertility of native women has been lower than that of foreign women."[11]

New England's perceived decline was regarded as particularly tragic in light of its proud role in national history. Social scientists citing demographic evidence of this region's plummeting birthrate often emphasized its symbolic significance. Daniel Webster and others in the antebellum period popularized the notion of a literal bloodline connecting the Plymouth settlers to the Revolutionary founders, making New England the nucleus of American genealogy. At the turn of the twentieth century, many Americans wondered, "Is the Puritan Race Dying Out?"[12] Richmond Mayo Smith commented in 1888 on new citizens' inauthentic relationship to the founders: "One-half of the people of Massachusetts can no longer speak of the constitution as the work of the Fathers except in an adoptive sense; and it is scarcely possible to conceive of the Fathers adopting the mass of Catholic

Irish and French-Canadians and beer-drinking Germans who make up the foreign-born."[13] Smith indicates that "natives" of Massachusetts hold the filial relationship to the founders that constitutes real Americanness, a national identity based literally in biological inheritance, not a symbolic or "adoptive" legacy. Similarly, as Thomas Gossett explains, Harvard English Professor Barrett Wendell argued in his *Literary History of America* (1900) "that the greatness of New England letters from 1830 to 1860 was to be attributed to the fact that the region was then almost racially homogeneous."[14] Thus the "woman's movement," with its emphasis on opportunities for women beyond the home and the attendant curtailment of reproduction, seemed to threaten the very character of American identity and its basis in white ancestral blood.[15] As an article in the *Medical Times* put it: "As the lineal stock of our representative families is becoming voluntarily more limited . . . the unrestricted progeny of the underfed ignorant toilers . . . the encroaching offspring of the prolific Negro, of the stoic foreign representatives of recent immigration [are] more and more profusely encumbering our shores . . . the jargon of foreign tongues, the dense stare of foreign eyes, appeal to our sense of concern for the future of the home of the brave of the past."[16] Academic studies of New England's decline in the late nineteenth century provided the basis of the race suicide panic and subsequent eugenic programs to control both immigration and sexual reproduction with the aim of preserving and perpetuating white supremacy in the United States.

The accusation of race suicide was lobbed at women who advocated any form of civic equality. For instance, the *LA Times* reported in 1910 that a Catholic priest had denounced "those of the weaker sex who seek to vote, for advocating race suicide. Calls them murderers."[17] In the face of such outrageous attacks, women reformers responded with a variety of rhetorical strategies. Some marshaled their own scientific data to prove that equality was not detrimental to women's reproductive capacity. Others embraced the idea that reproduction must be used to biologically engineer a more desirable national stock. Most famously, Margaret Sanger couched her arguments for contraception in the assertion that it would "assist materially in the improvement of the race stock. . . . Given Birth Control, the unfit will voluntarily eliminate their kind."[18] A litany of scholarship has averred that the ideology of the New Woman relied on racist reproductive politics: "nearly all feminist activism of the late 1800s to early 1900s was intertwined with the social purity movement and often with eugenics."[19] The reactionary familialism employed against women's rights undeniably drove many white feminists into an alliance with eugenics in an attempt to theorize how the curtailment of reproduction might actually benefit national strength. But critical accounts have focused so exclusively on this eugenic turn in first-wave feminism that we have neglected to see a conflict between the demands of white nationalism and women's antifamilial political desires in this period. Other strains of late-nineteenth-century feminist thought refused to bow to pronatalist logic, insisting that the value of women's lives did not rest entirely on their reproductive capacities.

According to historian Linda Gordon, the race suicide controversy marked a turning point in the relationship between American feminism and the family. Feminists were forced to "reject the cult of motherhood, which they had previously shared with more conventional women."[20] While earlier discourses of republican motherhood and domestic feminism affirmed women's importance within their traditional roles in the home and family, women acknowledged for the first time that these roles were actually the primary obstacles to their advancement. Gordon concludes that "the most radical response to the race-suicide attack was one that reinterpreted woman's role and 'duty' altogether" and asserted elective childlessness for women who wished to be socially useful in other ways.[21] Indeed, some defiantly enumerated the demerits of motherhood in their arguments for equal access to public life. For example, a writer identifying herself only as a happy and successful but "Childless Wife" explains: "we believe that to have children would be detrimental to our usefulness as members of society, detract from the happiness of our marriage and make us lower, not nobler, people."[22] Although this woman clings to the title of wife, she explains that she wants to continue to pursue a career in social work that benefits a multitude of people rather than shut herself up at home as the mother of a few children. Another woman responding directly to Roosevelt suggested not only that the birthrate was not yet low enough but also that men had no right to talk about it: "The greatest trouble is that there are too many unwelcome children born into the world. Men should leave the discussion of this matter to women —women who put their life in danger in bringing children into the world."[23]

The ideology of sexual equality achieved in part through the control of reproduction was not entirely new at the turn of the twentieth century; it had long been central to the agendas of Free Lovers, Fourierists, Perfectionists, and other utopian socialists that foregrounded the oppression of women in their arguments to abolish monogamy. Faced with accusations that they sought to destroy the family, many radicals readily acceded to this position. Victoria Woodhull, for example, delivered an address to as many as 250,000 people in cities across the United States in 1874 in which she declared her commitment to "relentless warfare against marriage." "It is a fraud upon human happiness. . . . I enter the fight, meaning to do the institution all possible harm in the shortest space of time; meaning to use whatever weapons may fall in my way with which to stab it to the heart, so that its decaying carcase [sic] may be buried."[24] She describes marriage as a "terrible curse," "the bane of happiness," and "the most consummate outrage on women" that has been "gilded over by priestcraft and law . . . to mildew and poison their lives." Specifically, she asserts that marriage "invests men with the right to debauch women, sexually, against their wills."[25] This view of the conjugal family as the site of women's sexual violation, rather than the sanctified sphere of their influence and protection, reveals a radical alternative to "domestic feminism," even before the Civil War. Writing in 1852, Marx Edgeworth Lazarus, an anarchist Free Lover from Alabama, stripped the veil from sentimental discourses of domesticity and motherhood: "To have a house of one's own to keep, or even superintend, is a systematic slavery, an immolation of one's personal predilections and pursuits on the altar of the family and domestic comfort."[26] In their 1854 tome against marriage in favor of Free Love and Fourierism, Thomas and Mary Gove Nichols state, "Marriage, with its almost invariable attendant, and involuntary, compulsory, often repugnant, and almost always, painful maternity, is the cause of disease, suffering, and premature death to both mother and offspring. . . . When women are set free from the domestic servitude of marriage . . . no man will have the power to force them to have children."[27] For these reformers, women's roles in the domestic family are the most egregious form of oppression, a lifelong affront to bodily integrity that must be abolished if eventual sociopolitical equality is to be achieved.

Nineteenth-century feminism with an antinatalist edge also found its way into fiction. In George Noyes Miller's novella *The Strike of a Sex* (1890), the narrator, Rodney Carford, finds himself in a strangely dilapidated town populated exclusively by men, the opposite in many ways of the hyperfunctional all-female utopia of Charlotte Perkins Gilman's *Herland*. He observes that the men's tattered clothes have no buttons, the houses are in disrepair, and the smells of burning rags and rotting food fill the air. A man on the street tells him that all the women, of every age and class, have been on strike for more than three months, that they have quit their habitations with men and are living together in a commune overlooking the town. He reports: "They say that the chains which have bound them for unnumbered ages, although artfully garlanded with flowers and called sentimental and endearing names, are older and more galling than those of any bondspeople on the globe."[28] Carford assumes the women are striking to gain property rights, suffrage, and equal wages. His new acquaintance, Justin Lister, informs him that those rights were granted within the first two weeks of the strike. Their fundamental grievance is not civic or economic but rather "they demand, as an inalienable right, that man shall give them an irrevocable, perpetual guarantee, that no woman from this time forth and forever, shall be subjected to the woes of maternity without her free, specific consent."[29] In other words, they want a system of "voluntary motherhood," advocated not only by radicals but even the most mainstream first-wave feminists. If this demand is not met, the women "will allow the race to lapse from the face of the earth."[30]

The narrator reads a copy of the newspaper the women print every morning called the *Bitter Cry*. The first article tells the story of Timothy Totten, an unwanted child and eventual burden to society, doomed to failure from the moment of his undesired conception. Another article headlined "WHY I HATE CHILDREN" observes, "Poetically speaking, children are the rosebuds of life; practically they are the torments of existence." Seeming preemptively to discount any objections based on the idea that many women choose and enjoy their womanly duties, the author insists that "if there be now and then a woman who is content to become a mere propagative drudge, the great majority of them are not."[31] Like Dickinson's *What Answer?*, this novel concludes not with a marriage, but with a vote. The men agree that women will henceforth have the power to control the frequency of pregnancy as they see fit. In the sequel, *Zugassent's Discovery*, Miller offers lengthy verbatim passages on the practice of "male continence" from the writings of John Humphrey Noyes, founder of the Oneida Perfectionists, to explain how men might prevent sexual intercourse from resulting in conception.[32]

Although Miller does not specify the location of this town in which the women have segregated themselves in a birth strike, the gloomy, childless place he depicts might put one in mind of the depopulated New England towns described by social scientists analyzing the "race suicide" phenomenon. In both *The Strike of a Sex* and *Zugassent's Discovery*, Miller makes use of the conventions of local color fiction to depict women who have realized that their freedom and equality depends on curtailing reproduction. Indeed, the canonical imaginative literature of late-nineteenth-century New England displays even more pronounced affinities with the sociological discourse of regional and racial decline. As in the writings of early "race suicide" alarmists, a preoccupation with the composition and reproduction of populations animates the representations of seemingly homogenous white communities in local color fiction. Stephanie Foote argued that this genre is marked by "a general concern over origins and nativity" and an exploration of how communities are formed through exclusion: "ostensibly coherent regions are the products of suppressed relationships between natives and strangers."[33]

In addition to its investment in constructing a homogenous New England, this genre is characterized by its focus on old women who represent the dwindling of noble ancestral stock and a peculiar relationship to marriage. The stories of Mary Wilkins Freeman, for example, are often built around a perversion of the marriage plot. "A New England Nun" ends with Louisa Ellis's resolve to live as an "uncloistered nun" because she prefers "serenity and placid narrowness" to marriage.[34] Stories like "Two Old Lovers" make romantic love pathetic and grotesque, even asserting outright that "there was something laughable" about the decades-long courtship of the elderly characters Maria and David. This tale concludes with a deathbed proposal of marriage, which will never be realized.[35] The main character of "A Humble Romance" claims "inheritance from some far-off Puritan ancestor," but her physical description suggests the decay of this proud national bloodline: "Her finger joints and wrist bones were knotty and out of proportion, her elbows, which her rolled-up sleeves displayed, were pointed and knobby, her shoulders bent, her feet spread beyond their natural bounds—from head to foot she was a little dischordant note."[36] She is married then abandoned then rejoined by a tin-peddler who was already married. Although the story ends with the hint that the couple will finally be united legally, just as "Two Old Lovers" ends with a proposal, both stories rely on this traditional plot structure only to present romantic love and marriage as ludicrous. Freeman focuses instead on the industry, resourcefulness, and resilience of New England women, portraying men as clumsy, slow, disruptive, unreliable, and ineffectual.

The most canonical work of New England regionalism, Sarah Orne Jewett's *The Country of the Pointed Firs* (1896) accords in many interesting ways with anxious arguments about race suicide. Set in a formerly prosperous but now exhausted seafaring town, this novel describes two funerals and notes a number of recent deaths among the elderly residents, but there are no children or young couples to signify this community's continuation into a future generation. It depicts New England in its dotage, nostalgic about its past racial greatness. Jewett's postfamilial, postreproductive world empowers women, but the consequence is that the community will not be reproduced biologically. In fact, the novel ends with three scenes that seem to prefigure the community's death and disappearance. Jewett's depiction of a moribund Maine town dovetails with contemporary sociological and political concerns about the diminishing reproductive output of New England and its relationship to the health of the nation at large. Balancing nativist anxiety with feminist utopianism, her work offers a complex appraisal of what it would mean for American women to abandon the imperatives of the family and the racial teleology it supports. *Country* exemplifies the inevitable conflict between white nationalism modeled on reproductive futurity and early feminism's antifamilial political desires.

Classic critical accounts of *The Country of the Pointed Firs* often dwell on its gloominess. Werner Berthoff pronounced in 1959 that the book leaves "an indelible impression of a community that is inexorably, however luminously, dying." He observed that Jewett's New England towns, peopled only by "the old, the retired, the widowed, the unmarrying, the sick, the mad, the 'uncompanioned,'" exhibit the effects of a "creeping decay."[37] Ann Douglas Wood found the genre to be so overwhelmingly bleak that she disparaged Jewett and other regionalist writers for delighting in the abnormality of women who are "barren and childless . . . alone, superannuated, almost deformed."[38] The second-wave feminist critics who reclaimed *The Country of the Pointed Firs* and vaunted it to its now canonical status largely ignored or denied its dark qualities, constructing the text instead as a celebration of vigorous women inhabiting "a realm of mystical female powers."[39] These critics lauded the text's emphasis on women's community and natural healing, its circuitous narrative structure, and its departure from heterosexual gender norms.[40] In the 1990s, considerations of gender were largely supplanted when Jewett scholarship took an important turn toward reevaluating the novel's racial politics, and the critical tone changed accordingly from adulating to censorious. In her introduction to *New Essays on The Country of the Pointed Firs*, June Howard explains that the collection "deliberately revisit[s] the familiar landscape of Jewett criticism" to expose "how deeply racialized and nationalist are the categories through which Jewett constructs her local solidarities," a project that aims to temper earlier feminist zeal.[41] Gauging the excesses of this swing of the scholarly pendulum, Marjorie Pryse contends that "critics who fault Jewett for racism and classism have attempted to 'overwrite' feminist criticism of her work."[42] Indeed, renewed attention to the analytics of gender and sexuality in *The Country of the Pointed Firs* can help clarify the novel's confounding racial politics.

In reconsidering Jewett's conception of community, critics have diagnosed the novel's affirmations of racial dominance and American imperial strength while ignoring its strangely decrepit representation of whiteness. A relatively recent reading by Heather Love was the first to confront fully the negativity of Jewett's representation of women living outside the family matrix: "The community that she imagines exists outside traditional narratives of marriage and biological reproduction; its beauty and singularity are linked with its fragility—and it can fail."[43] Furthermore, if we consider what Karen Sanchez-Eppler calls the "analogy between nation and nursery" in the nineteenth century—that is, the "similitudes between the national projects of raising good, white, middle-class, Christian, American children and that of raising an economic and cultural American empire"— then Dunnet Landing's elderly, uncoupled population takes on ominous political significance.[44] Positioning whiteness as simultaneously preeminent and exhausted, this overwhelmingly barren novel is a dystopic vision of demographic crisis, a forecast of imperiled American political futurity through reproductive sterility. Jewett's depiction of an aging women's community suggests that increased autonomy from the family contradicted the reproductive imperative of white nationalism.

Feminist critics rightfully rejected misogynist associations of local color fiction with pathological spinsterism and sterility, but when considered alongside contemporaneous writings about the decline of white New England, the emphasis on social decay in older readings of *The Country of the Pointed Firs* takes on new meaning.[45] Wood notes that in local color writing, "women appear a breed destined to extinction: the possibility hovers . . . that after the death of the last old lady in the last old house, there will be no women at all."[46] If we consider women not as themselves a separate "breed" but rather in terms of their duty to breed for the continuation of races and nations, their impending extinction in the region's literature bears striking similarities to the nativist paranoia that New England's unconventional, unreproductive women would bring about the extinction of racial whiteness.[47] Jewett offers an ambivalent account of the conflict between women's autonomy and the reproductive imperative of white nationalism without yielding to the demand that the social order must survive.

Rather than offering *The Country of the Pointed Firs* as another straightforward example of the insidious coalition of turn-of-the-century feminism with racist national futurism, I want to suggest instead that this text portrays the demands of white nationalism and feminism as conflicting and not easily reconcilable.[48] Racial nationalism characteristically stresses the importance of fecundity to ensure a political future; thus a community that allows women to live alone without having children is in opposition to this project. While some feminist discourses of this time asserted the centrality of the maternal function to civilization and seized upon the political significance granted to reproduction in eugenic thought, Jewett imagines women empowered by curtailing reproduction.

It would be possible, however, to overstate the radical intentions of Jewett's antinatalist feminism. Returning to Caroline Gebhard's discussion of local color's association with spinsters, Judith Fetterley and Marjorie Pryse recently suggested that in the context of Roosevelt's America, "we might understand the refusal of white women regionalists to place their fiction in

the service of reproducing 'true Americanism' or white Anglo-Saxon masculinity as a form of antiracist work, a form of white critique."[49] I maintain
that the convergences of *The Country of the Pointed Firs* with nativist discourse limit the extent to which we can consider it resistant to racist ideologies. This novel neither advocates a childless women's community to
undermine whiteness nor promotes a revised gender scheme to revitalize
white America's future. Rather Jewett conceives of a world in which unmarried and childless women like herself are happy, productive, and more
powerful than the men in their community, and simultaneously registers
that the result of this lifestyle is the end of reproductive futurity.

Sarah Orne Jewett, a lifelong Mainer and the descendant of two old New
England families, devoted her life to her career as a writer and never married or had children. Critics have described her long relationship with An-
nie Fields as "a classic, or perhaps *the* classic, 'Boston marriage.'"[50] Her
firsthand knowledge of small communities in coastal Maine and of women
whose lives were not centered in men and families formed the core of her
literary project. Jewett's first novel, *Deephaven* (1877), depicts "a quaint old
place which has seen better days."[51] Although "it was impossible to imagine
any children" in this traditional New England town, populated as it is with
elderly folks, the narrator pointedly observes that at least "there was no
disagreeable foreign population."[52] The young female protagonists attend
"a free lecture on the Elements of True Manhood." During its delivery, they
are barely able to contain their laughter because the talk "was directed entirely toward young men, and there was not a young man there." Indeed,
the most prominent male in the audience is "a deaf little old man with a
wooden leg."[53] Although the scene seems to ridicule the contemporary cult
of masculinity, it also illustrates precisely the situation advocates like Roosevelt were seeking to address, namely the absence of "true" men.

The Country of the Pointed Firs is similarly devoid of young men. In the
town cemetery, the narrator notes, most of the "graves were those of
women," since many of the town's men died away from home, "some lost at
sea, and some out West, and some who died in the war."[54] This observation,
ostensibly about the town's dead, soon turns to those who have elected to
live and die elsewhere, thus aligning other forms of depopulation with
death. In his 1917 article on race suicide, Thompson claimed that in rural
New England, "the more active, wide-awake, and ambitious men and
women have either gone west to new lands or they have migrated to the
cities to seek their fortunes. This has had a detrimental effect upon country
life and is probably responsible in large measure . . . for the decadent population now to be found in the rural districts of these states."[55] With the Civil

War long over, the closing of the frontier proclaimed by Frederick Jackson Turner in 1893, and the shipping industry greatly diminished, the narrator's allusion to the men of Dunnet Landing who had once fought wars, settled the land, and fished the seas resonates with the 1890s fear that white men, with no arena remaining in which to test their masculinity, were contributing to the decline of white American culture.

The narrator's sketches of the elderly men she encounters in the tale's rural Maine setting support Roosevelt's fear that men's lack of opportunity for exerting their masculinity would render them effeminate and sterile. She finds Captain Littlepage to be "delicate." Elijah Tilley cries and knits; he assumes his departed wife's gendered behaviors, like keeping house and showing the tea things to visitors. William Blackett, described as "son an' daughter both" to his mother (39), is criticized by his sister, Almira Todd, for lacking "snap an' power" (48). Not surprisingly, in this nonheterosexual, indeed noncoupling, world, the narrator reports that "he ain't disposed to be very social with the ladies" (40). Noting the narrator's ambivalence about these enervated characters, Susan Gillman observes that "their pathetic lives suggest that such gender reversal, and the freedom imagined along with it, are disturbing in the context of present social and economic conditions in Dunnet Landing."[56]

Aside from a few doddering men, Jewett's New Englanders are characteristically older, unmarried women. A scene in *Deephaven* describes the hobbling approach of "Widow Ware and Miss Exper'ence Hull, two old sisters . . . under the shadow of the two last members of an otherwise extinct race of parasols."[57] The comic description of their antiquated accessories cloaks the darker implication that the women are themselves among the few remaining relics of a dying race, a conclusion underscored by the repeated characterization of other elderly female townspeople as "the last of her generation" or "the last survivor of one of the most aristocratic old colonial families."[58] Jewett's depiction of the vanishing town, which clearly resonates with contemporary fears about the decline of New England's "natives" and the putative loss of their way of life, is particularly interesting for its conflicted view of the role of unconventional women. Although Jewett's fiction imagines women freed from reproductive obligations and thus capable of pursuing their own creative interests, it suggests that the achievement of personal productivity at the expense of familial reproductivity is not without cost to the community.

The Country of the Pointed Firs extends *Deephaven*'s concern with the relationship between New England's decline and the empowerment of childless women. With the exception of the middle-aged narrator, the town seems to be inhabited solely by elderly people, particularly women. The narrator, a writer who has traveled to Dunnet Landing from Boston to spend the summer practicing her craft, is an unmarried New Woman who describes herself as "no longer young." She lodges with Almira Todd, a hardy, long-widowed herbalist of advanced middle age. Other characters include Todd's mother, Mrs. Blackett, a spry, elderly woman living on a nearby island even more remote than Dunnet Landing, and Susan Fosdick, "a serious-looking little bit of an old woman," a prolix visitor and the last member of a large seafaring family (57). Far from an unmitigated celebration of these resilient women, however, the text's anxiety about their non-reproductivity suggests that their unconventional social order is valiant but not viable. Defiance of patriarchal, heteronormative gender differentiation and marriage allows women unprecedented personal freedom but does not ensure the continuation of families, races, or society itself. The novel depicts a community "actually diminishing in numbers" due to its lack of "good breeders," just as Roosevelt feared.

The narrator's ambivalence about the female culture she temporarily inhabits is perhaps most obvious in her treatment of "poor Joanna." In one of the many storytelling sequences that structure the novel, Mrs. Todd shares with the narrator the tale of Joanna, a woman who lived and died alone in self-imposed exile. Having moved into a tiny cabin on deserted, inhospitable Shell-heap Island after her plans for marriage collapsed, Joanna shunned human contact for the rest of her life. The novel's attitude toward Joanna, who carries the New Woman's ethos of independence to the extreme, oscillates between encomium and cautionary tale. Although Mrs. Todd is appalled that Joanna chose to live out her life in conditions of physical and emotional deprivation, the narrator, reflecting "upon a state of society which admitted such personal freedom," is at first captivated by Joanna's heroism (69). Soon, however, the narrator challenges her own initial assessment: "My thoughts flew back to the lonely woman on her outer island; what separation from humankind she must have felt, what terror and sadness" (73).

These contradictory interpretations of Joanna's behavior mirror myths concerning the island's earlier inhabitants, as conveyed by Mrs. Todd: "Some said 't was a great bangeing-place for the Indians, and an old chief resided there once that ruled the winds; and others said they'd always heard that once the Indians come down an' left a captive there without any bo't, an' 't was too far to swim across to Black Island, an' he lived there till he perished" (63). Joanna is both the chief, a powerful figure with the ability to control nature, and also the captive, a prisoner removed from his community and left for dead on the isolated island. These descriptions reiterate the narrator's indecision about whether Joanna's exile is an act of protest that affords her admirable autonomy or one of social exclusion, which she must painfully endure to the end of her days. The narrator concludes her reflections on Joanna with the puzzling assertion that in every person "there is a place remote and islanded, and given to endless regret or secret happiness" (83). Again, this contradictory appraisal assures that both interpretations of Joanna remain actively in play.

The key to this interpretive ambivalence might be found in Joanna's alignment with Native Americans, the people who once populated her island but who are now, in the characters' imaginations at least, an extinct race, replaced by the white townspeople.[59] Joanna, who dons moccasins and adorns her cabin with the relics of Indians' stone tools, recalls an unconventional old woman in *Deephaven* who "wore a man's coat, cut off so that it made an odd short jacket, and a pair of men's boots" and was "so wild and unconventional . . . that it was like taking an afternoon walk with a good-natured Indian."[60] The confluence of Jewett's "native" white women and Native Americans symbolizes an imagined relationship between the two groups as theorized by Walter Benn Michaels, who argues that Native Americans typify an American identity that is both natural and authentic, unlike the merely technical citizenship of naturalized immigrants. In nativist works, "the Indian, embodying an American identity that explicitly antedated his own legal citizenship, could figure as an exemplary counterinstance to these aliens." Moreover, the "extinction" of Native Americans represents a defiant and extreme form of racial purity insofar as their "disappearance" poses a noble alternative to interracial mixing. As Michaels argues, marriage is always fraught in the nativist imagination with the fear of interracialism because "the exogamous requirements of marriage (that the woman leave her family) conflict with the endogamous requirements of the race (that the woman be kept in the family)."[61]

We can understand, then, why the narrator finds Joanna's lifestyle both frightening and admirable. Her radical break from the social order marks her as the type of woman who occasioned fears about the end of whiteness. Although her "willful sterility" would make her a "race traitor" according to Roosevelt, her radical departure from marriage may also be interpreted as a sacrifice on behalf of blood purity, guarding against the threat of contamination, even at the cost of racial extinction.[62] Her figurative status as a Native American is loaded with anxiety that she is a harbinger of racial annihilation but also with a pervading pride in whiteness, even in this enervated form, as racially pure and natively American.

Celibacy is not the only form of willful sterility *The Country of the Pointed Firs* explores; it also hints at other methods of deliberately avoiding childbirth. Dunnet Landing's thriving older women inhabit a luxuriant natural world; beyond its titular trees and crashing ocean, the novel catalogues an abundance of herbs, flowers, and vegetables. Many readers have observed that the herb pennyroyal seems to be particularly abundant, most notably in the patch on Green Island, which, as Howard notes, "takes on virtually sacred significance."[63] Pennyroyal is, in fact, a natural abortifacient, as Maine's white settlers learned from Native Americans.[64] Early in the novel, "the Indian remedy" is named as one of the herbal medicines that Almira Todd dispenses to townspeople who "came at night as if by stealth" to hear the "whispered directions" for its use (4).[65] The plant's ubiquity, especially insofar as it is associated with a race the text figures as extinct, raises the specter of race suicide and serves as a pervasive reminder of the community's failure, or refusal, to reproduce. As Gordon notes, "nearly all those involved in the race suicide controversy, on all sides, asserted or assumed that birth control practices were widespread."[66] Although liberal feminists and radical Free Lovers alike championed voluntary motherhood rather than contraceptive devices or abortion, many race suicide alarmists accused white women of terminating pregnancies. As one doctor wrote: "The patriotic enterprise of recruiting American population with the blood of American citizenship is being gradually shifted to the lusty sexual output of foreign breeders, Americanized, who have not grown 'smart' in the limitation of family births."[67] He asserts unambiguously that abortion is making the white birthrate lower, not celibacy or biological changes due to education. "This backward lapse of national progress hinges on the fact that our educated, restless, esthetic American women have preached to womanhood the subtleties of emulating manhood in the guise of worldly spheres, and have developed among the masses an ethical, almost a constitutional reluctance to pregnancy." He details a range of "educated, restless" white women he has attended who have procured abortions and induced miscarriages.[68] The knowledge of herbal medicine that Jewett associates with New England women might be understood as one traditional regional technique for limiting reproduction at will. Although the women of Dunnet Landing seemingly have aged past the need for contraception, Mrs. Todd's admission that pennyroyal always reminds her of a secret kept from her late husband intimates a connection between women's autonomy and antinatal practices.

Perhaps surprisingly, despite its focus on childless and solitary women, *The Country of the Pointed Firs* endorses the belief that the family is the natural basis of the social order: "Clannishness is an instinct of the heart,—it is more than a birthright, or a custom," the narrator maintains, and the most powerful adhesive for any group is its "claim to a common inheritance" (110).

By defining the community's insiders and outsiders in terms of blood relatedness, the novel renders the health of the family equivalent to the health of society. Almira Todd explains: "when you call upon the Bowdens you may expect most families to rise up between the Landing and the far end of the Back Cove. Those that are n't kin by blood are kin by marriage" (98). Sandra Zagarell claims that the text "actively *produces* Dunnet as a pure and homogenous community" in part by "mapping 'community' onto 'family.'" Moreover, the correlation between this particular family and the nation is made explicit when the narrator compares their reunion to "the great national anniversaries which our country has lately kept" (110). Zagarell comments: "America itself, in this formulation, is a 'clan,' both familial and racial. Citizenship, by implication, is natural and inborn."[69] Because the perpetuation of a homogenous community relies on the reproduction of its constituent families, the climactic family reunion depicts the consequences of individual infertility on larger social formations, specifically the nation.[70]

Although marriage is conspicuously absent in *Country*, the family is solemnly, even ritualistically celebrated in the chapters devoted to the Bowden reunion.[71] Readings of this scene have served as the cornerstone of critical arguments decrying Jewett's racism. For example, Elizabeth Ammons argues that "the Bowden reunion is about racial purity and white cultural dominance. It celebrates white ethnic pride, the extended Bowden family's Anglo-Norman lineage, which is militantly asserted and religiously affirmed in all the orderly marching and solemn worshipping."[72] Gillman similarly declares that "the Bowden family might as well be one of the many fraternal organizations—among them the Knights of Columbus and the Ku Klux Klan—that flourished during this period."[73] But this apparent veneration of white national genealogy seems at odds with the novel's disinterest in the hetero-reproductive conjugal family. In the genealogical matrix of American identity, racial continuity depends on endogamous marriage and ongoing births. Clearly, this posed a conflict for late-nineteenth-century reformers cognizant of women's naturalized inequality in their capacities as wives and mothers. But to turn away from these duties meant to undermine the perpetuation of race and nation, a particularly audacious path in light of the alleged demographic crisis in New England. The Bowden reunion certainly celebrates the white family, although not by asserting its strength, as these critics suggest, but rather by eulogizing its former greatness and symbolically enacting its decline and eventual demise. The end of bloodlines is the inevitable result of antinatalist feminism, which Jewett depicts as cause for commemoration, but not distress.

The pomp and circumstance of the reunion scene is undercut first by Sant Bowden, the leader of the march. "He was imperative enough," the narrator says of the grand marshal, "but with a grand military sort of courtesy, and he bore himself with solemn dignity of importance" (101). The closest thing to a "good fighter" in Dunnet Landing is an alcoholic who has a reputation of being "good for nothing" (102). Despite the military bearing that so impresses the narrator, Bowden has never been a soldier. He tried repeatedly to enlist in the Civil War, but according to Almira Todd, "he ain't a sound man," and the army "wouldn't have him" (102). The real veterans, she explains, do not object to him wearing the uniform, and they "invite him to march on Decoration Day, same as the rest, [because] he comes of soldier stock." From his lineage, Bowden has inherited the appearance of authority, but it is his only qualification for participating in military-style parades. The family parade, which Ammons describes as "a bunch of white people marching around in military formation ritualistically affirming their racial purity, global dominance, and white ethnic superiority and solidarity," is strangely headed up by an emasculated, laughable, and mentally unsound man, an empty figurehead of white dominion.[74] The contrast between Bowden's commanding appearance and his underlying inadequacy serves to deflate the ritual, showing it to be an empty display of a once powerful whiteness, now spent.

The consumption of family identity enacted in the reunion scene is not limited to the Bowdens' funereal march but becomes literal during the community's ingestion of desserts with "dates and names . . . wrought in lines of pastry and frosting on the tops" (108). The Bowdens celebrate their genealogy by publicly recording and then eating it.[75] The narrator and Mrs. Todd together consume an apple pie decorated with the words "Bowden Reunion." They eat "precept upon precept," suggesting that this feast of family identity also entails digesting an ideology. At the height of the family's gustatory revels, the women present a cake formed into a "model of the old Bowden house made of durable gingerbread, with all the windows and doors in the right places, and sprigs of genuine lilac set at the front." The narrator reports that "there was a general sigh when this fell into ruin at the feast's end, and it was shared by a great part of the assembly, not without seriousness, and as if it were a pledge and token of loyalty" (108). After spending the day affirming its pure white lineage, the family symbolically enacts the falling into ruin of their own ancestral home. If, as Wood observes, the "empty, nearly pestiferous old house which dominated the Local Colorists' imagination" holds "iconographical links with the diseased and barren womb," the Bowdens' ravaged familial home is linked to the community's decline.[76] With no prospect of a future generation, the Bowden line will come to an end at the hands of these childless women.[77]

From "The Fall of the House of Usher," *The House of the Seven Gables*, and *Incidents in the Life of a Slave Girl* to "The Yellow Wall-Paper" and *Absalom,*

Absalom!, houses appear throughout American literature as symbols of familial onus, tainted inheritance, and claustrophobic domesticity. In this sense, Jewett's fallen gingerbread house is a kind of antifamilial gesture in the midst of a family reunion. It clearly symbolizes New England lineage on the verge of collapse, but it might be interpreted either as a translation of antifeminist descriptions of the effects of women's rights agitation, or of radical feminist calls for the abolition of atomized domestic units. Furthermore, this scene calls to mind a striking image from "Immigration and Degradation" (1891), a foundational work of race suicide theory by Frances Amasa Walker.[78] This landmark essay offered the first comprehensive account of demographic data to posit a causal relationship between immigration and the falling "native" birthrate, namely that white couples did not want to bring children into the world to compete with immigrants.[79] Walker represents white New Englanders' superior quality of life through the metaphor of a house "kept in order, at whatever cost, the gate hung, the shutters in place, while the front yard had been made to bloom with simple flowers." Jewett's account of the gingerbread house mimics Walker's characterization of the proper New England home. Her observation that "all the windows and doors [were] in the right places" echoes his concern that shutters and gates be neatly hung, and the cake's sprig of "genuine lilac set at the front" of the home reproduces his image of a front yard "made to bloom with simple flowers." In Walker's report, the influx of foreigners drags down New England's traditional standard of living, and as a result, the formerly tidy homes degenerate into "houses that were mere shells for human habitations, the gate unhung, the shutters flapping or falling, green pools in the yard."[80]

The metaphor of the American nation as a white family home vulnerable to foreign interlopers had been circulating for years when *The Country of the Pointed Firs* was published. An 1888 article entitled "Our National Family" declares, "here is our great American home; it is a big establishment, three thousand miles from front door to back; but it is our home; and under God it belongs to us Americans." The author addresses the problem of "hordes of foreigners flocking to our shores," "entering our doors without knocking, and lounging in our parlors and making familiar with our furniture." He speaks for Americans who "regard with undisguised aversion" the consequence of "our national home cluttered up and its sacred privacy dishonored by a mass of foreign stuff." Making his xenophobia explicit, he states, "we want one seamless garment, not a coat of many colors; one integral people, not tribal patchwork nor ethnological crazy quilt."[81] In light of works like "Our National Family," Jewett's representation of an American home falling into ruin, not corrupted by foreigners but rather devoured by white women, provides an evocative climax to her narrative of decline.

On the other hand, the reunion ritual cements this community's survival by a means that does not mire women in traditional family roles. To understand the narrator's ingestion of words in this scene, we must remember that she is a writer who had come to Dunnet Landing to work but spends her time listening to the townspeople instead. At first she finds them tiresome, wishing she could focus on her writing, but soon becomes fascinated with the locals and their way of life. In this climactic scene, they feed her their family identity in a communion feast in which genealogy is transubstantiated from blood into pure text: she is served the word "Bowden" on a piece of pie. Along with the townspeople's stories and culture, which she has absorbed all summer, their family identity becomes part of her. She soon leaves Maine and presumably pens this account of her summer visit—the text of *The Country of the Pointed Firs*. The Bowdens survive in this narrative rather than through a bloodline by means of sexual reproduction. Jewett offers print culture, a textual archive, or perhaps specifically imaginative literature as a non-familial vehicle for cultural transmission.

The unnamed narrator's experience alone unifies the circuitous narrative structure of this work that eschews the heteroteleology of conventional literary forms. Her only development over the course of the plot, if we can call it that, is to become the chronicler of this place, ultimately taking on the role of perpetuating it after the death of the townspeople who will not achieve this continuity biologically. While race suicide alarmists denounced the people of this region for their willful refusal to reproduce, some New England women perpetuated this culture to posterity in a public mode that also advanced their intellectual and professional pursuits. Local color fiction both memorializes and immortalizes a culture that experts declared well on its way to extinction, offering their writing as the afterlife to a dead civilization. This genre constructs a sympathetic regional character, but it is neither a jingoistic contribution to mythicizing this region of national nascence nor a call for the violent protection and resuscitation of a vulnerable, embattled white culture. Rather, they dwell on the sickly, the eccentric, and the non-normative, chronicling a culture disinterested in reproductive futurity even though this lifestyle seemed to have global political repercussions.

The novel concludes with two more symbolic enactments of the characters' and the town's demise. At the end of the summer, as the narrator prepares to leave town, she anticipates her own death. Looking around her bedroom, once again empty as she had found it, she reflects: "so we die before our own eyes" (129). Dunnet Landing is a community dying before its own eyes, obsessively recounting in its twilight years memories of a stronger, more glorious past. In the final sentence of the novel, Dunnet Landing suddenly disappears from sight as the narrator's boat rounds a bend, headed for Boston. The moment recalls Captain Littlepage's tall sea tale of "a strange sort of country 'way up north . . . and strange folks living in it . . . a place where there was neither living or dead . . . a kind of waiting-place between this world an' the next" (22–24). The New England Jewett portrays is just such a place, a strange northern country with "fog-shaped" people suspended between life and death that will soon exist only as a story (22). Although in many ways *The Country of the Pointed Firs* privileges a lifestyle that defies the traditional insistence on marriage and childbirth, Dunnet Landing's disappearance echoes anxieties that the racial order so intrinsic to America's national identity might fail to reproduce itself. The novel's pairing of a nostalgic vision of vanishing homogeneity with a progressive portrayal of female independence not only reveals meaningful links between the tradition of New England local color literature and contemporary sociological writings from and about the region but also complicates our understanding of the relationship between turn-of-the-century feminism and racist discourses of the national future. Many white women reformers of this period undeniably traded in despicable eugenic ideologies, but it is important to recognize the complex racial politics of this turning point in American feminism when women reevaluated the meaning and costs of marriage, childbearing, and domesticity. If Jewett's Dunnet Landing is a feminist utopia, it is not despite but *because* it is also a harbinger of demographic collapse.

CHAPTER 6

⌒∿⌒

Another Long Bridge

Textual Atavism in Hagar's Daughter

A woman escapes at dusk from a slave pen in Washington, D.C., sprints across the Long Bridge toward the woods on the other side of the Potomac, finds herself caught between approaching captors on both sides, clasps her hands, lifts her eyes to heaven, and leaps into the river to her death in view of the White House and the Capitol building. This narrative was written by Seth M. Gates, a Congressman from New York, and published under the headline "Slavery in the District" in the *New York Evangelist* on September 8, 1842.[1] The author presented it as an eyewitness description of an event that he observed with a number of other onlookers. For at least sixty years, this scene circulated in American print culture as anecdotal evidence of the perversity of slavery and the desperate desire for freedom among the enslaved. It was reprinted in other periodicals, including 1845 issues of the *Herald of Freedom* and *Prisoner's Friend*.[2] It was retold in poems by Sarah J. Clarke and John Kemble Laskey, published in the *Liberator* in 1844 and 1845, respectively.[3] Frederick Douglass recounted the story in an address delivered in Boston on May 28, 1844.[4] Even after Emancipation, this scene retained its appeal, resurfacing in diverse works including the autobiography *Half a Century* (1880) by journalist activist Jane Grey Cannon Swisshelm, Frances E.W. Harper's novel *Iola Leroy; Or, Shadows Uplifted* (1892), and an 1897 history of African Americans by Reverend Norman B. Wood.[5]

Of course, this narrative's position in literary history was cemented eleven years after its original publication when William Wells Brown gave the woman on the Long Bridge a name, a back story, and a Revolutionary genealogy, reproducing this excerpt verbatim as the climactic scene of *Clotel; Or, The President's Daughter*, discussed at length in Chapter 2. His rendering of this tale in the chapter "Death Is Freedom" has come to emblematize not only this foundational novel but also the durable "tragic mulatta" trope with which it is routinely associated, serving as a revealing and pivotal image in the tradition of the African American novel that it inaugurated.

Conveying this magnetic narrative into the twentieth century, Pauline Hopkins reused it nearly in its entirety and original expression as the cornerstone of her first serialized novel, *Hagar's Daughter*, published in *The Colored American Magazine* from March 1901 to March 1902. From 1874, when Brown, by then a celebrity author and orator, awarded the fifteen-year-old Hopkins ten-dollars as a prize for a high school essay, her literary oeuvre abounds with homage to this antecedent author, including a trail of unattributed quotations from Brown's fiction, drama, and non-fiction.[6] In an excellent recent biography of Hopkins, Lois Brown holds that Hopkins's liberal and uncredited use of these antecedent texts "raise the issue of plagiarism in *Hagar's Daughter*, even as they confirm the deep respect that Hopkins had for Brown's work."[7] Far from unoriginality, the striking reproduction of the Long Bridge scene marks an instance of intertextual suturing that contributed to the establishment of an African American literary tradition and typifies Hopkins's signature strategy as a writer of politically engaged historical romance. While this retelling itself serves as a bridge uniting the two novels in a tradition of African American literature spanning the century, Hopkins ultimately utilizes this duplication to foreground the failure of Reconstruction to facilitate a bridge into freedom for African Americans. Her repetition constructs a tragic a loop, creating for readers the sense of déjà vu that Hopkins and her contemporaries describe as central to black experience at the turn of the twentieth century.

Although classic studies of African American women's writing of this period have emphasized the security and advancement of the black family centered in the construction of a genteel but politically engaged free black womanhood, the deconstruction of the white family as both sentimentalized private institution and politicized public phenomenon is equally important to Hopkins's oeuvre.[8] Intervening into the broader cultural preoccupation with theories of racial ancestry and national futurity, *Hagar's Daughter* interrogates women's role in the transmission of identity.[9] She identifies white genealogical nationalism as a chief ideological structure impeding black advancement.[10]

Paired with concerns about the declining white birthrate and "race suicide," theories of black atavism and morbidity at the turn of the century formed what Felipe Smith calls "an increasingly paranoid discourse of race,

AMEN!"

An owner of a slave in the District, who from losses at the gaming table or race course, from extravagance, improvidence, or other cause, determines upon the sale of his slave, will most assuredly, from motives of shame, make a *secret sale* to Mr. Joshua Staples. The first notice the poor slave has of his sale for a Southern plantation may be, that he or she is suddenly drawn and locked into that private "PEN," as it is called, having been sent there, perhaps, under pretense of carrying a letter, or doing an errand! Occasionally an incident occurs, which affords a glimpse at the deeds of darkness and infamy practised there, and of the keenness of the misery, and the desolation of hopes, experienced by the captives who are shut within it. For the truth of the following occurrence, I might refer to at least one member of Congress, as well as to many of the citizens of the District, who saw and heard of the transaction at the time.

A smart and active female slave was placed in this prison, having been sold for the Southern market, and the time of her departure was at hand. Her particular history I cannot give. Whether it was the dread of the cruelties and starvation of a Southern cotton plantation; the dread of the abuse and violence of some licentious purchaser; or the grief of being suddenly and forever separated from husband, children, and the friends of her youth, that drove the unhappy woman to adopt, not only in theory, but in practice, the sentiment of Patrick Henry—"Give me liberty, or give me death," I know not. Whatever was the cause, the sentiment was adopted; and at dusk of the evening previous to the day when she was to be sent off; as the old prison was being closed for the night, she suddenly darted past her keeper, and ran for her life. It is not a great distance from the prison to the long bridge, which passes from the lower part of the city across the Potomac, to the extensive forests and woodlands of the celebrated Arlington Place, occupied by that distinguished relative and descendant of the immortal Washington, Mr. GEORGE W CUSTISS. Thither the poor pursued fugitive directed her flight. So unexpected was her escape, that she had quite a number of rods the start before the keeper had secured the other prisoners, and rallied his assistants in pursuit. It was at an hour when, and in a part of the city where horses could not readily be obtained for the chase; no bloodhounds were at hand to run down the flying woman; and for once it seemed as though there was like to be a fair trial of speed and endurance, between the slave and the slave catchers. The keeper and his forces raised the hue and cry on her pathway, close behind; but so rapid was the flight along the wide Avenue, that the astonished citizens, as they poured forth from their dwellings to learn the cause of alarm, were only enabled to comprehend the nature of the case, in season to fall in with the motley mass in pursuit, or, (as

Figures 6.1 and 6.2

"Slavery in the District" by Seth Gates, *New York Evangelist*, September 8, 1842. Incorporated verbatim into Brown's *Clotel* in 1853 and Hopkins's *Hagar's Daughter* in 1901. Image courtesy of the American Antiquarian Society.

her enemies.

But God by his Providence had otherwise determined. He had determined that an appalling
tragedy should be enacted that night, within plain
sight of the President's House and the Capitol of
the Union, which should be an evidence wherever
it should be known, of the unconquerable love of
liberty the heart of the slave may inherit; as well
as a fresh admonition to the slave dealer, of the
cruelty and enormity of his crimes. Just as the
pursuers crossed the high draw for the passage of
sloops, soon after entering upon the bridge, they
beheld in the distance, three men slowly advancing
from the Virginia side. They immediately called
to them to arrest the fugitive, whom they proclaimed a runaway slave. True to their Virginia instincts, as she came near, they formed in line across
the narrow bridge, and prepared to seize her.
Seeing escape impossible in that quarter, she stop-
ped suddenly, and turned upon her pursuers. On
came the profane and ribald crew, faster than ever,
already exulting in her capture, and threatening
punishment for her flight. For a moment she
looked wildly and anxiously around, to see if there
was no other hope of escape. On either hand, far
down below, rolled the deep loamy waters of the
Potomac, and before and behind the rapidly approaching step and fierce and noisy shout of pursuers, showed how vain would be any further ef
fort for freedom. Her resolution was taken. She
clasped her *hands* convulsively, and raised *them,*
as she at the same time raised her *eyes,* towards
heaven, and begged for that mercy and compassion
there, which had been denied her on earth ; and
then, with a single bound, she vaulted over the
railing of the bridge, and sunk forever beneath the
waves of the river! !

Slave trader! "thy prey hath escaped thee," and
if thou comest up to the judgment without deep
repentance for thy damnable traffick, as thy deeds
of wickedness shall one after another be passed in
review before an assembled universe, and thou
shalt be driven away from the presence of God and
the Lamb, will not all created intelligences cry out.
Amen, to thy sentence, when they shall see that
thou didst persist in buying and selling the bodies
and souls of thy fellow-men, after being warned of
the tendency and cruelty of thy villainous trade,
by the self-destruction of the poor hunted fugitive
upon the "Long Bridge?"

A MEMBER OF CONGRESS.

Figures 6.1 and 6.2 *(continued)*

combining the wish for black race extinction with the fear of white race extinction."[11] A body of social scientific thought claimed that people of African descent enjoyed a modicum of advancement under slavery but had failed with freedom. Chief among these prophesies of black extinction, Frederick L. Hoffman's *Race Traits and Tendencies of the American Negro* (1896) argues that since Emancipation, "in vital capacity, the most important of all physiological characteristics, the tendency of the race has been downward."[12] Hoffman popularized the view that "the colored population is gradually parting with the virtues and the moderate degree of economic efficiency developed under the regime of slavery. . . . It is merely a question of time when the actual downward course, that is, a decrease in the population, will take place."[13] He predicts that in the near future, inborn black "traits and tendencies must in the end cause the extinction of the race."[14] Social Darwinist notions of race competition for survival reinforced the longstanding genealogical determinism of American culture. Despite discourses of individualism and contractualism that ostensibly formed the ideological core of the Revolution, the precept that the quality of ancestral "blood" limits the prospects of future generations survived even into the twentieth century.

These theories foreclosed the possibility that African Americans might be safely integrated into American society because even the most remote generation would transmit the threat of regression to a savage ancestral type. For example, Paul Brandon Barringer, the faculty chair at the University of Virginia, argued, "Every day of slavery seems to have counted for their benefit, as we will see if we compare the records of this generation with that of those whose boast it is that they were born free."[15] He concludes that African Americans are "reverting through hereditary forces to savagery. Fifty centuries of savagery in the blood cannot be held down by two centuries of forced good behavior if the controlling influences which held down his savagery are withdrawn as they have been in this case."[16] In a 1902 work published by the American Economic Association, Joseph Alexander Tillinghast declared that "this people, considered as a whole, is slowly but surely tending to revert . . . the Negro finds it surpassingly difficult to suppress the hereditary instincts that do not harmonize with American social organization."[17] The concept of atavism, or devolution to the condition of remote forebears, epitomizes how, long after the end of hereditary enslavement, American scientific, legal, and sociological discourses entrenched people of color in genealogical paradigms to exclude them from the realm of contractual relations that supposedly defines American citizenship.

The shackle of ancestral identity was forced on people of African descent not only to deny their self-determination but to tie them forever to an inborn and transmissible status definitively excluded from blood-based American identity. The scientific theory of atavism found practical expression in the "one drop" logic of the *Plessy v. Ferguson* decision, which upheld segregation by ancestry, and policies like the "grandfather clause," enacted by a number of Southern states starting around 1898 to prohibit African Americans from exercising the right to vote granted by the Fifteenth Amendment. This practice effectively limited suffrage to those whose ancestors had the right to vote before the Civil War. In other words, beyond the mere cultural amnesia associated with sectional reunification, certain fin-de-siècle policies sought practically to efface the Civil War and Reconstruction, saddling African Americans at the turn of the twentieth century with a sociopolitical status all too similar to their antebellum predecessors.

We know that ancestral determinism and savage regression were central topics of literary naturalism in this period, but this was not necessarily a new direction inspired by Charles Darwin and Emile Zola. The continued preoccupation with ancestral manses, the power of testation, misdirected inheritance, and the end of white family lines in the literature of this period indicates ongoing engagement with the genealogical paradigms that were central to antebellum works. Although critics have traditionally focused on the importance of domesticity and family formation to racial uplift in postbellum, pre-Harlem novels, this tradition also addresses white supremacy rooted in aristocratic blood pride as a violation of republican principles, investigating the white American family as the biological and rhetorical mechanism for the reproduction of the conditions of slavery. They indict a social system built on hereditary distinctions for barriers to black advancement, not an atavistic return to hereditary tendencies.

For example, in *The Wife of His Youth and Other Stories of the Color Line*, Charles Chesnutt addresses the reappearance of suppressed antebellum relationships in the lives of both black and white Americans long after the abolition of slavery.[18] "The Wife of His Youth" concerns Mr. Ryder, a formerly enslaved man who has reinvented himself after Emancipation, becoming a prominent member of the "Blue Veins," an exclusive club of mixed-race social Darwinists who believe that their "fate lies between absorption by the white race and extinction in the black" and that "self-preservation is the first law of nature." Ryder's coming marriage to a very light-skinned woman "would help to further the upward process of absorption he had been wishing and hoping for."[19] But his long-lost wife, from whom he was separated during slavery, appears on his doorstep looking for Sam Taylor, the antebellum identity Ryder has tried to jettison. She is described in racialized terms as everything the Blue Veins reject and also as an "ancient," "old-fashioned" remnant of a bygone era: "she looked like a bit of the old plantation life, summoned up from the past."[20] With the return of this anachronistic character, Ryder accepts that he cannot fully escape the antebellum past, which entails his identification with a degraded social position. In opposition to the idea that fin-de-siècle African Americans were biologically reverting to a previous condition, Chesnutt portrays them as hamstrung by the far-reaching afterlife of slavery from achieving upward mobility as defined by white society.

The Marrow of Tradition (1901) tackles accusations of black atavism more directly, contextualizing them alongside white anxieties about African American ascendency in the wake of universal suffrage. In three intertwining plots lines, Chesnutt describes how the persistence of antebellum culture delimits African American progress at the turn of the century. The novel begins with the aristocratic Major Carteret, "the last of his line," who returned home from the Civil War to Wellington, North Carolina, to find his "family, one of the oldest and proudest in the state, hopelessly impoverished by the war, even their ancestral home swallowed up in the common ruin."[21] In the novel's funereal opening scene, his wife prematurely gives birth to a son, Theodore Felix Carteret, renewing this diminishing family line. The doctor cautions Carteret to take good care of his son, adding, "your wife can never bear another."[22] Significantly, after his birth is brought on prematurely by his mother's shock at seeing her black half-sister, the baby's life is endangered three more times over the course of the novel, all in connection with his black relatives.

This unacknowledged branch of Olivia Carteret's family tree, the product of her father's relationship with his enslaved housekeeper, threatens her only son and more generally the mythic whiteness of her proud Southern lineage. *Marrow* portrays the legacy of slavery—not the proverbial drop of black blood—as a hereditary condition that reappears for generations: "Such relations . . . had been all too common in the old slavery days, and not a few of them had been projected into the new era. Sins, like snakes, die hard. The habits and customs of a people were not to be changed in a day, nor by the stroke of a pen." The day after his son's birth, Carteret returns to his newspaper office with renewed vigor for the cause of protecting white privilege for future generations: "His regret had been more than personal at the thought that with himself an old name should be lost to the State; and now all the pride of race, class, and family welled up anew, and swelled and quickened the current of his life."[23] This "more than personal" connection between family lines and the public enforcement of white supremacy leads Carteret and his cronies to unleash a race riot on the community.

Pseudoscientific accounts of atavistic decline used to justify the restriction of African American rights appear as an important context for this narrative: "Statistics of crime, ingeniously manipulated, were made to present a fearful showing against the negro. Vital statistics were made to prove that he had degenerated from an imaginary standard of physical excellence which had existed under the benign influence of slavery."[24] Echoing the rhetoric of Hoffman and his followers, Chesnutt's white characters regard African Americans as a "race of weaklings" soon to be "eliminated by the stress of competition." They view even the most benign family servants, like Sandy Delamere, with anxious suspicion: "No one could tell at what moment the thin veneer of civilization might peel off and reveal the underlying savage." When he is falsely accused of a crime, they conclude that, "left to his own degraded ancestral instincts, Sandy had begun to deteriorate, and a rapid decline had culminated in this robbery and murder."[25]

In a reversal of the accusation of devolution into savagery, it is the aristocratic white families, the Cartarets and the Delameres, indeed the entire white community, who demonstrate barbaric, animalistic tendencies. As a white horde threatens to lynch Sandy and murder any black person they can find, the nadir culture of terror turns "the whole white population into a mob of primitive savages." Chesnutt portrays lynching as an atavistic return to primal violence: "White men, the most favored of races, the heirs of civilization, the conservators of liberty, howling like red Indians around a human being slowly roasting at the stake."[26] Seeming to revert to primitive practices, white people "carried off the fragments of his mangled body as souvenirs, in much the same way that savages preserve the scalps or eat the hearts of their enemies."[27] Chesnutt crystallizes his point about white, rather than African American, atavism with the revelation that the murder was committed by a "degenerate aristocrat," the dissolute remnant of the proud white Delamere lineage, whose grandfather declares, "we have no more family honor."

The Delamere patriarch soon dies, willing all of his money to Sandy and to the African American community's new hospital. After his death, however, his will is put aside with the understanding that "Mr. Delamere's property belonged of right to the white race, and by the higher law should remain in the possession of white people."[28] His estate passes to his biological heir, a known murderer, making clear the injustice of the traditional practice of shoring up unearned wealth within the bloodline. By the end of the race riot that soon follows, the African American hospital, a symbol of black progress and health, "lay smouldering in ruins, a melancholy witness to the fact that our boasted civilization is but a thin veneer, which cracks and scales off at the first impact of primal passions."[29] The criminal protection of white family property paired with mob violence that destroys black public works underscores how white allegiance to blood paradigms, rather than for the rule of law, bars black advancement.

A third plotline also concerns the continuity of antebellum wrongs in the nadir period. Captain McBane, a newly moneyed white supremacist still characterized by his ancestral status as "white trash," seems to represent new socioeconomic developments in the postwar South. In fact, this son of an overseer is merely a replication of his hereditary type, a member of the Klan who sells convict labor, a reproduction of the slave system. Chesnutt presents Josh Green's plot to avenge McBane's crimes against his parents as evidence of "the continuity of life, how inseparably the present is woven with the past, how certainly the future will be but the outcome of the present." During the riot, Green kills him with "a huge bowie-knife, a relic of the civil war," residue from a previous era, like so much else in this novel.[30] Chesnutt and many of his contemporaries reject the idea that the Civil War, Emancipation, and Reconstruction marked a sea change in American race relations. In the African American novel of this period, the turn of the twentieth century seems less like the dawn of a new era than another installment of a long hereditary struggle.

For writers of both fiction and non-fiction, the pages of *The Colored American Magazine* provided a forum for African American rebuttal to theories of racial decline. Like Chesnutt, many of the magazine's writers flipped the accusation of reversion, positing white savagery and criminality in the nadir period as an inheritance from, or a return to, the conditions under slavery. A September 1901 article that shares a page with an installment of *Hagar's Daughter* explains that after the Civil War, the Southern people "immediately set to work with their great ability, influence and power, to defeat the emancipation act of the Nation, and return the Freedmen to a new and far more cruel slavery. They brought to their aid, those characteristics of cruelty and injustice, rooted and cultivated in them and their ancestors during slavery."[31] These characteristics, according to the author, manifested in a "system of barbarism, cruelty and injustice, in constant practice during the past thirty-five years; educating the children, the youth and young manhood of that white people, into the savagery of past ages."[32] In other words, the descendants of slaveowners were reverting to a savage ancestral condition. This writer points to a combination of hereditary viciousness and family training in old racist ideologies underlying white attempts to resurrect the conditions of slavery.

An August 1902 article in *The Colored American Magazine* similarly reverses accusations of atavism, arguing that the long experience of absolute sovereignty over the enslaved had a deleterious effect on white Americans, producing "characteristics [that] were transmitted and educated into the children of that . . . people from generation to generation during that long period of slavery, until they became fixed and established characteristics."[33] This African American reverse discourse theorizes racial traits and tendencies as the cause of white savagery and degeneration. The article concludes that these regressive white Southerners aim to enforce the effective reversion of African Americans: "it has become evident to the close observer that the intent was and now is to return the Negroes to a peon slavery, more galling than the one from which they have been relieved."[34]

With similar outrage against barriers to black progress, Hopkins's fiction articulates a powerful antiracist response to popular theories of black reversion and decline. In her novels, the struggles of post-Reconstruction African Americans indict the failed progress of racial equality after the Civil War. She uses a split plot structure in *Contending Forces* (1900), for example, to explore the relationship between institutional slavery and nominal freedom in black experience. As Hopkins explains in the novel's preface, "the atrocity of the acts committed one hundred years ago are duplicated today, when slavery is supposed no longer to exist."[35] She declares that the difference between the experience of antebellum slaves and African Americans at the beginning of the twentieth century "is so slight as to be scarcely worth mentioning."[36] Historical recursivity, the duplication of the atrocities of slavery and the imperceptibility of any progress toward true equality and freedom for African Americans stands as Hopkins's primary characterization of the post-Reconstruction nadir.

In *Of One Blood* (1902–1903), Hopkins uses gothic conventions like ghostly visitations and second sight to depict the uncanny return of antebellum conditions. Utilizing a genre that allows for a penetrable boundary between life and death, Hopkins breaks down the racial binary and the strict separation of the past from the present. For example, an inscription on a sphinx in the hidden city of Telassar reads: "that which hath been, is now; and that which is to be, hath already been."[37] This refers specifically to the Ethiopianist prediction of a millennial return to greatness for people of African descent, but more broadly it underscores the novel's cyclical model of temporality, an antiprogressive understanding of history underlying the depiction of American slavery as undead. This logic not only guides the plot from the United States to Africa, but also from Boston to an ancestral Southern plantation where antebellum roots branch into a twisted genealogy of incest, murder, and suicide.

This disjunctive mode of history informs her attention to sexual as well as textual reproduction. In the social Darwinist racial discourse of this period, notions of historical progress were inextricable from hereditarian theories of inheritance and race survival. Hopkins strategically returns to antebellum texts, manipulating a widespread white American preoccupation with black ancestral regression at the turn of the twentieth century. Responding to white writers who forecasted African American decline and even extinction in the aftermath of Emancipation, Hopkins portrays a fin-de-siècle culture in which the inherited legacy of slavery enforces the immobility and even regression of African Americans, and in which an irrational clinging to the ancestral past degrades white American families and the nation they represent.

Hagar's Daughter's byzantine, multipart plot structure implements an abortive teleology that resists the linear, progressive conventions of the novel in its exploration of the relationship of family structures to national history.[38] The first chapter orients the reader in 1860, opening at a Confederate convention that includes a long speech by Jefferson Davis, where we meet St. Clair Enson and a slave trader named Walker. Enson receives a letter informing him that his brother has married and had a daughter, which eliminates any chance of his inheriting the valuable family estate. The trader claims that he can help St. Clair resecure his inheritance and travels with him to Enson Hall in Maryland. Walker presents St. Clair's brother, Ellis Enson, with a bill of sale and claims his wife, Hagar, and their infant daughter as his "stolen property," supplying proof that Hagar had been a slave adopted by a rich white family and raised as their own child.[39] The exposure of this seemingly white woman's African heritage wreaks havoc on the transmission of property and on the Enson family identity.

Although Ellis pays off Walker, he explains to Hagar that he must end their marriage not only to abide the law but to save his family from dishonor: "I feel it my duty as a Southern gentleman, the representative of a proud old family, to think of others beside myself and not allow my own inclinations to darken the escutcheon of a good old name. I cannot, I dare not, and the law forbids me to acknowledge as my wife a woman in whose veins courses a drop of the accursed blood of the Negro slave" (59). His horror at the prospect that Hagar might "darken the escutcheon" of the "proud old family" of the Ensons, in other words reveal as interracial an emblematic white family obsessed with its pure genealogy, drives the plot and proves to be the downfall of not only the Ensons but the nation that they represent.

The danger that Hagar is perceived to pose to the Enson family highlights the position of women as both the cornerstone and the greatest threat to white racial purity. Perhaps not surprisingly, the discourse of black morbidity theorized racial identity as determined by maternal inheritance, so that the protection of white blood depended on the control of white women's sexuality while the sexual license of white men held no consequences for racial integrity. For example, William Benjamin Smith insists that white men who sire mixed-race children do not compromise white purity: "however degraded and even unnatural, they in nowise, not even in the slightest degree, defile the Southern Caucasian blood. That blood to-day is absolutely pure."[40] Underscoring his double standard for the transgression of interracial sex, he posits that "the offense of the man is individual and limited, while that of the woman is general, and strikes mortally at the existence of the family itself."[41] His indeterminate use of "family," seemingly to describe both the immediate kin relations of the woman in question and also the entire "racial family" of whites, positions white women as the safeguard of the survival of both inextricable formations.

Hagar's Daughter troubles the very idea of white womanhood, arguing that a woman of mixed racial heritage can function seamlessly as the white wife of an elite plantation owner and "would have remained in this social sphere all her life, beloved and respected by her descendants, her blood mingling with the best blood of the country if untoward circumstances had not exposed her ancestry" (62). In other words, Hagar's "one drop" of "black blood" would have circulated in the country's "white" gene pool, making no difference as long as it went undetected, as this passage implies that many other cases surely do. But in the white imagination, "the one drop of black blood neutralized all her virtues, and she became, from the moment of exposure, an unclean thing. Can anything more unjust be imagined in a republican form of government whose excuse for existence is the upbuilding of mankind" (62)? Rather than positively re-signifying black blood, Hopkins emphasizes instead that the discourse of racial blood is not only irrational but blatantly undemocratic, a violation of basic republican principles.

At the end of this first plot, Ellis changes his mind and goes away to make plans for his new life with Hagar abroad. However, the family is soon informed that Ellis has committed suicide, his disfigured body found at the edge of the property gripping a pistol. St. Clair takes control of the estate and gives Hagar and her daughter to Walker to sell. National history is again interspersed with family history, as the evil brother's usurpation of Enson Hall is coincident with the formation of the Confederate States of America, drawing on familial metaphor to cast the Civil War as a white fraternal schism.

Significantly, it is at the stark break between the antebellum and postbellum plots that Hopkins's extended near-verbatim reiteration of William Wells Brown's *Clotel* appears. When Hagar escapes captivity, the narration notes, "It was not far from the prison to the long bridge which passes from the lower part of the city, across the Potomac, to the forests of Arlington Heights. Thither the fugitive directed her flight" (73–74). Compare this to the description of Clotel's escape: "It is not a great distance from the prison to the Long Bridge, which passes from the lower part of the city across the Potomac, to the extensive forests and woodlands of the celebrated Arlington Place . . . Thither the poor fugitive directed her flight" (Brown 205). Both novels describe "the hue-and-cry" of her pursuers and the "astonished citizens" that "poured forth from their dwellings" to join in the chase (Hopkins 74, Brown 205).

In both novels, just when the woman thinks she will make it across, men approach from the Virginia side of the bridge so that she is trapped in the middle. The heroines decide that death is the only "freedom" available. Both novels declare that "her resolution was taken" and conclude, respectively, as follows: "[Clotel] raised her eyes toward heaven, and begged for . . . mercy and compassion . . . and then, with a single bound, she vaulted over the railings of the bridge, and sunk for ever beneath the waves of the river" (Brown 207)! In Hopkins's account, "[Hagar] raised her tearful, imploring eyes to heaven as if seeking mercy and compassion, and with one bound sprang over the railing of the bridge, and sank beneath the waters of the Potomac River" (75).

Why would Hopkins, writing in the first years of the twentieth century, revisit, indeed repeat, a novel published half a century earlier, that was itself a reproduction of a narrative published a decade before that, aimed at significantly different goals, namely the abolition of slavery? Hanna Wallinger suggests that "since this leap and similar acts of mothers who would rather kill their children than have them grow up as slaves were most certainly familiar to her readers, Hopkins's repetition of such a well-known scene not only points out the longevity of the African American memory but also reminds the reader of the legacy of a past that will haunt the national memory."[42] Moreover, the formal reappearance of antebellum texts is central to Hopkins' refutation of white pundits who blamed atavistic devolution for the failure of black sociopolitical advancement after Reconstruction.

Dana Seitler theorizes the concept of atavism in fin-de-siècle America as "a 'reproduction' and a 'recurence' of the past in the present, [bringing] the ancestral past into conjunction with the modern present."[43] *Hagar's Daughter* broadcasts its engagement with atavism in a number of ways, perhaps most conventionally in the remarks of a white character who narrowly escapes marriage to a mixed-race woman: "The mere thought of the grinning, toothless black hag that was her foreparent would forever rise between us" (271).[44] This passage reveals how fears of atavism shaped antimiscegenation discourse. In the racist imagination, people of African descent carried the threat of a savage ancestral past that might resurface in the modern American population. According to Seitler, "atavism offers up a notion of time as multidirectional and of the body as polytemporal . . . it brazenly pushes the past onto the present, materializing the pressing force of history on our lives . . . atavism suggests not simply genetic continuity but historical and corporeal recursivity."[45] In this case, Hopkins represents this experience through textual recursivity so that "the gap between past and present, between history and prehistory, becomes bridgeable."[46] In bridging the 1850s and the twentieth century with the scene on the Long Bridge, Hopkins twists the phobic white preoccupation with black regression into a literary strategy that we might call textual atavism. Denying the narrative of national progress, specifically that the Civil War and Reconstruction had effected change, Hopkins indicts a white cult of genealogy for catalyzing a reversion to the savage practices of slavery and disallowing black political evolution.[47]

The Long Bridge meme instructs us in the ways that images, anecdotes, and passages circulate through print, bridging texts and serving as connective tissue to build discourses, movements, and even identities. Although this seems to confirm our understanding of how literary traditions work, it shakes our reliance on traditional conceptions of this process as a progressive flow of inheritance and innovation. To wit, Hopkins's citation of Brown is not mere writerly homage but a rueful representation of stunted historical evolution. This scene affirms African American literature as an intertextual tradition, but far from celebrating the continuity between these epochs in black experience, Hopkins presents it as a tragic impasse.

The citation chain of the Long Bridge narrative inserts *Hagar's Daughter* anachronistically back into the nexus of the antebellum culture of reprinting. As Meredith McGill notes of this prior moment in American print culture, "In the multiplicity of their formats and points of origin, and in the staggered temporality of their production, reprinted texts call attention to the repeated acts of articulation by which culture and its audiences are constituted."[48] In her practice of textual atavism, Hopkins asserts exactly this kind of relationship to the authors and activists of the antebellum period but also simultaneously challenges the assumption that generational continuity is desirable.

The projects of the Reconstruction period designed to aid the transition of the formerly enslaved into the full exercise of citizenship were imagined as "a bridge from slavery to freedom," as Charles Sumner described the Freedmen's Bureau in 1864. In the pages of *The Colored American Magazine* surrounding the publication of *Hagar's Daughter*, there is frequent reference to the path or journey of progress that African Americans must complete. These accounts point to a variety of obstructions on this path, making the bridge to freedom impassable. A July 1902 article denounces attempts "to blockade the Negro's road of progress with the frowning barriers of distinction and discrimination . . . stifling their ambitions, smothering their aspirations, strangling their loftiest desires, suffocating their determination to succeed."[49] The passage to freedom can be completed, this author declares, only if Americans "batter down all walls and limitations—remove all obstructions from the Negro's thorny pathway of advancement."[50] A poignant example of this metaphor, Hopkins's retelling of the Long Bridge narrative modifies the meaning of its original incarnations, written before the abolition of slavery, so that Hagar's tragically foiled passage to freedom represents a failed transition between Emancipation and her own early twentieth-century moment.

Despite its seeming fidelity to the source texts, Hopkins's refashioning of Clotel's suicide offers repetition with significant differences. Foremost, she has an infant in her arms, underscoring the fact that her death not only registers her refusal to endure enslavement but also severs the transmission of that condition to future generations. In her only substantive addition to Gates's original rendering of this scene (or Brown's reproduction of it), Hopkins imagines these final words from mother to child: "Alas, poor innocent, there is one gift for thee yet left for your unfortunate mother to bestow,—it is death. Better so than the fate reserved for us both" (75). Ultimately, however, Hopkins's characters are not granted the freedom of death. Unlike Clotel, Hagar and Jewell survive and resurface after the Civil War, representing the survival of slavery in the post-Reconstruction United States.

The break of twenty years in the plot immediately following this scene typifies Hopkins's disruptive narrative mode and its opposition to notions of linear, progressive national history.[51] Indeed, this interruption of the progress of the serialized plot, seeming to stop the forward action and start again with unrelated material, registers the failure of historical progress that constitutes the subject of the novel as a whole.[52] Echoing *Clotel*'s structure of multigenerational repetition, the second, seemingly separate plot that begins after Hagar's leap from the Long Bridge is revealed to be the continuation, as the title indicates, of the story of Hagar's daughter.

The narrative reopens in 1882 with a conversation between two seemingly new characters, General Benson, the head of the Federal Treasury Department, and Major Madison. These characters introduce Senator Zenas Bowen, an unconventional Western multimillionaire, his beautiful wife Estelle, his daughter from a previous marriage, Jewell, and her boyfriend

Cuthbert Sumner, the son and heir of a rich New England family. Benson and Madison hatch a plot to gain both the Bowen and Sumner family fortunes by breaking up the young couple. After a tangled courtship plot, Benson murders Elise Bradford, a woman working in his office who is the mother of his illegitimate child, and pins the crime on Sumner, who is apprehended and jailed. Distraught, Jewell seeks the help of a detective, Chief Henson of the Secret Service. The ensuing trial reveals that nearly all of the characters have two identities. Madison is revealed as the slave trader, Walker, and General Benson as St. Clair Enson, who is wanted as a conspirator in the Lincoln assassination. Chief Henson is actually his brother, Ellis Enson, and Estelle reveals herself to be Hagar. Soon thereafter, Jewell, whom Sumner had described as his "white angel of purity," is actually Hagar's daughter, the interracial Enson heir who had apparently died with her mother in the jump from the Long Bridge (103).

In this second plot, the setting returns to the Enson plantation, and social relations clearly revert to their antebellum structure. As Kristina Brooks observes, "There are just three characters whose names and racial identities remain constant over the twenty-year span of the novel, thus providing continuity between the two narratives."[53] She continues, "Aunt Henny, Marthy, and Isaac are static characters incapable of development. . . . Stuck in a time warp and in plantation culture, the mammy, wench, and buck are not subjects but objects for the reader's gaze."[54] Brooks holds that these objectified caricatures offer a minstrel "side show" to the novel's "main act" of light-skinned, mixed-race characters. Instead, we might read the odd reappearance of antebellum stock characters in this early twentieth-century novel as another instance of textual atavism. Chesnutt's *The Marrow of Tradition* similarly juxtaposes plantation tropes—Sandy, Mammy Jane, and her grandson Jerry (who is made to fetch "Calhoun cocktails," another nod to the white characters' antebellum fixation)—with a new generation of free African Americans. The Carteret's young black nurse, a paid employee with no pretense of emotional connection to the white family, regards these characters with disdain: "these old-time negroes, she said to herself, made sick with their slavering over the white folks."[55] These characterizations overlay the past with the present, indicating the coexistence of two supposedly separate epochs. Because antebellum conditions did not instantly evaporate with formal abolition, Chesnutt describes this era as an "imperfect blending of old with new, of race with race, of slavery with freedom."[56] Both authors respond to the theory of black atavism by representing the persistence of ancestral "types" as an effect of slavery's long cultural aftereffects. These anachronistic characters represent a kind of "temporal drag," to borrow Elizabeth Freeman's phrase, further signaling the novel's focus the uncomfortable persistence of the antebellum past in the post-Reconstruction present through the recurrence of ancestral texts.[57]

Through a double plot structure that folds back on itself, Hopkins slowly reveals that American society after Reconstruction is merely a repetition and continuation of a tragic past, with only the names and surface details changed. Expressing the same conclusion in *The Marrow of Tradition*, Chesnutt describes Emancipation as only a temporary solution that had not secured black freedom in the nadir: "the weed had been cut down, but its roots remained, deeply imbedded in the soil, to spring up and trouble a new generation."[58] Despite the official narrative of Reconstruction, Hopkins insists that there has been no progress for African Americans, no successful crossing of the bridge into freedom and a new national era, only the sinister blossoming of antebellum slavery into fin-de-siècle racist violence. The transformation of the Enson brothers into Benson and Henson signifies the splintering of the family identity so rigorously protected, even fetishized, in the first plot. Importantly, the disclosure of concealed identities reveals that none of the women in the novel are white. All of the seemingly white families turn out to be interracial due to these mixed-race women's role as the transmitters of racial identity. Furthermore, this novel has a preponderance of dead mothers, namely Cuthbert's mother, Aurelia's mother, Jewell's putative white mother, the Enson brothers' mother, Elise Bradford, the mother of the illegitimate Enson heir, and Hagar's putative white mother. The absence of mothers suggests the impossibility of securing the pure matrilineal racial heritage required to uphold the sanctity of whiteness and therefore of a racially defined American identity. This novel constructs maternal inheritance as ultimately inaccessible and mysterious, flouting the culture's obsession with white women as the safeguards and vessels of American national identity through white racial purity. In the white imagination, women carry the threat of racial impurity, a cultural fear that Hopkins explored repeatedly through representations of women with mysterious genealogies. Hopkins debunks the white woman at the center of the myth of the white family whose sexual and racial purity served as the justification for the long campaign of racist terrorism in the nadir that garishly illustrated the failure of Reconstruction.

Hopkins ironically reproduces the alarmist antimiscegenation rhetoric in a fictionalized newspaper response to the revelation that a Senator's wife was a mixed-race woman passing as white: "This story, showing, as it does, the ease with which beautiful half-breeds may enter our best society without detection, is a source of anxiety to the white citizens of our country. At this rate the effects of slavery can never be eradicated, and our most distinguished families are not immune from contact with this mongrel race" (266). With this assertion that if present conditions prevail, "the effects of slavery can never be eradicated," Hopkins restates the antiracist message of the novel from the perspective of whites concerned that the genealogical repercussions of slavery will taint the national future. The editorial ends with the proclamation "we cannot . . . unlock the gates of caste and bid her enter. Posterity forbids it" (267). This passage voices white anxiety about the damage that a mixed-race woman functioning as white could do to "our most distinguished families" and to white reproductive futurity, pointing to the disciplinary function of "posterity." The atavistic paradigm of fin-de-siècle racism imagined that traces of black ancestry would cause biopolitical crisis in the future American population. This novel capitalizes on precisely this paranoia, appropriating the discourses of "miscegenation," atavism, and racial death to deconstruct the oppressive myth of the white family.

Through a constellation of racial revelations, *Hagar's Daughter*'s white characters come to realize that "black blood is everywhere—in society and out, and in our families even; we cannot feel assured that it has not filtered into the most exclusive families" (160). Just as the antebellum Enson family was exposed as racially mixed, so is the Bowen family at the heart of post-Reconstruction political society. Earlier in the novel, one of the characters declares that "the Bowen family is *white* right through" (224, original emphasis). As it turns out, the Bowens are neither white nor a "family" in the way it first seems. Zenas is described as having "the hair and skin of an Indian" and Estelle and Jewell, apparently a white woman and her white stepdaughter, are revealed to be biologically mother and daughter, and both African American according to the laws of hypodescent. As Hazel Carby notes, "the threads of black inheritance and heritage extend to the Washington elite, to the heart of the white power structure," providing another important link to *Clotel*.[59] Furthermore, Zenas and his daughter are not biologically related, so these white families are further deconstructed by the revelation that relationships previously thought to be biological and natural are actually adoptive and constructed, disrupting the hereditarian paradigm.

Shocked that Ellis Enson plans to remarry the recently widowed and racially revealed Hagar, Sumner asks, "ought we not, as Anglo-Saxons, keep the fountain head of our racial stream as unpolluted as possible? . . . I am willing to allow the Negroes education, to see them acquire business, money, and social status within a certain environment. I am not averse even to their attaining political power" (271). Enson is dissatisfied with Sumner's white liberal prejudice, pointing out that he is willing to concede "every privilege but the vital one of deciding a question of the commonest personal liberty which is the fundamental principle of the holy family tie" (271). This exchange clarifies the novel's position that only the willingness to interracialize the family, or rather to accept the interracial character of the American family, will truly mean that African Americans are the acknowledged equals of whites. Hopkins refuses to segregate sociopolitical matters from sexual and familial mores, revealing instead the inextricability of these considerations.

We might understand this position as a reaction against not only white prejudice but also prominent models of black accommodation. In his famous "Atlanta Compromise" address in 1895, Booker T. Washington acquiesced to white fears of social integration to promote a vision of black economic progress that he described as a continuation of race relations under slavery:

> As we have proven our loyalty to you in the past, in nursing your children, watching by the sick bed of your mothers and fathers, and often following them with tear dimmed eyes to their graves, so in the future in our humble way, we shall stand by you with a devotion that no foreigner can approach, ready to lay down our lives, if need be, in defense of yours, interlacing our industrial, commercial, civil and religious life with yours in a way that shall make the interests of both races one. In all things that are purely social we can be as separate as the fingers, yet one as the hand in all things essential to mutual progress.[60]

Washington describes a twentieth-century black workforce of humble servants with a long history of service to white families. He assures the white audience that African Americans will continue to be as loyal as they were to previous generations of white slaveholders, harboring no grudge for centuries of enslavement: "you can be sure in the future, as you have been in the past, that you and your families will be surrounded by the most patient, faithful, law-abiding and unresentful people that the world has seen." Most importantly, Washington separates interracial intimacy from national progress, suggesting that segregation can be maintained as long as black economic progress is allowed. Striking a more menacing note, he threatens white America with the image of black backwardness that they feared, suggesting that obstacles to black progress will mire white Americans in the same primitive morass: "we shall prove a veritable body of death, stagnating, depressing, retarding every effort to advance the body politic."[61]

Hopkins, on the other hand, clearly argues that segregation in "purely social" matters has derailed the process of black civic empowerment and specifically pinpoints the family as the ultimate frontier of integration. She refuses to concede sexuality or the family as private or purely "social" considerations.

Hagar's Daughter analogizes the "impassable social chasm" enforced between blacks and whites in the service of protecting the purity of "white blood" to an impassable bridge into freedom and a new historical era, suggesting that even in the twentieth century, African Americans were stuck in the hereditarily subordinate status that defined the condition of the enslaved. Rather than trading in socioscientific suggestions of black morbidity, she ultimately suggests that the white family is reverting and declining instead.

Although Ellis and Hagar reunite, and the good brother regains possession of the patrimonial estate, seemingly restoring the order that the Civil War disrupted, the novel ends with a powerful symbol of the degraded future of the Enson family and the nation that it represents. The happy ending of this interracial couple is compromised by the fact that their child, the title character, has died prematurely of a sudden illness, foiling the marriage plot.[62] Hopkins rejects the heterofamilial teleology of novelistic conventions that would turn again to the institution of the family for narrative conclusion.

The only Enson child remaining symbolizes the degraded status of this formerly proud and fiercely protected white line: "Across the lawn of Enson Hall a child—a boy—ran screaming and laughing. . . . It was the child of St. Clair Enson and Elise Bradford, the last representative of the Enson family. . . . In him was embodied, a different form, a lesson of the degradation of slavery" (284). Hopkins describes this unnamed bastard with the Faulknerian epithet "the motherless and worse than fatherless child" (253). This last white child, or "end son" that the family name itself seems to presage, exemplifies not the taint of interracialism perverting a white dynasty but rather the decay and corruption of whiteness, its failure to evolve and progress. The proud Enson line, so strenuously protected from the taint of blackness, continues only in illegitimacy and violence, hobbled by its own maniacal attempts to deny and exclude the blackness that it already contains. In a radical reversal of popular discourses of postbellum black decline, Hopkins depicts whites meeting that end instead. Far from extinction, "black blood is everywhere," plentiful, if unacknowledged, in the white families understood to constitute and represent the nation.

Despite reformist zeal in the early republic that aimed to root out the remnants of a society based on blood inheritance and permanent aristocratic distinctions, "race" and related conceptions of nationalism gave Americans throughout the nineteenth century a scientifically sanctioned way of talking about ancestry, blood distinctions, natural heirs, and interloping outsiders. In historical romances of American racial formation like *The House of the Seven Gables*, a marriage that once would have been regarded as a violation of social taboos ultimately obliterates blood distinctions. The descendants of formerly segregated peoples become joint inheritors of family estate and ensure its transmission to the future. African American literature throughout the nineteenth century contends that American blood is racially "mixed," that if national identity is a heritable property, then many people who are enslaved or otherwise marginalized also hold a natural claim to it, that there is no stable blood difference on which to build a system of social relations. But rather than imagining a future integrated ideal in which whites have finally acknowledged their African American relatives, who in turn have eagerly joined the family, authors like Brown, Hopkins, and Chesnutt explore the value of repudiating this inheritance.

The Marrow of Tradition culminates with Janet Miller (a kind of Hagar's daughter, the dispossessed child of a white patriarch and his servant) refusing her legitimate claim to a white family estate. With the Carteret heir dying, in need of an operation that only Dr. Miller can perform, Olivia begs for help from the half-sister she has always shunned, although Janet's own child has been killed in the riot. Olivia consciously manipulates her with the language of shared blood, kinship, family obligation, and responsibility, but although Janet sends her husband to the dying child out of human decency, she is not moved by the tactics of familial pathos. Indeed, she pointedly rejects the white family inheritance and identity that Olivia has finally offered: "all my life you have hated and scorned and despised me . . . you have robbed me all these years. . . . Now, when this tardy recognition comes, for which I have waited so long, it is tainted with fraud and crime and blood, and I must pay for it with my child's life. . . . I throw you back your father's name, your father's wealth, your sisterly recognition. I want none of them,—they are bought too dear" (329)! This scene suggests that even when one has a lawful claim to an inheritance, there may be significant ethical reasons to renounce and terminate that inheritance, to stop the past from continuing and to resist entanglement with those who have perpetuated it. For Chesnutt, Hopkins, and Brown, assertions of kin relation across the color line do not inspire hopes for a happy reunion, but instead serve as the basis of their rejection of the white American family as a drag on republican ideals.

CODA

cᐱつ

Writing in Blood

Print Kinship?

The search for descent is not the erecting of foundations: on the contrary, it disturbs what was previously thought immobile; it fragments what was thought unified; it shows the heterogeneity of what was imagined consistent with itself.

> —Michel Foucault, "Nietzsche, Genealogy, History," in *The Foucault Reader*, ed. Paul Rabinow (New York: Pantheon, 1984), 82.

Human beings are the only creatures on the planet who reproduce through archives.

> —Wai-Chee Dimock, *Through Other Continents: American Literature through Deep Time.* (Princeton: Princeton UP, 2008), 58.

What is kinship? Definitions not only vary but conflict: the biogenetic substance of common descent, a set of roles and performances, the coordination of social with sexual reproduction that mandates gender and heterosexuality, a sense of affinity that is not necessarily genealogical, the social structure that makes hominids into human beings. In response to a culture that reified the family, regarding it as the stable basis for scientific and legal discourses of personhood, the works addressed in the preceding chapters utilize literary techniques to assert that the family is, above all, a fiction. Kinship is a collection of overlapping stories about relatedness and its meanings that assume certain forms in relation to cultural and historical context. It rests on metaphors like "blood," texts like marriage licenses and birth certificates, formulaic narratives, and ritual retellings. Family histories, even genealogical charts researched with scholarly precision, are creative texts, not positive records. But is fiction a family? What is the relationship between ancestral lineage and literary "inheritance" or traditions? For those attempting to think a way out of politicized familialism, is print finally opposed to blood or simply another technology for extending its logic?

This book aims to debunk two myths about the post-Enlightenment family. First, contrary to the prevailing view that domestic intimacy supplanted traditional patriarchal verticality in this period, the nineteenth century saw the intensification of blood inheritance as the basis of two totalizing concepts: race and nation. Genealogical and conjugal paradigms were not strictly successive or oppositional, though this is precisely how modern forms of family and governance represent themselves as modern.[1] Second, far from being universally venerated in the nineteenth century, the domestic family was a site of contention across the ideological spectrum. Its perceived decline was welcomed by radicals and utilized by conservatives as an argument against social change. The authors addressed in the preceding chapters, mostly liberal reformers, portray the family not only as the site of disciplinary intimacy but also as the stronghold of a naturalized rhetoric of exclusion based on a principle of blood inheritance that is antithetical to republicanism. A third argument, implicit in my methodology, is that imaginative literature is a vital source of evidence about the history and meaning of the American family, and more specifically, that the novel has been a primary medium for critiques of the very familial context that gave rise to the form.

In the prevailing critical accounts, the domestic family created the novel, and the novel helped to create the nation. According to Jürgen Habermas, this literary form emerged as both the product and the record of a new kind of subjectivity produced in the private sphere of the conjugal family, a guarded realm cordoned off from economic considerations where relations were regarded as purely human. The confessional communications within this sphere, especially the emotive family letter, gave voice to a new consciousness that formed the core of the novel's sensibility.[2] From their intertwined beginnings, these new forms have worked in tandem. In the eighteenth-century, the novel spread the Enlightenment view of parental authority as tyrannical, offering the orphan as the representative modern subject and associating the ancestral family with gothic monstrosity.[3] In the nineteenth-century, the marriage plot and sentimental novels eroticized the conjugal realm, advertising the model of family relations appropriate for upholding and representing the modern nation-state. Novel plots thematically insisted that the family was the yardstick of both personal development and societal health, and the experience of reading novels gave rise to models of temporality and imaginary interpersonal connections necessary for national consciousness.[4]

In the United States, however, the relationship between the novel, the family, and the political community was never seamlessly symbiotic. Michael Warner argues that in the early republic, publication was synonymous with civic virtue and public action, so that the rise of a literary form encouraging private, imaginary identifications represented a crisis in republicanism and hastened the transition to nineteenth-century nationalism.[5] Warner suggests that a true novel tradition did not emerge in the eighteenth-century United States because republican discourse so firmly associated print with the public that American authors were not comfortable in the inward world of the novel. Indeed, he holds that American novels before Cooper are characteristically at war with their own generic conventions, retaining a sense that publication intrinsically entails a duty to the public good: "Americans to a surprising degree, and even in aesthetic discourse, understood their engagements with print as activities in the republican public sphere subject to its norms."[6]

American Blood presents the nineteenth-century American novel's unruly representations of the family as evidence that this literary form did not monolithically abet the rise of nationalism. Indeed many novels call for a return to republican wariness of the family, even up to the turn of the twentieth century. Although a number of the works treated in this study are didactic and indifferent to aesthetics in a way that Warner regards as non-novelistic, classic studies have long held that even the most "literary," seemingly apolitical American novels are averse to the marriage plot and the private realm of heterosexuality, preferring instead interracial male friendship and outdoor adventure.[7] If the scarcity of American novels that adhere to the traditional form reveals the legacy of republicanism, it is not only in a preference for direct public participation but also in relation to the family. In the supposed golden age of both nationalism and the domestic family, American literature displays a wariness of inherited legacies that restrain self-determination and social equality, a republican desire to curtail the power of private institutions that endanger public life, and a resistance to the tyranny that both the dead and the unborn can exert over the living generation. The novel is the product, indeed the chief art form of the domestic family epoch, but it has an unpredictable relationship to it. Rather than assuming that this form aligns with the modern family, we would do better to regard it is as an analytical discourse of this institution, dense with information about its workings, its limitations, its objectives, and results. Moreover, as Nancy Bentley notes, kinship in the American context provides a signifier for the nation that is unstable at best, and this misfit "is actually a boon for the novel, a resource for writing beyond and against the stories preferred by the state. . . . Against the singular story told again and again by national allegory, the epistemology of the novel uncovers multiple mutations of an ongoing history at once traumatic, creative, and generative."[8] For this reason, the authors in this study utilize the novel as a uniquely advantageous form for critiquing the family-nation analogy.[9]

Indeed, some of these texts seem to test the possibility of literature itself as a postfamilial project that might unseat certain aspects of conventional kinship structures. In the work of Washington Irving, for example, Warner has detected the desire for imaginative literature to provide "generational continuity that would be social and public rather than merely private and familial."[10] Perhaps especially in the American context, Warner suggests, where republican ideology opposed the perpetuation of the self in estates and noble lineages, authors may "pursue mortality-transcendence through other means," namely, immortalizing their names to "literary posterity."[11] In addition to lineal propagation, literature can foster the sense of connection and community that kinship ostensibly offers. Along these lines, Fanny Fern's autobiographical novel *Ruth Hall* (1854) portrays the relationship between an author and the reading public as a superior third family form after consanguineous and conjugal models have failed. The protagonist escapes her unhappy childhood for a marriage dominated by tyrannical, disapproving in-laws. Her household is largely ambivalent about the birth of her first child, which soon dies, as does her husband. Once she is widowed, her relatives by both birth and marriage refuse to provide for her financially or emotionally. When she starts writing periodical articles, she discovers not only an independent way to support herself but also a purified kinship network. Ruth's writing seems to forge direct relationships with readers that open possibilities for real interdependencies, not the passive, imaginary identifications by which novels foster nationalism. For instance, one fan letter from a mother convinced she will soon die in childbirth asks Ruth to become the guardian of her child. Ruth, who never reunites with her blood relatives or remarries, entrusts the care of her own children to her editor, Mr. Walter: "if he *really* felt such a brotherly interest in her, how sweet it would be to have him for a brother; a—*real, warm-hearted, brotherly brother*, such as she had never known."[12] Ruth has had a "real" biological brother all her life but apparently not a "*brotherly brother*." Periodical culture provides her with a kin network more familial than the family.[13]

Thus in novels that seem to chafe against the novel form, American authors have tested the possibility that literature might function as a queer kinship system of the kind Elizabeth Freeman has described as "a replicative system, but not a heterosexually reproductive one."[14] Focusing on the transmission of corporeal movements and rituals, she observes how physical tropes are "'passed on' and modified," linking the performers in a chain of influence and homage, an embodied but not familial way to "'be *long*,' to endure in corporeal form over time . . . to 'hold out' a hand across time and touch the dead or those not born yet, to offer oneself beyond one's own time."[15] As a technology for "being long," one of the most fundamental functions of writing is to record and transmit things that might be lost if entrusted only to private interpersonal transmission. Laurel Thatcher Ulrich observes that writing offers "a way of extending one's identity beyond death. When we are dead and in the grave and all our bones are rotten, perhaps some of the things we create will remain."[16] Texts might survive indefinitely while human memory is imperfect and human bodies die. Like sexual reproduction, authorship offers the hope of a kind of earthly existence after death.[17]

Extending this vision to the largest possible scale, Wai Chee Dimock theorizes the long history of global literature as a kinship network. She describes the relationships between seemingly disparate textual traditions as a Wittgensteinian family resemblance that branches through all of human history, defying traditional periodization or national taxonomy.[18] This theory rests on a mathematical rather than biological conception of kinship that she calls a "periodic rate of return." She holds that in a large enough population over a long enough time, there will be individuals who are similar, "not necessarily a genealogical connection, but, just as often, a broad spectrum of affinities."[19] She celebrates what she views as a uniquely human capacity to "have 'kin' above and beyond what biology permits," so that oppressive blood paradigms are overthrown by statistics: "biological reproduction is not the only game in town. . . . The tyranny of biology, in other words, has been upstaged by a mathematical law that performs the same reproductive function."[20]

But the problematic qualities of kinship inevitably creep into even this utopian design for textual-numeral connection and longevity. Reproduction shifts from metaphor to ideology, becoming just as compulsory and inescapable as in traditional forms of family: "it reduces us to nothing; but, in reproducing us, perhaps against our will, it gives us a deep field of kinship."[21] Dimock views intergenerational continuity as an inflexible obligation; merely being alive entails the responsibility to "pick up where the dead leave off, though we are bound to fall short," which in turn compels "future humans to act on our behalf."[22] This model of relatedness insists on strict generational continuity, a procreative logic suggesting that the most profound duty of the present is to connect the past to the future. Dimock's "endless kinship" is an important assertion of common humanity through the shared project of literature, but its familial template hamstrings its vision of anti-identitarian human connectivity. Christopher Peterson, perhaps the most stalwart critic of discourses of alternative kinship, reminds us, "Insofar as queer affiliation mimes the conventional belief that kinship can supercede alterity, it remains implicated in a violent reduction of the other to the same."[23] Rather than expanding the discourse of familial sameness from the nation to the globe, there is value in imagining most of the world as a place outside one's family and cultivating an ethics of public life that can deal with difference. Indeed, reading and writing might help to facilitate a relation to the world outside the family that does not require a conviction of homogeneity. The importance of nonfamilial relationships— students and teachers, readers and writers, civic coalitions, meaningful contact with strangers—is underestimated as a consequence of kinship's vaunted status as the foundation of both human life and civilization. Metaphors notwithstanding, these relationships are not reducible to kinship nor are they necessarily reflections or reproductions of family dynamics.

Kinship metaphors may allow us to see imaginative literature as a queer paradigm that can replace and in some ways outperform the family, but insisting on this comparison acquiesces to an encroaching familial logic, grafting onto texts the very system they may seek to deconstruct. Furthermore, fiction writing is not always done for posterity or as an attempt to "be long," to return to Freeman's useful phrase. Harriet Beecher Stowe, William Wells Brown, Anna Dickinson, and Pauline Hopkins used fiction to address urgent sociopolitical crises, calling not for an improved situation for future generations, but for immediate, sweeping change for the living. Even Sarah Orne Jewett's work, despite its ambivalence about the ramifications of deemphasizing the family, explores a way of life at odds with heterosexuality and reproduction, tacitly privileging writing, along with stasis and noncontinuity, over marriage and motherhood. Jewett's fictionalization of her regional culture, though it is available to future generations of readers, is not comparable to reproduction through the descent of genes, bodies, real or symbolic estate in a bloodline.

Indeed, the antifamilial perversions of form and content this study has examined are not as anomalous as they first seem. While they run counter to specific ideologies of race and nationalism in mainstream American culture, these works align with a broader literary historical trend. They corroborate Edward Said's account of "something like an event, near the end of the nineteenth century, in the life of the novel itself."[24] In authors like Gustave Flaubert, Joseph Conrad, and Thomas Hardy, he senses "a revulsion from the novelist's whole procreative enterprise," a recognition "that the dynastic principles of traditional narrative now seemed somehow inappropriate."[25] Over the course of the century, Said posits, as the form came to focus on lives that are exceptional precisely in their departure from normative family structures, the novel assumed "a compositional integrity which is ironically based on sterility, celibacy, and eccentricity."[26] Critical definitions of literary forms, genres, and traditions steeped in familial discourse train us to see linear development, dynastic causality, inheritance, and continuity, but Said's commonsense assertion that genealogical continuity plainly differs from the novel's "radical internal discontinuity as well as its disjunctive relations with reality" offers a divergent understanding of the form.[27] Rather than mirroring procreation, nineteenth-century novels may aim to be "productive at exactly those points where life is not."[28]

We might view the woman on the Long Bridge as both a model of politicized queer negativity and also, paradoxically, a figure for the longevity of stories, especially in print. While writers and readers have been captivated precisely by her choice of death over life and reproduction, the print medium nonetheless ensures her a kind of unquiet survival. In her citation of this anecdote, Hopkins seems to embrace her genealogical relationship to Brown and the narratives that precede her, even as she rejects the white fixation on ancestry as irrational and stultifying. Her overt reutilization of an episode that was already poached from a newspaper might be said to enact a print genealogy free from the chauvinisms of the family. This formal practice undercuts traditional associations of authorship with paternity, originality, and conception, transforming an outdated anecdote in a disjunctive new context.

While it is tempting to think of print as a utopian space of homage, cooperative meaning making, and inheritance beyond blood, Hopkins's use of this meme expresses instead a galling sense of stasis, condemning her generation's forced continuity with Brown's. These works do not idealize print or the novel form as a purified kin matrix or a new technology for reproduction. Indeed, they utilize the medium in part to deal with aspects of the past that rightfully should be terminated, archiving experiences that are unredeemable in individual lives but indispensable to the record of human history.[29] *American Blood* has focused primarily on a tradition of reform fiction in the United States that disrupts genre conventions to unmoor the novel from the blood logic that also motivates racial nationalism. These works are not outliers but exemplars of an overlooked impulse in the nineteenth-century novel that calls into question the assumed heteronormativity of the form more broadly.[30] Contrary to the nationalist familial ideal of unbroken succession, they work against the reproductive tendencies of textuality to model the value of disruption.

NOTES

INTRODUCTION

1. Alexis de Tocqueville, *Democracy in America* Vol. 2 (New York: Colonial Press, 1900), 202.
2. Ibid.
3. See Jay Fliegelman, *Prodigals and Pilgrims: The American Revolution against Patriarchal Authority, 1750–1800* (Cambridge: Cambridge UP, 1982).
4. This project affirms what scholars working to erode the "separate spheres" model of nineteenth-century history have suggested for the past decade: there never was a private sphere, but the fantasy of a vulnerable, embattled private sphere has been a durably effective way to mobilize an exclusionary American nationalism. See *No More Separate Spheres!* eds. Cathy Davidson and Jessamyn Hatcher (Durham: Duke UP, 2002).
5. "Disciplinary intimacy" is Richard Brodhead's term. See *Cultures of Letters: Scenes of Reading and Writing in Nineteenth-Century America* (Chicago: U of Chicago P, 1995), 17–18.
6. In addition to the genealogical discourses in literature, science, law, and political culture treated more extensively in this study, the mid-nineteenth-century United States also saw the inception of anthropological kinship studies with Lewis Henry Morgan's *Systems of Consanguinity and Affinity of the Human Family*, begun in 1858 and published in 1871. Morgan, a New York state senator, was influential to later theorists of kinship and the family including Marx and Engels, Darwin, Freud, and Levi-Strauss. Morgan's interest in kinship was inspired by his study of the Iroquois. As Trautmann notes, "kinship had to be discovered, and it was discovered the discordant, noncommonsensical kinship of the cultural other." Thomas R. Trautmann, *Lewis Henry Morgan and the Invention of Kinship* (Berkeley: U of California P, 1988), 3.
7. Many excellent literary studies make note of consanguinity rhetoric in the Revolutionary era. Betsy Erkkila argues that "anxious appeals to blood kinship underwrite the language of the founding documents," and in the nation-state that these documents established, "blood became a national fetish, a means of affirming political community, kinship, citizenship, and union at the same time that it became the grounds for exclusion, expulsion, negation, and extermination." She notes that the founders' extensive use of the language of "common kindred," "consanguinity," and "common blood," framed "the federal republic as a national family of blood kin." Betsy Erkkila, *Mixed Bloods and Other Crosses: Rethinking American Literature from the Revolution to the Culture Wars* (Philadelphia: U of Pennsylvania P, 2005), 2, 7, 5.

Jared Gardner similarly observes that "the early novel, Federalist tracts, and racial science inaugurated in 1787 a particularly American preoccupation with breeding." In other words, American literature, national identity, and racial biologism have been imbricated in the construction of a blood-based national identity since their simultaneous beginnings. Jared Gardner, *Master Plots: Race and the Founding of American Literature, 1787–1845* (Baltimore: Johns Hopkins UP, 1998), 23. On republican motherhood, see Linda Kerber, "The Republican Mother: Women and the Enlightenment—An American Perspective." *American Quarterly* 28.2 (Summer 1976), 187–205.

8. Furthermore, classical republicanism theorized citizenship as a definitive departure from ancestral groupings, a move from blood relations to civic relations. Ivan Hannaford explains: "previously order had depended on the observation of hierarchical rules pertaining to household, family, clan, and tribe," but with the invention of the ideal of citizenship in ancient Greece, society underwent a "transition from kith and kin to polity, from blood relationship to political relationship." Ivan Hannaford. *Race: The History of an Idea in the West* (Baltimore: Johns Hopkins UP, 1996), 10.

9. On the problem of a perpetual state produced from a revolution, see Hannah Arendt, *On Revolution* (New York: Penguin, 1965), 232.

10. My treatment of "nation" as a concept rooted in the idea of a homogenous population with a common ancestral origin counters Benedict Anderson's influential claim that the nation was imagined through print discourses, replacing older social forms based on the dynasty or the clan: "from the start the nation was conceived in language, not in blood." Benedict Anderson. *Imagined Communities: Reflections on the Origin and Spread of Nationalism*. (New York: Verso, 1983), 145.

   For other critical sources holding that nationalism assumes blood homogeneity, see the following: Paul Gilroy, *There Ain't No Black in the Union Jack: The Cultural Politics of Race and Nation* (London: Routledge, 2002), 144–45; Alys Eve Weinbaum, *Wayward Reproductions: Genealogies of Race and Nation in Transatlantic Modern Thought* (Durham: Duke UP, 2004), 38.

11. Historian George B. Forgie has detailed a number of factors that mark this decade as the dividing line between the revolutionary era and the subsequent generation characterized by filial piety to the founders. For instance, the first five American presidents had all directly contributed to the nation's founding. The sixth, John Quincy Adams, took office in 1825, representing the transition of power to the next generation, in this case literally a son's rise to the former office of his father. The following year, the deaths of Jefferson and John Adams coincided with the fiftieth anniversary of the adoption of the Declaration of Independence, marking a moment of commemoration and reflection on the founders' legacy. See George B. Forgie, *Patricide in the House Divided: A Psychological Interpretation of Lincoln and His Age* (New York: Norton, 1981), 49–53.

12. Catharine Maria Sedgwick, *The Linwoods; Or, "Sixty Years Since" in America* (Hanover, NH: UP of New England, 2002), 41.

13. Sedgwick, *The Linwoods*, 25. *American Blood* examines the relationship of imaginative literature to the culture of political familialism in the period from 1850 to 1900, when the ideological fusion of family, race, and nation was well established. The literature of the transitional period of the 1820s and 30s demands further study.

14. For an excellent account of the language of national consanguinity in Webster's Bunker Hill address and the Senate debates of the Compromise of 1850, see Gregg

Crane, *Race, Citizenship, and Law in American Literature* (New York: Cambridge UP, 2002), 47–48.

15. Daniel Webster, *A Discourse, Delivered at Plymouth, December 22, 1820. In Commemoration of the First Settlement of New-England*, 3rd ed. (Boston: Wells and Lilly, 1825), 9.

16. Webster, *A Discourse*, 53.

17. Ibid., 58.

18. Ibid., 7.

19. Ibid., 33.

20. Ibid., 39.

21. Ibid., 34.

22. Ibid., 74.

23. Ibid. Mark Rifkin also analyzes the language of national genealogy in Webster's address at Plymouth: "American history appears as the diachronic extension of bloodlines, situating the present as a moment in a relentlessly procreative push toward the future in which identification with the past is a function of filiation to a long line of dead fathers." Mark Rifkin, *When Did Indians Become Straight?: Kinship, The History of Sexuality, and Native Sovereignty* (New York: Oxford UP, 2011), 104.

24. François Weil notes, "Because New England held dominion over the fledgling enterprise of antiquarianism, its proponents were able to argue successfully that the region's local history was the history of the nation in the making." See Weil for an account of Farmer's relationship to the foundation of the Massachusetts Historical Society and the New England Historic Genealogical Society. François Weil, "John Farmer and the Making of American Genealogy," *New England Quarterly* 80.3 (September 2007), 414.

25. Daniel Webster, *A Discourse*, 75.

26. Weil, "John Farmer and the Making of American Genealogy," 433.

27. Ibid., 409.

28. For more on Farmer's role in the birth of American genealogical research, see Francesca Morgan, "Lineage As Capital: Genealogy in Antebellum New England," *New England Quarterly* 83.2 (June 2010): 250–282.

29. Weil, "John Farmer and the Making of American Genealogy," 409.

30. Weil, "John Farmer and the Making of American Genealogy," 420. Morgan, "Lineage As Capital," 259.

31. Farmer's book does not focus exclusively on the descendants of the Mayflower passengers but rather on the early settlers of New England more broadly. Weil suggests that Farmer and his colleagues were directly inspired by Webster's oration at Plymouth. Weil, "John Farmer and the Making of American Genealogy," 416–18.

32. *The Art of Family: Genealogical Artifacts in New England*, ed. D. Brenton Simons (Boston: New England Historic Genealogical Society, 2002), 100.

33. Moreover, these family records present ordered lineages that efface the unstable and multiple family forms that characterize the New World. Nancy Bentley observes that life in the Americas has long been associated with "the threat of a transformative disorder in human kinship" (97). Nancy Bentley, "Creole Kinship: Privacy and the Novel in the New World." *The Oxford Handbook of Nineteenth-Century American Literature*, Ed. Russ Castronovo (New York: Oxford UP, 2012) 97–114.

34. On Webster's role in constructing the Pilgrims as the origin of American history, see Paul D. Erickson, "Daniel Webster's Myth of the Pilgrims," *New England Quarterly* 57.1 (March 1984): 44–64.

35. *The Art of Family*, 75.

36. Elizabeth Povinelli, "Notes on Gridlock: Genealogy, Intimacy, Sexuality," *Public Culture* 14.1 (Winter 2002), 214.

37. "As lineal kinship, solidarity between generations and the economic functions of the extended family dissolve, what takes their place is . . . a nationalization of the family, which has as its counterpart the identification of the national community with a symbolic kinship." Etienne Balibar and Immanuel Wallerstein, *Race, Nation, Class: Ambiguous Identities* (New York: Verso, 1991), 101–102.

38. The title of this project focuses attention on "blood" not only because it was the organizing principle of national identity, but also because it is the metaphor through which the modern conception of "race" was mapped onto the family. "Blood" has served as an exceedingly effective schema for biologizing racial difference because this metaphor has long naturalized the culturally constructed power relations of the family. "Race" is the most vivid example of how the fetter of ancestral identity gives the lie to American discourses of individualist self-making.

39. Frederick Douglass, *My Bondage and My Freedom*, ed. John David Smith (1855; New York: Penguin, 2003), 30.

40. Lindley Spring, *The Negro at Home*, (New York: published by the author, 1868), 115.

41. Ibid., 187.

42. Rifkin, *When Did Indians Become Straight?*, 11–12.

43. Ibid., 102.

44. Elizabeth Povinelli, *The Empire of Love: Toward a Theory of Intimacy, Genealogy, and Carnality* (Durham: Duke UP, 2006), 226.

45. In her autobiography, Zora Neale Hurston writes, "The Negroes who claim that they are descendants of royal African blood have taken a leaf out of the book of the white ancestor-hounds in America, whose folks went to England with William the Conqueror, got restless and caught the *Mayflower* for Boston, then feeling a romantic lack, rushed down the coast and descended from Pocahontas. From the number of her children, one is forced to the conclusion that that Pocahontas wasn't so poky, after all." Zora Neale Hurston, *I Love Myself When I Am Laughing*, (New York: Feminist Press, 1993), 66.

46. John Winthrop, "A Defense of an Order of Court," 1637, in *The Puritans in America: A Narrative Anthology*, eds. Andrew Delbanco and Alan Heimert (Cambridge: Harvard UP, 1985), 164.

47. Thomas Paine, *Common Sense*, 1776 (London: Penguin Classics, 1986), 84.

48. Ibid.

49. Ibid., 85.

50. Ibid., 90.

51. Michael Grossberg, *Governing the Hearth: Law and the Family in Nineteenth-Century America* (Chapel Hill: U of North Carolina P, 1985), 10.

52. William Aikman, *Life at Home; Or, The Family and Its Members* (New York: Samuel R. Wells, 1870), 7.

53. Ibid., 28

54. "The Family is threatened and all men North or South who love and revere it, should be up and a doing." George Fitzhugh, *Cannibals All! Or, Slaves without Masters* (Richmond, VA: Morris, 1857), 293.

55. Ibid., 281.

56. Lisa Cochran Higgins, "Adulterous Individualism, Socialism, and Free Love in Nineteenth-Century Anti-Suffrage Writing," *Legacy* 21.2 (2004), 194. One hundred

years later in the 1970s, debate of the proposed Equal Rights Amendment to the Constitution revealed that the rhetorical yoking of gender equality and the endangerment of the family remained an effective antifeminist strategy.

57. Roddey Reid, "Death of the Family,' or Keeping Human Beings Human," *Posthuman Bodies*. ed. Judith Halberstam (Bloomington: Indiana UP, 1995), 185. Reid notes that a posture of weakness is the modus operandi of this familial politics: "the handwringing and expressions of alarm over the decline or death of The Family [have] always been a tactic for reinscribing and protecting the so-called normative 'humanity' of (straight) upper-middle-class whites through stigmatizing social others for lack of 'family'" (186).

58. Alexis de Tocqueville, *Democracy in America* Vol. 1 (New York: Appleton, 1899), 407.

59. William Benjamin Smith, *The Color Line: A Brief in Behalf of the Unborn* (New York: McClure, Phillips, and Co., 1905), ix.

60. Ibid., 7.

61. While it is true that the American family weathered particularly dramatic upheavals and challenges in the nineteenth century, my larger point is that this institution is in fact constituted by anxiety, inseparable from the fear of disintegration, decline, and doom. Like masculinity and whiteness, the American family has been "in crisis" in not only this but in every period of American history because its power is derived in part from the assertion of a threatened or vulnerable pose despite the reality of its hegemonic position.

62. Thomas and Mary Gove Nichols, *Marriage: Its History, Character, and Results* (New York: T.L. Nichols, 1854), 378.

63. Ibid., 299.

64. Victoria Woodhull, "The Scarecrows of Sexual Slavery: An Oration" (New York: Woodhull and Claflin Publications, 1874), 21.

65. "Although the ideology of the home as a haven in a heartless world gained its ascendancy during the antebellum period, its route to acceptance was anything but uncontested." David M. Lubin, *Picturing a Nation: Art and Social Change in Nineteenth-Century America* (New Haven: Yale UP, 1994), 163–64.

66. Indeed, Fitzhugh supports his claim that free society is a failure by pointing out how many groups in the North were restless to overthrow it: "Why have you Bloomer's and Women's Right's men, and strong-minded women, and Mormons, and anti-renters, and 'vote myself a farm' men, Millerites, and Spiritual Rappers, and Shakers, and Widow Wakemanites, and Agrarians, and Grahamites, and a thousand other superstitious and infidel Isms at the North?" Fitzhugh, *Cannibals All*, 103.

67. Steven Mintz and Susan Kellogg, *Domestic Revolutions: A Social History of American Family Life* (New York: Simon and Schuster, 1989), 64.

68. Carl J. Guarneri, *The Utopian Alternative: Fourierism in Nineteenth-Century America* (Ithaca, NY: Cornell UP, 1991), 3.

69. John Humphrey Noyes, *American Socialist* 1.2 (Oneida, NY), 1.

70. Albert Brisbane, "Association and a Social Reform" *The Boston Quarterly Review* 5.8 (Boston, 1842), 24.

71. M. Edgeworth Lazarus, *Love vs. Marriage* (New York: Fowler and Wells, 1852), 144.

72. Ibid., 126.

73. This feminist thesis is most often attributed to Gayle Rubin's celebrated essay, "The Traffic in Women: Notes on the 'Political Economy' of Sex," in *Toward an Anthropology of Women*, ed. Rayna Reiter (New York: Monthly Review Press, 1975). If

Rubin's analysis echoes nineteenth-century radical feminism in some fundamental ways, the antifeminist opposition was also unchanged in wielding alarmist familial endangerment rhetoric to block women's rights. At the time Rubin was writing "The Traffic in Women," Phyllis Schlafly and other antifeminist opponents of the proposed Equal Rights Amendment trumpeted the view that sociopolitical equality would destroy the American family and usher in an era of rampant homosexuality, abortion, and compulsory "unisex" bathrooms.

74. *Love, Marriage, and Divorce, and the Sovereignty of the Individual: A Discussion between Henry James, Horace Greeley and Stephen Pearl Andrews*, 1853 (New York: M & S Press, 1975), 49.

75. Michele Barrett and Mary McIntosh, "The Anti-Social Family" in *Families in the U.S.: Kinship and Domestic Politics*. eds. Karen V. Hansen and Anita Ilta Garey (Philadelphia: Temple UP 1998), 221.

76. Ibid., 227–28.

77. *Slavery and Marriage: A Dialogue* (Oneida, NY: 1850), 13–14.

78. Michael Warner, *The Trouble with Normal: Sex, Politics, and the Ethics of Queer Life* (Cambridge: Harvard UP, 2000), 89.

79. Herman Melville, *Pierre; Or, the Ambiguities*, in *The Writings of Herman Melville*, vol. 7, eds. Harrison Hayford, Hershel Parker, and G. Thomas Tanselle (Evanston and Chicago: Northwestern UP and the Newberry Library, 1971), 268.

80. Ibid., 13.

81. Carole J. Singley, *Adopting America: Childhood, Kinship, and National Identity in Literature* (New York: Oxford UP, 2011), 3.

82. Jane Tompkins, *Sensational Designs: The Cultural Work of American Fiction, 1790–1860* (New York: Oxford UP, 1986), 277.

83. Shirley Samuels, *Romances of the Republic: Women, the Family, and Violence in the Literature of the Early American Nation* (New York: Oxford UP, 1996), 19.

84. Ibid.

85. Elizabeth Barnes, *States of Sympathy: Seduction and Democracy in the American Novel* (New York: Columbia UP, 1997), 3.

86. Ibid., 4.

87. Cindy Weinstein, *Family, Kinship, and Sympathy in Nineteenth-Century American Literature* (New York: Cambridge UP, 2004), 12.

88. Claudia Tate, *Domestic Allegories of Political Desire: The Black Heroine's Text at the Turn of the Century* (New York: Oxford UP, 1992), 7. Also see Anne duCille, *The Coupling Convention: Sex, Text, and Tradition in Black Women's Fiction* (New York: Oxford, 1993).

89. Ibid.

90. Hortense Spillers, *Black, White, and in Color: Essays on American Literature and Culture* (Chicago: U of Chicago P, 2003), 219.

91. Ibid., 229.

92. Pauline Hopkins, *Hagar's Daughter* in *The Magazine Novels of Pauline Hopkins* (1901–1902: New York: Oxford UP, Schomberg Library of Nineteenth-Century Black Women Writers, 1988), 160.

93. *American Blood* focuses primarily on the literature of the northeast, the region enduringly regarded as the locus of the American bloodline, thanks in part to nineteenth-century New Englanders like Daniel Webster and John Farmer. However, the nineteenth-century South had an equally fascinating relationship to the discourse of national blood, a rich literary tradition of family romances, and its own iterations of "family values" rhetoric, represented here primarily in the writings of George Fitzhugh. In the decade before the Civil

War, secessionists challenged the metaphor of the national family that Northern compromisers like Webster were constructing to affirm the nation's historical unity and political destiny as one people. As the nation seemed increasingly
likely to disband, the idea that the North and South had never shared common
ancestral blood gained traction. Edward Blum notes, "For decades preceding
the war, northern and southern whites had come to view themselves as fundamentally different peoples with distinct origins, traits, cultures, and economic
systems. Origin myths, which suggested that austere Puritans had populated
the North while hot-blooded Cavaliers had settled the South, emerged to explain sectional differences." Edward Blum, *Reforging the White Republic: Race,
Religion, and American Nationalism, 1865–1898* (Baton Rouge, LA: Louisiana
State UP, 2005), 4.

94. Harriet Beecher Stowe. *A Key to Uncle Tom's Cabin* (London: Sampson Low,
1853), 323.

CHAPTER 1

1. John V. Orth, "After the Revolution: 'Reform' of the Law of Inheritance," *Law and
History Review* 10 (1992): 33.
2. Entail (or fee tail) is an inheritance practice that keeps property within a family for
generations by disallowing the owner to sell an estate or will it away from his heirs.
3. James Kent, *Commentaries on American Law* (New York: O. Halstead, 1830), 4:20.
4. Thomas Jefferson, *The Works of Thomas Jefferson*, ed. Paul Leicester Ford, 12 vols.
(New York: Putnam, 1904–5), 1:77.
5. U.S. Const. art. III, § 3, cl., 2. For more on the framers' desire to curtail the negative ramifications of parental history, see Michael Grossberg, "Citizens and Families: A Jeffersonian Vision of Domestic Relations and Generational Change," in
Thomas Jefferson and the Education of a Citizen, ed. James Gilreath (Washington,
D.C.: Library of Congress, 1999), 3–27.
6. Jefferson to James Madison, 6 September 1789, *Works of Thomas Jefferson*, 6:3–4.
7. Ibid., 6:8–9.
8. Thomas Paine, *Common Sense* (London: D. Jordan Picadilly, 1792), 16, 18.
9. Herbert Sloan, "The Earth Belongs in Usufruct to the Living" in *Jeffersonian Legacies*, ed. Peter S. Onuf (Charlottesville: U of Virginia P, 1993), 303.
10. Ibid., 282.
11. Jefferson to Madison, *Works of Thomas Jefferson*, 6:5.
12. Ibid., 6:8.
13. Jefferson to John Wayles Eppes, 24 June 1813, *Works of Thomas Jefferson*, 11:298.
14. Ayelet Shachar and Ran Hirschl point out that the standing practice of "birthright" citizenship unequally distributes rights and life chances at birth based
on an otherwise discredited system of blood: "reliance on automatic and hereditary transfer of membership entitlement resembles some of the most
deeply criticized, and ultimately abolished, feudal mechanisms of inheritance: the entail. Whereas the archaic institution of hereditary transfer of
landed estates has been discredited in the realm of property, in the most un-
likely of places, we still find a structure that resembles it: that is, in the con-
ferral of political membership" (273). Ayelet Shachar and Ran Hirschl,
"Citizenship as Inherited Property." *Political Theory.* Vol. 35, No. 3 (June
2007), pp. 253–287.
15. Alexis de Tocqueville, *Democracy in America* (1835; New York: Bantam, 2000), 54.

16. Ibid., 56.
17. In Edgar Allan Poe's "The Fall of the House of Usher" (1839), the Usher estate has been transmitted by default according to the principle of primogeniture so that, echoing Tocqueville's description, the house is understood to be the physical analog of the family itself: "It was this deficiency, perhaps, of collateral issue, and the consequent undeviating transmission, from sire to son, of the patrimony with the name, which had, at length, so identified the two as to merge the original title of the estate in the quaint and equivocal appellation of the 'House of Usher'—an appellation which seemed to include, in the minds of the peasantry who used it, both the family and the family mansion" (399).

   Just as Tocqueville posits that this model of property transmission and the form of kinship that rests upon it will come to an end in the United States, the spectacular fall of this house, both the family and the domicile, at the story's end represents the collapse of an uncanny anachronism, presumably "ushering" in a new era. Edgar Allan Poe, "The Fall of the House of Usher," in *Collected Words of Edgar Allan Poe*, vol. 2, *Tales and Sketches 1831–1842*, eds. Thomas Ollive Mabbott et al. (Cambridge: Harvard UP, 1969, 1978), 392–422.
18. George Fitzhugh, *Sociology for the South; Or, The Failure of Free Society* (1854; New York: Burt Franklin, 1965), 236, 189, 192.
19. Ibid., 175.
20. Ibid.,184.
21. Ibid., 190–91, 237.
22. These examples come from *Ishmael* (1863–4), which is also discussed in the next chapter, but a number of Southworth's novels concern cursed female inheritance, like *Retribution* (1849) and *The Family Doom* (1869), which could be read fruitfully in relation to Hawthorne's canonical tale of a blood curse.
23. Herman Melville, *Pierre; Or, the Ambiguities*, in *The Writings of Herman Melville*, vol. 7, eds. Harrison Hayford, Hershel Parker, and G. Thomas Tanselle (Evanston and Chicago: Northwestern UP and the Newberry Library, 1971), 9.
24. Ibid., 9.
25. Ibid., 10.
26. Ibid.
27. Ibid., 11.
28. Ibid.
29. Nathaniel Hawthorne, *The House of the Seven Gables*, eds. William Chavart et al., *The Centenary Edition of the Works of Nathaniel Hawthorne*, vol. 2 (Columbus: Ohio State UP, 1965), 23; hereafter cited parenthetically.
30. For more on Jefferson, inheritance, and French radicalism, see Stanley N. Katz, "Republicanism and the Law of Inheritance in the American Revolutionary Era," *Michigan Law Review* 76 (November 1977), 22–24. Tocqueville also remarks on this shortcoming in the American reform of inheritance that renders it all but symbolic: "the Americans have yet to conceive, as we have done in France, of depriving fathers of one of the principal elements of their power by denying them the freedom to dispose of their property after death. In the United States, there are no limits on what a man may do with his will." Tocqueville, *Democracy*, 336 n.1.
31. Jefferson to Madison, *Works of Thomas Jefferson*, 6:10.
32. Ibid., 6:8–9.
33. Amy Schrager Lang makes a similar point about Holgrave, but in her account, "the answer to class conflict lies in the purified relations of gender." (460) See Amy

Schrager Lang, *The Syntax of Class: Writing Inequality in Nineteenth-Century American Literature* (Princeton: Princeton UP, 2003).

34. Gillian Brown, "Hawthorne, Inheritance, and Women's Property," *Studies in the Novel* 23 (1991): 108.

35. See Michael T. Gilmore, "The Artist and the Marketplace in the House of the Seven Gables," *ELH* 48 (1981): 172–89.

36. Indeed, Hawthorne's Preface insists that the very form of this Romance indicates a preference for purely metaphorical property and eschews any concrete relationship to material reality, as opposed to the novel, as "a house, of materials long in use for constructing castles in the air" (4).

37. As a recurrent symbol in American literature, the ancestral manse concretizes the intangible essence of family identity, making "real" the family property that anthropologists have described as "symbolic estate." Daniel Craig argues that kinship relationships are valued for "transmitting one's 'substance' on to successive generations" (95). To define this "substance," he relies on Bernard Farber's concept of "symbolic family estate," which refers to the nonmaterial aspects of inheritance. Literary works that concern the hereditary transmission of real family property must also be understood to take aim at the deeper issue of the persistence of family identity and its sociopolitical meanings. See Daniel Craig, "Immortality Through Kinship: The Vertical Transmission of Substance and Symbolic Estate," *American Anthropologist* 81 (1979): 94–96. See Bernard Farber, *Kinship and Class: A Midwestern Study* (New York: Basic Books, 1971).

38. T. Walter Herbert, *Dearest Beloved: The Hawthornes and the Making of the Middle-Class Family* (Berkeley: U of California P, 1993), 90. Scholars of historical family dynamics in *The House of the Seven Gables* have focused primarily on the role of a particular construction of femininity in the formation of a middle-class domestic ideal. Herbert describes this work as "Hawthorne's parable of the transition to a domestic family ideology: a family is grounded not in an ancestral establishment but in the mutual love between a self-sufficient man and a 'true woman.'" Joel Pfister agrees that "Hawthorne thematizes . . . the feminization of class." For Pfister, Phoebe "exemplifies the ideological uses to which the 'feminine' was put by the middle class in its class struggle." See Joel Pfister, *The Production of Personal Life: Class, Gender, and the Psychological in Hawthorne's Fiction* (Stanford: Stanford UP, 1991), 161. Similarly, Teresa Goddu argues that "through Phoebe, his Victorian woman, Hawthorne contains the lawless forces of this new order within the boundaries of love and the family." See Teresa Goddu, "The Circulation of Women in *The House of the Seven Gables*," *Studies in the Novel* 23 (1991): 125. While these readings have highlighted middle-class identity formation as represented in *The House of the Seven Gables* and its reliance on Phoebe's femininity as the core of a new family ideal, I argue that this historical reconfiguration of American kinship was crucially reliant on a new model of whiteness and the intensified concern beginning around 1850 with the racial family, its composition, governance, and reproductive capacity.

39. Michael Grossberg, *Governing the Hearth: Law and the Family in Nineteenth-Century America* (Chapel Hill: U of North Carolina P, 1985), 5.

40. Stephanie Coontz, *The Social Origins of Private Life: A History of American Families, 1600–1900* (New York: Verso, 1988), 26.

41. Carroll Rosenberg-Smith, "Sex as Symbol in Victorian Purity: An Ethnohistorical Analysis of Jacksonian America," in *Turning Points: Historical and Sociological Essays on the Family*, eds. John Demos and Sarane Spence Boocock (Chicago: U of Chicago P, 1978), S220.

42. Michel Foucault, *The History of Sexuality: An Introduction*, vol. 1 (New York: Vintage, 1990), 149.

43. Etienne Balibar, "The Nation Form: History and Ideology," in *Race, Nation, Class: Ambiguous Identities*, eds. Etienne Balibar and Emmanuel Wallerstein (London: Verso, 1991), 102, 100.

44. John H. Van Evrie, *Negroes and Negro "Slavery,": The First, an Inferior Race—the Latter, Its Normal Condition* (Baltimore: John D. Toy printer, 1853), 20, 21, 23 (original emphasis).

45. Thomas Paine, *Common Sense*, 12.

46. See Josiah Nott and George Gliddon, *Types of Mankind* (Philadelphia: Lippincott, 1854).

47. Cheryl Harris, "Whiteness As Property," *Harvard Law Review* 106 (1993): 1724.

48. Eva Saks, "Representing Miscegenation Law," in *Interracialisms: Black-White Intermarriage in American History, Literature, and Law*, ed. Werner Sollors (New York: Oxford UP, 2000), 70–72.

49. For an excellent treatment of the role of inheritance in Morgan's work, see Yael Ben-zvi, "Where Did Red Go?: Lewis Henry Morgan's Evolutionary Inheritance and U.S. Racial Imagination," *CR: The New Centennial Review* 7 (Fall 2007) 201–229. As Ben-zvi observes, Morgan did not consider Africans to be members of the single human family he set out to chart, despite his ostensible stance against polygenesis.

50. Lewis Henry Morgan, *Systems of Consanguinity and Affinity of the Human Family* (Washington, D.C.: The Smithsonian Institution, 1871), 14.

51. As David Schneider has pointed out, Morgan's system is resolutely biologist even in the face of viable alternative explanations. A man cannot feel a preference for his "own" son under a system that does not reserve the designation "son" for his direct descendant unless the preference for one's biological offspring is a preexisting natural instinct, which would mean that kinship systems are not ultimately cultural formations. See David M. Schneider, *A Critique of the Study of Kinship* (Ann Arbor: The U of Michigan P, 1984).

52. On Scipio's dialect, see Lloyd Pratt, "Dialect Writing and Simultaneity in the American Historical Romance," *Differences: A Journal of Feminist Cultural Studies* 13 (Fall 2002): 121–42.

53. David Anthony observes: "Scipio's 'Africanist presence' [is] deployed mainly as a means of introducing race into the encounter between the Maules and the Pyncheons. . . . Scipio demarcates the distinctions between upper-class and lower-class white blood so central to the class struggle between the two families." See David Anthony, "Class, Culture, and the Trouble with White Skin in Hawthorne's *The House of the Seven Gables*," *Yale Journal of Criticism* 12 (1999): 261.

54. Anthony, "Class, Culture, and the Trouble with White Skin," 251–54.

55. Smith argues, "In order to challenge the aristocratic conceits of blood purity, Hawthorne calls upon the proof of inherited character upheld by biological racialists and eugenicists." See Shawn Michelle Smith, *American Archives: Gender, Race, and Class in Visual Culture* (Princeton: Princeton UP, 1999), 41. Robert Levine counters that "the Pyncheons' 'eugenicism' . . . must be taken as one of the novel's *subjects*, not its donnée. Rather than advocating blood thinking in the manner of the Pyncheons, Hawthorne takes pains throughout *House* to raise questions about the very notion of blood purity and superiority that the Pyncheons deploy to legitimate their power over others." See Robert S. Levine, *Dislocating Race and Nation: Episodes in Nineteenth-Century American Literary*

Nationalism (Chapel Hill: U of North Carolina P, 2008), 137. In many respects, my reading echoes Smith's excellent treatment of Hawthorne's embrace of racial scientific discourse and its visual technologies to celebrate the ascendancy of the white middle class. However, while Smith and others have emphasized gender as the organizing principle of this racialized class formation at mid-century, I see these gender roles as epiphenomenal to the historical emergence of the modern domestic family, the stanchion of white nationalism that replaced the aristocratic blood paradigm.

56. Paul Gilmore describes the Jim Crow gingerbread as "a commodified representation of racial difference and slavery," and argues that for Hawthorne, "blackness comes to represent the market revolution's potential disruption to gender and class identities and its commodification of everything, including literature." See Paul Gilmore, *The Genuine Article: Race, Mass Culture, and American Literary Manhood* (Durham: Duke UP, 2001), 126.

57. Susan Mizruchi, *The Power of Historical Knowledge: Narrating the Past in Hawthorne, James, and Dreiser* (Princeton: Princeton UP, 1988), 86.

58. Kyla Wazana Tompkins writes of this scene: "black bodies, here rendered in the most extreme representation of objectification and dehumanization, must . . . enter into and change the white body (and thus the white body politic) if it is itself to enter into modernity" (207). See Kyla Wazana Tompkins, "'Everything 'Cept Eat Us': The Antebellum Black Body Portrayed as Edible Body," *Callaloo* 30 (2007): 201–24.

59. Balibar, "The Nation Form," 100.

60. Elizabeth A. Povinelli, *The Empire of Love: Towards a Theory of Intimacy, Genealogy, and Carnality* (Durham: Duke UP, 2006), 177.

61. Coontz, *The Social Origins of Private Life*, 126.

62. Downing declares that heritable family estates have no place in American society "because they are contrary to the spirit of republican institutions; because the feelings upon which they are based can never take root, except in a government of hereditary rights: because they are wholly in contradiction to the spirit of our time and people." He asserts that a "true American" should hope to establish "a home in which humanity and republicanism are stronger than family pride and aristocratic feeling." See Andrew Jackson Downing, *The Architecture of Country Houses* (New York: Appleton and Co., 1850), 267–70.

63. Keiko Arai writes, "Joined by Hepzibah and Clifford, this newly constituted family abandons patriarchal aristocracy, capitalism, and radical reformism, all linked with Europe, thus suggesting an alternative social vision for America." See Keiko Arai, "'Phoebe Is No Pyncheon': Class, Gender, and Nation in *The House of the Seven Gables*," *Nathaniel Hawthorne Review* 34 (Spring/Fall 2008): 40–62.

64. Walter Benn Michaels, "Romance and Real Estate," in *The American Renaissance Reconsidered*, ed. Donald Pease (Baltimore: Johns Hopkins UP, 1985), 179 n.3.

CHAPTER 2

1. "An Oration upon the Death of General Washington" Gouverneur Morris, December 31, 1799. New York, New York. Quoted in Forgie 38. Ten years earlier, Washington offered his childlessness as a primary qualification for the presidency. In a draft of his first inaugural address, he writes, "Divine Providence hath not seen fit, that my blood should be transmitted or my name perpetuated by the endearing, though sometimes seducing channel of immediate offspring. I have no child for

whom I could wish to make a provision—no family to build in greatness upon my
country's ruins." His suspicion that parenthood carries the seductive threat of
lineally transmitted status exemplifies a strain of eighteenth-century political
thought that viewed the traditional blood family as potentially ruinous to the new
republic. "Undelivered First Inaugural Address: Fragments," The Papers of George
Washington. Available at: http://www.gwpapers.virginia.edu. Alderman Library,
University of Virginia.

2. For example, he declares, "May our children, and our children's children, for a thousand generations, continue to enjoy the benefits conferred upon us by a united
country, and have cause yet to rejoice under those glorious institutions bequeathed
us by Washington and his compeers!" *Harper's Weekly* (October 25, 1862), 686.

3. Abraham Lincoln, "First Inaugural Address, March 4, 1861," in *Great Speeches*, ed.
John Grafton (Toronto: Dover, 1991), 55.

4. Ibid., 60.

5. Ibid., 55.

6. Stuart Hall, *The Hard Road to Renewal: Thatcherism and the Crisis of the Left* (New
York: Verso, 1988), 96.

7. Michael F. Holt, *The Political Crisis of the 1850s* (New York: Wiley, 1978), ix.

8. Russ Castronovo, *Fathering the Nation: American Genealogies of Slavery and Freedom* (Berkeley: U of California P, 1995), 175. George Forgie has dubbed Lincoln's
generation the "post-heroic age" and historicizes antebellum politics in relation to
a feeling of belatedness and inferiority in relation to the founders. George B. Forgie, *Patricide in the House Divided: A Psychological Interpretation of Lincoln and His
Age* (New York: Norton, 1981), 6.

9. Lincoln, "The Perpetuation of Our Political Institutions: Address Before the Young
Men's Lyceum of Springfield, Illinois, January 27, 1828," in *Great Speeches*, 2.

10. Ibid., 8.

11. Nathaniel Hawthorne, *The Scarlet Letter* (1850; New York: Norton, 2004), 61.

12. Harriet Jacobs, *Incidents in the Life of a Slave Girl*, ed. Jean Fagan Yellin (1861;
Cambridge: Harvard UP, 1987), 59.

13. Frederick Douglass, *My Bondage and My Freedom*, ed. John David Smith (1855;
New York: Penguin, 2003), 42.

14. Herman Melville, *Moby-Dick* (1851; New York: Random House [Modern Library
Paperbacks], 2000), 1. For more on the orphaned heroines of "women's fiction,"
see Nina Baym, *Women's Fiction: A Guide to Novels by and about Women in America,
1820–70* (Ithaca, NY: Cornell UP, 1978; reissued by the U of Illinois P, 2003).

15. Walt Whitman, "Poem of Procreation" in *Walt Whitman: Selected Poems 1855–1892,
A New Edition*, ed. Gary Schmidgall (New York: St. Martin's Press, 1999), 150 ln.
32, 36–40.

16. Lauren Berlant, *The Queen of America Goes to Washington City: Essays on Sex and
Citizenship* (Durham: Duke UP, 1997), 18.

17. Berlant, *Queen of America*, 18.

18. Noting the interdependence of national identity and the racial make-up of the
population, Raimon declares, "the 1850s marked the precise moment of U.S. racial
and national identity formation when the status of American nationalism and the
nation's racial composition were at once in crisis." See Eva Allegra Raimon, *The
"Tragic Mulatta" Revisited: Race and Nationalism in Nineteenth-Century Antislavery
Fiction* (Rutgers: Rutgers UP, 2004), 2.

Jeffory Clymer's recent book reminds us that "The criminalization of interracial
marriage and the strict limitation of the family's legal parameters should be

understood as an economic policy as much as a racial strategy." Jeffory Clymer, *Family Money: Property, Race, and Literature in the Nineteenth Century* (New York: Oxford, UP 2013), 22.

19. *American Journal of the Medical Sciences*. Volume 6, Issue 11 (July 1843), 252–256; *The Boston Medical and Surgical Journal*. Volume 29, No. 2 (August 16, 1843), 29–32.

20. Josiah C. Nott and George R. Gliddon, *Types of Mankind* (Philadelphia: Lippincott, Grambo & Co., 1854), 373 (original emphasis).

21. Ibid., 407.

22. See Thomas Gossett, *Race: The History of an Idea in America* (New York: Oxford UP, 1997), 65.

23. John Van Evrie, *Subgenation: The theory of the normal relation of the races: an answer to Miscegenation* (New York: John Bradburn, 1864), 27 (original emphasis).

24. Werner Sollors, *Neither Black Nor White Yet Both: Thematic Explorations of Interracial Literature* (New York: Oxford UP, 1997), 132. Lawrence R. Tenzer provides compelling evidence that government practice was affected by this racial scientific theory. He suggests that the category of "mulatto" was added to the census due to the widespread interest in Nott's theory of hybrid infertility. Among the many legislators pushing for inclusion of the category of mulatto, he notes, Thomas L. Clingman of North Carolina, urged the census board to gather official data on the longevity and reproduction of interracial people. In a letter, Clingman declared, "Whether the mulatto deteriorates physically . . . is the question of the highest importance, considering the ratio in which this portion of our population is increasing" (qtd. in Tenzer 48). See Lawrence R. Tenzer, *The Forgotten Cause of the Civil War: A New Look at the Slavery Issue* (Manahawkin, NJ: Scholars' Publishing House, 1997), 25.

25. Werner Sollors, *Beyond Ethnicity: Consent and Descent in American Culture* (New York: Oxford UP, 1987), 224. We might also think of the disruption mixed-race descendants represent to "white" bloodlines in terms of Sara Ahmed's theory of the heterosexual gift transmitted vertically in the family, which each individual is expected to return by passing it down the line. See Sarah Ahmed, "Orientations: Toward a Queer Phenomenology," *GLQ* 12 (2006): 543–74.

26. Orlando Patterson, *Slavery and Social Death: A Comparative Study* (Cambridge: Harvard UP, 1985), 5.

27. Ibid., 7.

28. Aliyyah I. Abdur-Rahman, "'The Strangest Freaks of Despotism': Queer Sexuality in Antebellum African American Slave Narratives," *African American Review* 40 (Summer 2006), 223.

29. Ibid., 224. Furthermore, Abdur-Rahman holds that the nation-state's investment in the regulation of both interracial sex and homosexuality ultimately serves the goal of reproducing a specific racial family structure as the basis of the economic and political system: "Prohibitions on same-sex and interracial desire support the evolution and multiplication of the white family as both the basic unit of capitalist acquisition and as a microcosm of the US" (235, n.7).

30. Lee Edelman, *No Future: Queer Theory and the Death Drive* (Durham: Duke UP, 2004), 3.

31. Sharon Holland, "Bill T. Jones, Tupac Shakur, and the (Queer) Art of Death," *Callaloo* 23 (Winter 2000): 391.

32. "The Late Slave Case at Cincinnati," *National Era*, March 20, 1856: 56.

33. "The Cincinnati Slaves: Another Thrilling Scene in the Tragedy," *The Liberator*, March 21, 1856: 47. A third account suggested that Garner tried to jump into a rescue boat with the child in her arms but had fallen short.

34. Edelman, *No Future*, 30–31.
35. The "mulatto" trope manifests Edelman's claim that queerness represents the refusal "of every substantialization of identity, which is always oppositionally defined, and, by extension, of history as linear narrative." See Edelman, *No Future*, 4.
36. Sterling Brown qtd. in Sollors, *Neither Black Nor White*, 280.
37. Hazel Carby, *Reconstructing Womanhood: The Emergence of the Afro-American Woman Novelist* (New York: Oxford UP, 1987), 89.
38. Theresa C. Zackodnick, *The Mulatta and the Politics of Race*, (Jackson: UP of Mississippi, 2004), xi.
39. Raimon, *"Tragic Mulatta" Revisited*, 4.
40. Cassandra Jackson, *Barriers Between Us: Interracial Sex in Nineteenth-Century American Literature* (Bloomington: Indiana UP), 2, 3.
41. Robert Reid-Pharr, *Conjugal Union: The Body, the House, and the Black American* (New York: Oxford UP, 1999), 48.
42. Raimon, *"Tragic Mulatta" Revisited*, 7.
43. Reid-Pharr, *Conjugal Union*, 62.
44. Harriet Wilson, *Our Nig: Sketches from the Life of a Free Black*, ed. Henry Louis Gates, Jr., and Richard J. Ellis, (1859; New York: Vintage, 1983) 30.
45. See Lois Leveen, "Dwelling in the House of Oppression: The Spatial, Racial, and Textual Dynamics of Harriet Wilson's *Our Nig*," *African American Review* 35 (2001): 561–80.
46. Frank J. Webb, *The Garies and their Friends* in *Frank J. Webb: Fiction, Essays, and Poetry*, ed. Werner Sollors (New Mitford, CT: The Toby Press, 2005), 152–54. Reid-Pharr describes this stillborn child "the very emblem of interracialism," representing the impossibility of an interracial future. See Reid-Pharr, *Conjugal Union*, 88.
47. Webb, *The Garies and their Friends*, 375–76.
48. Reid-Pharr argues that in the early African American novel, "only the black household, properly constituted, can produce the black body while interracial households produce only anomaly." See Reid-Pharr, *Conjugal Union*, 7.
49. William Wells Brown, *Clotel; or, The President's Daughter*, ed. Robert S. Levine (1853; Boston: Bedford/St. Martin's, 2000), 81; hereafter cited parenthetically.
50. Raimon, *"Tragic Mulatta" Revisited*, 68; Robert S. Levine, Introduction to *Clotel; or The President's Daughter*, 7.
51. Reid-Pharr, *Conjugal Union*, 61–62.
52. See D. Brenton Simons and Peter Benes, *The Art of Family: Genealogical Artifacts in New England* (Boston: New England Historic Genealogical Society, 2002), 76.
53. Elizabeth A. Povinelli, "Notes on Gridlock," 223.
54. Judith Roof, *Come as You Are: Sexuality and Narrative* (New York: Columbia UP, 1996), xxiv. For other genealogical readings of *Clotel*, see Robert S. Levine, *Dislocating Race and Nation* (Chapel Hill: U of North Carolina P, 2008), and Castronovo, *Fathering the Nation*, 215–28.
55. Krister Friday notes that depictions of interracialism disrupt linear temporality as well as white family lines. He argues, "miscegenation often marks a temporal crisis and a consequent disruption of linear time and identity," and more specifically, it "undermines the white historical imagination and its desire for continuity." See Krister Friday, "Miscgenated Time: The Spectral Body, Race, and Temporality in *Light in August*," *Faulkner Journal* 16 (Fall 2000/Spring 2001): 41–63.

56. Clotel's suicidal leap from the Long Bridge also counters Eliza Harris's famous escape in *Uncle Tom's Cabin* by jumping across ice floes over the Ohio River, which another character calls "Lizy's Bridge." With this scene, Stowe suggests that even supernatural acts of endurance and survival are made possible by maternal love. However, Stowe's novel acknowledges queer tactics comparable to those of Brown's heroine and Margaret Garner in her descriptions of two enslaved women who jump into rivers to commit suicide, one holding an infant, as well as Cassie's murder of an infant to save it from slavery.

57. Chapter 6 provides a fuller account of this finding and the print history of the Long Bridge narrative.

58. William Andrews asserts that "fictive and natural discourses dovetail and can easily be made to look the same. Instead of clarifying distinctions between the real and the fictive in his text, the narrator leaves the reader to ponder the basis on which one distinguishes between the real and the fictive in any text." See William L. Andrews, "The Novelization of Voice in Early African American Narrative," *PMLA* 105 (January 1990), 32. Raimon agrees that Brown's mixing of fact with fiction ultimately reveals the discursive production of identity categories: "the blurring of the boundaries of fictivity that is so insistent in *Clotel* joins with the project of blurring the boundaries of race and nation, revealed as their own brand of fiction." See Raimon, *"Tragic Mulatta" Revistied*, 70.

59. For a detailed account of antebellum reprinting and its implications, see Meredith McGill, *American Literature and the Culture of Reprinting, 1834–1853*, (Philadelphia: U of Pennsylvania P, 2002).

60. My attribution of this poem to Clarke is at odds with the established critical view that the final stanza was written by Brown and added to Grace Greenwood's 1851 poem, "The Leap from the Long Bridge." See Brown, *Clotel*, 209 n.8. The poet had previously published the poem, including this final stanza, as "The Escape" in the *Liberator* on September 20, 1844, under her original name, Sarah J. Clarke. This poem and "The 'Long Bridge'" by John Kemble Laskey, which appeared in the *Liberator* on August 22, 1845, seem to have been inspired by Gates's original 1842 account in the *New York Evangelist*, suggesting that the Long Bridge narrative was well known to abolitionist readers in the decade preceding the publication of *Clotel*.

61. Sarah J. Clarke, "The Escape," *Liberator*, September 20, 1844: 152 (original emphasis).

62. See Forgie, *Patricide in the House Divided*, 168–73.

63. Webb, *The Garies and their Friends*, 421.

64. Ibid.

65. *Clotel* copies this passage verbatim from Alvan Stewart's 1845 argument to abolish slavery in New Jersey. See Alvan Stewart, *A Legal Argument before the Supreme Court of the State of New Jersey, at the May Term, 1845, at Trenton, for the Deliverance of Four Thousand Persons from Bondage* (New York: Finch and Weed, 1845), 9.

66. Edelman, *No Future*, 30–31.

CHAPTER 3

1. Melville, *Pierre; Or, The Ambiguities*, 90.

2. Ibid., 197.

3. Ibid., 175.

4. Cindy Weinstein further argues, "Pierre's experiment suggests that reformers did little more than justify and, in some cases, institutionalize (in the name of progress) the incestuous impulses within the biological family." See Cindy Weinstein, *Family, Kinship, and Sympathy in Nineteenth-Century American Literature* (New York: Cambridge UP, 2004), 177.

5. Michael Rogin also considers *Pierre*'s relationship to contemporaneous discourses of romantic sibling love that render the family inescapable: "family reformers who feared licentious behavior in a world of strangers imported family inhibitions into society. William Alcott urged young men to see every woman as another man's sister when contemplating sexual relations with her. To obey that injunction would be to spread the incest taboo throughout society and, turning exogamy into endogamy, to paralyze all libidinal ties. . . . The incest taboo drives Pierre more deeply into his family; it does not free him from it." See Michael Paul Rogin, *Subversive Genealogy: The Politics and Art of Herman Melville* (Berkeley: U of California P, 1985), 181–82.

6. Elizabeth Dill, "The Damned Mob of Scribbling Siblings: The American Romance as Anti-novel in *The Power of Sympathy* and *Pierre*," *American Literature* 80 (December 2008): 714.

7. Brian Connolly, "Liberalism's Incestuous Subject: Private and Public Sex in the Nineteenth-Century United States," *History of the Present* 1 (Summer 2011): 39.

8. Michel Foucault, *The History of Sexuality*, vol. 1 (New York: Vintage, 1990), 108–109.

9. Elizabeth Barnes, *States of Sympathy: Seduction and Democracy in the American Novel* (New York: Columbia UP, 1997), 19.

10. Gillian Feeley-Harnik has suggested that Lewis Henry Morgan wrote his "genealogy of the human family," which inaugurated anthropological kinship studies, to prove that all people are biologically related, which would make incest the norm. Morgan was married to his first cousin, a practice that had once been socially acceptable but was coming to be viewed as incest at this time. See Gillian Feeley-Harnik, "'Communities of Blood: The Natural History of Kinship in Nineteenth-Century America," *Comparative Studies in Society and History* 41 (1999): 215–62. Conversely, Josiah Nott notes that Cain took his wife from a foreign land, insisting, "I do not believe that true religion ever intended teach a common origin for the human race." In this formulation, polygenesism becomes a rejection of incest and the logical outcome of exogamy. See Nott and Gliddon, *Types of Mankind*, 408.

11. *Ishmael; Or, In the Depths* was initially serialized in the *New York Ledger* in 1863–1864 and finally issued as a two-volume novel in 1876.

12. Susan Warner, *Wide, Wide World* (1850; London: G. Routledge & Co, Farrindon Street, 1853), 530.

13. Emily VanDette, "'A Whole Perfect Thing': Sibling Bonds and Anti-Slavery Politics in Harriet Beecher Stowe's *Dred*," *American Transcendental Quarterly* 22 (June 2008): 416.

14. Melville, *Pierre*, 7. See VanDette, "'A Whole Perfect Thing,'" 417.

15. Southworth considered *Ishmael* to be not only her best novel but also her most nationalistic, issuing it in book form in 1876 to mark the national centennial. See "Call Her Ishmael: E.D.E.N. Southworth, Robert Bonner, and the 'Experiment' of *Self Made*," in *Popular Nineteenth-Century American Women Writers and the Literary Marketplace*, ed. Kenneth Salzer et al. (Newcastle upon Tyne, England: Cambridge Scholars, 2007), 215–35.

16. The novel begins with the story of Ishmael's parents, Herman Brudenell and Nora Worth, the heir of an aristocratic family and a poor orphan girl who lives as a tenant on his land. The couple meets at Herman's lavish birthday, when all of the servants and tenants on the family's estate are invited to gaze upon the spectacle of the Brudenell coat of arms illuminated across the sky in fireworks. The impoverished, white Worth sisters are repeatedly aligned with African Americans, much like the early Maules in *The House of the Seven Gables*. The idea that one of them could marry a man of Herman's rank is regarded as preposterous and referred to as "the interdicted subject." Herman's mother will not even allow Nora to enter the front door of the patrimonial estate when she comes to pick up laundry. Herman protests, "Mother, this is a Republic!" She answers: "it is ten times more necessary to keep the lower orders down, in a Republic like this, where they are always trying to rise, than it is in a Monarchy, where they always keep their place." Faced with the same loyalty bind as Pierre Glendinning between consanguineous and conjugal families, Herman takes exactly the opposite course, legally marrying Nora but concealing it from his mother. This secret marriage is never revealed; Nora dies in childbirth, and Ishmael, the offspring of their cross-class relationship, i.e., the American product of the white national romance formula, is born into poverty and illegitimacy. Ishmael's story tracks the historical transition in the United States by which class distinctions were deemed artificial so that even an ill-gotten orphan can be recognized as "nature's nobleman." See E.D.E.N. Southworth, *Ishmael; Or, In the Depths* (New York: The Federal Book Company, 1884), 60, 572.

17. See Baym, *Women's Fiction*, ix. In her recent study of adoption in the nineteenth-century American novel, Carol Singley concedes that this practice is "fundamentally conservative" in that it shores up the traditional family form, even as it seems to allow for a more plastic and non-blood-based criteria for membership. See Carol Singley, *Adopting America: Childhood, Kinship, and National Identity in Literature* (New York: Oxford UP, 2011).

18. Weinstein, *Family, Kinship, and Sympathy*, 12, 10.

19. Barnes, *States of Sympathy*, 16.

20. Arthur Riss, "Racial Essentialism and Family Values in *Uncle Tom's Cabin*," *American Quarterly* 46 (December 1994): 513–44.

21. Weinstein, *Family, Kinship, and Sympathy*, 24.

22. Elizabeth Dillon, *The Gender of Freedom: Fictions of Liberalism and the Literary Public Sphere* (Palo Alto: Stanford UP, 2004), 233.

23. Riss, "Racial Essentialism," 534.

24. See Robert Levine, *Martin Delany, Frederick Douglass, and the Politics of Representative Identity* (Chapel Hill: U of North Carolina P, 1997), 83. See also Gregg Crane, *Race, Citizenship, and Law in American Literature* (New York: Cambridge UP, 2002), 243 n.41. The *Dred Scott* case gained interest as early as February 1856, and Stowe's novel was written over that summer. Noel Gerson's biography, *Harriet Beecher Stowe*, suggests that Stowe changed the name of the novel to correspond with the case. See Noel B. Gerson, *Harriet Beecher Stowe* (Westport, CT: Praeger Publishers), 1976.

25. Riss, "Racial Essentialism," 526.

26. Gossett, *Race: The History of an Idea*, 44.

27. Nott and Gliddon, *Types of Mankind*, 50–51. In "Claims of the Negro Ethnographically Considered," Frederick Douglas claims that legislation already demonstrated a reliance on a polygenesist model of racial difference: "the debates in Congress on

the Nebraska Bill during the past winter, will show how slaveholders have availed themselves of this doctrine in support of slaveholding. There is no doubt that Messrs. Nott, Glidden, Morton, Smith and Agassiz were duly consulted by our slavery propagating statesmen." Douglass assumes that elected officials read racial science and that these theories influenced national politics. See Frederick Douglass, "Claims of the Negro Ethnographically Considered" (Rochester, NY: Lee, Mann & Co., 1854), 16.

28. Nott and Gliddon, *Types of Mankind*, 404.
29. The Senate debates over the Compromise of 1850 returned to the founding generation's belief that democratic self-government was the unique heritage of Anglo-Saxons and that the cohesion of the national community relied upon its shared blood. Greg Crane explains that, in this context, both Northern and Southern senators wielded "the myth of a shared Anglo-Saxon identity to reunite the founders' fractious heirs." See Crane, *Race, Citizenship, and Law*, 48.
30. Nott and Gliddon, *Types of Mankind*, 79.
31. *Scott vs. Sandford*, 60 U.S. 393 (1857).
32. Ibid.
33. Castronovo, *Fathering the Nation*, 15.
34. Rogers M. Smith, *Civic Ideals: Conflicting Visions of Citizenship in U.S. History* (New Haven: Yale UP, 1997), 268.
35. John H. Van Evrie, "Introduction," *The Dred Scott Decision* (New York: Van Evrie, Horton, & Co., 1859), iv.
36. This pamphlet epitomizes Zackodnick's description of the "symbiotic relationship between science and the law as tools of a white supremacist ideology" in the nineteenth century: "legal and scientific pronouncements on race interacted to enable each other such that scientific 'evidence' affirmed the courts' decisions, and the codification of ever-more refined distinctions between blackness and whiteness validated the development of new theories and studies aimed at 'proving' inherent racial difference." See Zackodnick, *Mulatta and the Politics of Race*, 18.
37. Susan Ryan, "Charity Begins at Home: Stowe's Anti-Slavery Novels and the Forms of Benevolent Citizenship," *American Literature* 72 (December 2000): 772.
38. Harriet Beecher Stowe, *Dred* (1856; NY: Penguin/Putnam, Penguin Classics, 2000), 50, 274; hereafter cited parenthetically.
39. Dred's revolutionary fervor seems to be biologically inherited from his father, Denmark Vesey. Stowe crafts this black revolutionary lineage to show that the political vision of the founding fathers was not the result of an Anglo-Saxon insistence on self-government, as the American School suggested.
40. Crane, *Race, Citizenship, and Law*, 72.
41. Harriet Beecher Stowe, *Uncle Tom's Cabin* (1852; New York: Penguin/Putnam, Signet Classics, 1988), 26.
42. Riss, "Racial Essentialism," 513. Gillian Brown also notes that Tom's portrait depicts Washington "in blackface." See Gilliam Brown, *Domestic Individualism: Imagining the Self in Nineteenth-Century America* (Berkeley: U of California P, 1999), 48.
43. Riss, "Racial Essentialism," 513, 514.
44. Jeffory Clymer, *Family Money: Property, Race, and Literature in the Nineteenth Century* (New York: Oxford UP, 2013), 41.
45. Dillon, *The Gender of Freedom*, 227, 232.
46. Ibid., 228.
47. Elizabeth Duquette, "The Republican Mammy? Imagining Civic Engagement in *Dred*," *American Literature* 80 (March 2008): 19.

48. Judith Butler, "Is Kinship Always Already Heterosexual?" *Differences* 13 (2002): 34 (original emphasis).
49. Ibid., 15.
50. Christopher Peterson, *Kindred Specters: Death, Mourning, and American Affinity* (Minneapolis: UP of Minnesota, 2007), 16.
51. Barnes, *States of Sympathy*, 92.
52. Ibid., 4.
53. Peterson, *Kindred Specters*, 34. As Greg Crane explains, "marriage is a contract with a difference: once this contract is sealed, it becomes like a blood relation, permanent, non-consensual, hierarchic." See Crane, *Race, Citizenship, and Law*, 47.
54. Peterson, *Kindred Specters*, 34.
55. VanDette, "'A Whole Perfect Thing,'" 425–26.
56. Milly later raises a multiracial group of orphans. See Duquette, "The Republican Mammy?" 1–28.
57. Ryan, "Charity Begins at Home," 772.
58. VanDette, "'A Whole Perfect Thing,'" 422.
59. Ryan, "Charity Begins at Home," 772–73.
60. VanDette, "'A Whole Perfect Thing,'" 432 n.6.
61. Butler, "Is Kinship Always Already Heterosexual?" 14.
62. Ibid., 37.
63. By the end of the novel, Tiff lives with the grown-up Fanny, whose marriage and newborn child serve as Stowe's tip of the hat to traditional family and narrative forms.
64. See Kath Weston, "Forever Is a Long Time: Romancing the Real in Gay Kinship Ideologies" in *Long Slow Burn: Sexuality and Social Science* (New York: Routledge, 1998), 57–82.
65. Pierre Bourdieu, *The Logic of Practice* (Stanford: Stanford UP, 1980), 168.
66. Weinstein makes it clear that sentimental novels ultimately entertain only relatively minor edits to the family, like substituting adoptive parent-child relationships for biological ones. Many socialist groups were eager to make more radical moves like the separation of parents and children in favor of communal upbringing. See Weinstein, *Family, Kinship, and Sympathy*, 8.
67. Singley, *Adopting America*, 13.

CHAPTER 4

1. For an excellent account of the sacrifice of racial reform in the name of white reunion, see Edward J. Blum, *Reforging the White Republic: Race, Religion, and American Nationalism, 1865–1898* (Baton Rouge: Louisiana State UP, 2005). Nina Silber agrees that despite the ostensible legal gains that brought African Americans into citizenship, bringing the nation back together was accomplished through the further conflation of Americanness with white racial identity: "the new nationalism rested on the unity of Anglo-Saxons, namely, the bonds between southern whites . . . and northern whites. That which was 'truly American' was increasingly defined in racial terms." Nina Silber, *The Romance of Reunion: Northerners and the South, 1865–1900* (Chapel Hill: U of North Carolina P, 1993), 158.
2. Gregory Jackson, "'A Dowry of Suffering': Consent, Contract, Political Coverture in John W. De Forest's Reconstruction Romance," *American Literary History* 15 (Summer 2003): 282.
3. Silber, *Romance of Reunion*, 63.

4. Ibid., 63.
5. Kathleen Diffley, *Where My Heart Is Turning Ever: Civil War Stories and Constitutional Reform, 1861–1876* (Athens: U of Georgia P, 1992), 55.
6. David Blight, *Race and Reunion: The Civil War in American Memory* (Cambridge: Harvard UP, 2001), 217.
7. Silber, *Romance of Reunion*, 40.
8. Albion Tourgée, *Bricks without Straw*, (1880; Durham: Duke UP, 2009), 364.
9. To Tourgée's credit, the novel's final chapters—"what shall the end be?" and "how?"—allude to the open-endedness of the questions Reconstruction was supposed to resolve, much like *What Answer?*, the interrogative title of Anna Dickinson's novel. Tourgée proposes two classic republican solutions for the problems he had observed firsthand in the South—education and the township system—after the marriage plot ending.
10. Constance Fenimore Woolson, "Old Gardiston," *Harper's Magazine* 52, April 1876: 662–674.
11. Ibid., 664.
12. Ibid., 670.
13. Ibid., 672.
14. Ibid., 673–74.
15. Silber, *Romance of Reunion*, 157.
16. Ibid., 56.
17. Blight, *Race and Reunion*, 211.
18. Ibid., 237. Although Blight draws an opposition between literary realism and mimetic battlefield accounts on one hand and popular forms like the romance of reunion on the other, the most paradigmatic author of romances of reunion, John DeForest, was a veteran and some have pointed to his realistic descriptions of combat as the beginning of an ethos of realism in American fiction. Blight also calls attention to the speeches of Frederick Douglass, who was among the most vociferous critics of the Reconstruction culture of forgetting, insisting that the Civil War be remembered as the "Abolition War." Douglass and Dickinson worked closely together on a number of issues, including the Fifteenth Amendment.
19. Duquette, *Loyal Subjects*, 67.
20. As Diffley notes, "the few failed romances suggest what could hinder the transfer of affections at the altar of national allegiance." See Diffley, *Where My Heart Is Turning Ever*, 76.
21. Lyde Cullen Sizer, *The Political Work of Northern Women Writers and the Civil War, 1850–1872* (Chapel Hill: U of North Carolina P, 2000), 238.
22. Nancy Cott, *Public Vows: A History of Marriage and the Nation* (Cambridge: Harvard UP, 2000), 5.
23. Ibid., 98, 100.
24. Elizabeth Duquette notes that it is not simply marriage but "remarriage" that provides the model for sectional reconciliation in the romance of reunion plot. See Elizabeth Duquette, *Loyal Subjects: Bonds of Nation, Race, and Allegiance in Nineteenth-Century America* (New Brunswick: Rutgers UP, 2010), 64.
25. Anna Dickinson, *What Answer?* (1868; Amherst, NY: Humanity Books, 2003), 75; hereafter cited parenthetically.
26. See Elizabeth Young, *Disarming the Nation: Women's Writing and the American Civil War* (Chicago: U of Chicago P, 1999) and Sizer, *Political Work of Northern Women Writers*.

27. Sizer argues that Jim's logic here rests on the racist idea that white blood dominates other strains in a person's ancestry. See Sizer, *Political Work of Northern Women Writers*, 237.

28. Jackson, "'A Dowry of Suffering,'" 304.

29. The prospect of black suffrage was bleak in 1865. Eric Foner notes that the most successful proposal in this year was a referendum in Washington, DC, held among white voters in which 35 votes were cast in favor of black suffrage, with 6,951 against. See Eric Foner, *Reconstruction: America's Unfinished Revolution, 1863–1877* (New York: Harper & Row, 1988), 240.

30. Frederick Douglass, "Reconstruction," *Atlantic Monthly* 18 (1866): 761.

31. Ibid., 765.

32. Ibid., 761.

33. J. Matthew Gallman, "Introduction" to *What Answer?*, 15.

34. Drew Gilpin Faust, *This Republic of Suffering: Death and the American Civil War* (New York: Knopf, 2008), 269.

35. "New Publications: Anna Dickinson's 'What Answer?'" *Daily Evening Bulletin*, (San Francisco, CA), October 31, 1868.

36. Elizabeth Cady Stanton quoted in J. Matthew Gallman, *America's Joan of Arc: The Life of Anna Elizabeth Dickinson* (New York: Oxford UP, 2006), 93.

37. Foner, *Reconstruction*, 447.

38. See Louise Michelle Newman, *White Women's Rights: The Racial Origins of Feminism in the United States* (New York: Oxford UP, 1999), 62.

39. Susan B. Anthony quoted in Newman, *White Women's Rights*, 65.

40. Anna Dickinson quoted in Giraud Chester, *Embattled Maiden: The Live of Anna Dickinson* (New York: Putnam, 1951), 94.

41. Chester, *Embattled Maiden*, 94.

42. Frederick Douglass and Susan B. Anthony quoted in Chester, *Embattled Maiden*, 94.

43. Susan B. Anthony quoted in Gallman, *America's Joan of Arc*, 84.

44. Gallman, *America's Joan of Arc*, 93.

45. Timothy Morris, "'A Glorious Solution': Gender, Families, Relationships and the Civil War Story," *Arizona Quarterly* 51 (Spring 1995): 63.

46. Jackson notes that the focus on marriage in Reconstruction culture was used to argue against the women's suffrage discourse of female autonomy and empowerment. See Jackson, "'A Dowry of Suffering,'" 293. Critiques of the patriarchal family model were considered oppositional to national union.

47. Chester, *Embattled Maiden*, 94.

48. Gallman, *America's Joan of Arc*, 10.

49. Ibid., 84.

50. Karen Sánchez-Eppler, "Bodily Bonds: The Intersecting Rhetorics of Feminism and Abolition," in *The Culture of Sentiment: Race, Gender, and Sentimentality in Nineteenth-Century America*, ed. Shirley Samuels (New York: Oxford UP 1992), 95.

51. Anna Dickinson quoted in Chester, *Embattled Maiden*, 94.

52. Carolyn L. Karcher, *The First Woman in the Republic: A Cultural Biography of Lydia Maria Child* (Durham: Duke UP, 1994), 510.

53. Ibid., 511.

54. Ibid., 516.

55. Ibid., 527.

56. News, *Newark Advocate*, (Newark, OH), February 5, 1869.

57. News, *Daily Arkansas Gazette*, (Little Rock, AR), April 23, 1872.

58. See Sara deSaussure Davis, "Feminist Sources in the Bostonians," *American Literature* 50 (1979): 570–87. Gallman agrees that Verena Tarrant was based on Dickinson. See Gallman, *America's Joan of Arc*, 124.

59. Ann Brigham, "Touring Memorial Hall: The State of the Union in *The Bostonians*," *Arizona Quarterly* 62 (2006): 16.

60. Henry James, *The Bostonians* (1886; New York: Knopf Everyman's Library, 1992), 210.

61. Brigham, "Touring Memorial Hall," 11.

62. Chester, *Embattled Maiden*, 169, 292.

63. Anna Dickinson quoted in Chester, *Embattled Maiden*, 7.

64. Anna Dickinson quoted in Silber, *Romance of Reunion*, 157.

65. Quoted in Gallman, *America's Joan of Arc*, 175.

66. "Anna Dickinson," *Boston Daily Advertiser*, (Boston, MA), September 22, 1888.

67. There are many other examples of forgotten feminist pioneers of this era who challenge the current scholarly consensus that women's rights agitation in the nineteenth-century United States was inseparable from discourses of white supremacy. Stanton and Anthony's racist opposition to the Fifteenth Amendment met with much disapproval within the women's suffrage movement. Feminists like Lucy Stone and Julia Ward Howe formed the American Woman Suffrage Association to support the Reconstruction Amendments and disassociate the fight for women's rights from the suppression of African American rights. Abby Kelley, a Quaker and a radical supporter of both causes much like Dickinson, also supported the goal of securing black suffrage first, and therefore split with Stanton and Anthony. Moreover, many African American women were instrumental leaders in the women's suffrage movement, including Mary Church Terrell.

CHAPTER 5

1. Edward H. Clarke, *Sex in Education; Or, A Fair Chance for Girls* (Boston: Osgood and Co., 1874, 2nd ed.), 39.

2. Louise Michele Newman, *White Women's Rights: The Racial Origins of Feminism in the United States* (New York: Oxford UP, 1999), 93.

3. Ibid., 92.

4. Theodore Roosevelt, "National Life and Character" (1894), *American Ideals and Other Essays, Social and Political*, 2 vols. (New York: G. P. Putnam's Sons, 1897), 2:117. Quoted in Gail Bederman, *Manliness and Civilization: A Cultural History of Gender and Race in the United States, 1880–1917* (Chicago: U of Chicago P, 1995), 201. See also Theodore Roosevelt, "Duties of American Citizenship," (Buffalo, NY: January 26, 1883).

5. Theodore Roosevelt, "On American Motherhood," (Washington, DC: March 13, 1905).

6. Laura L. Lovett traces the term "race suicide" to a speech that Ross delivered on May 7, 1900, about the dangers of Asian immigration. See Laura L. Lovett, *Conceiving the Future: Pronatalism, Reproduction, and the Family in the United States* (Chapel Hill: U of North Carolina P, 2007), 82. The first instance of Roosevelt using the term in print can be found in his introduction to *The Woman Who Toils*, by Mrs. John Van Vorst and Marie Van Vorst (New York: Doubleday, Page & Co., 1903), vii.

7. Quoted in Linda Gordon, *The Moral Property of Women: A History of Birth Control Politics in America* (1976; Urbana: U of Illinois P, 2002), 96. See also Newman, *White Women's Rights*, 89.

8. See Gordon, *Moral Property of Women*, 87.

9. Edward A. Ross, "Western Civilization and the Birth-Rate," *American Journal of Sociology* 12 (March 1907): 607–32.

10. Warren S. Thompson, "Race Suicide in the United States," *Scientific Monthly*, (July 1917): 22, 23.

11. Joseph J. Spengler, "Has the Native Population of New England Been Dying Out?" *Quarterly Journal of Economics* 44 (August 1930): 639, 662.

12. See Albert Bushnell Hart, "Is the Puritan Race Dying Out?," *Munsey's Magazine* (May 1911): 252–55.

13. Quoted in Barbara Mill Solomon, *Ancestors and Immigrants: A Changing New England Tradition*, (Boston: Harvard UP, 1956), 78.

14. Gossett, *Race: The History of an Idea*, 134.

15. See Dr. William Leland Holt, "Economic Factors in Eugenics," *The Popular Science Monthly* (November 1913): 478.

16. George B. H. Swayze, "Reluctant Pregnancy," *The Medical Times* (November 1909): 321.

17. "Priests Flay Suffragists," *Los Angeles Times*, May 22, 1910.

18. Margaret Sanger, "A Better Race Through Birth Control, *The Thinker* (November 1923), 60.

19. Daylanne K. English, *Unnatural Selections: Eugenics in American Modernism and the Harlem Renaissance* (Chapel Hill: U of North Carolina P, 2004), 141.

20. Gordon, *Moral Property of Women*, 91.

21. Ibid., 94.

22. A Childless Wife, "Why I Have No Family," *The Independent* (Boston, MA), March 23, 1905: 654.

23. "Ridicules Race Suicide Talk: Mrs. McColloch Says Roosevelt Attack Was Unbecoming," *Chicago Daily Tribune*, May 2, 1910.

24. Victoria Woodhull, *Tried as by Fire: or, The True and the False, Socially* (New York: Woodhull and Claflin, 1874), 5.

25. Ibid., 7.

26. Marx Edgeworth Lazarus, *Love vs. Marriage, Part 1* (New York: Fowlers and Wells, 1852), 109.

27. T.L. Nichols and Mary Grove Nicholas, *Marriage: Its History, Character, and Results; Its Sanctities and Its Profanities; Its Science and Its Facts* (New York: Nichols, 1854), 306.

28. George N. Miller, *The Strike of a Sex* (New York: Twentieth Century Publishing Company, 1891), 22.

29. Ibid., 104.

30. Ibid., 37.

31. Ibid., 107, 11.

32. Noyes's writings on male continence excerpted by Miller can be found in "The Family and Its Foil," *Oneida Circular* (Oneida, NY), November 16, 1854; and "Egotism for Two" *Oneida Circular* (Oneida, NY), April 11, 1854: 219–20. They were ultimately collected in John Humphrey Noyes's volume *Male Continence* (Oneida, NY: Published by the Oneida Community, 1872).

33. Stephanie Foote, *Regional Fictions: Culture and Identity in Nineteenth-Century American Literature* (Madison: U of Wisconsin P, 2001), 18.

34. Mary E. Wilkins, "A New England Nun" in *A New England Nun and Other Stories* (New York: Harper, 1891), 17.

35. Mary E. Wilkins, "Two Old Lovers" in *A Humble Romance and Other Stories* (New York: Harper, 1887), 31.

36. Mary E. Wilkins, "A Humble Romance" in *A Humble Romance and Other Stories*, 6.
37. Werner Berthoff, "The Art of Jewett's Pointed Firs," *New England Quarterly* 66 (March 1959): 33, 37, 34.
38. Ann Douglas Wood, "The Literature of Impoverishment: The Women Local Colorists in America, 1865–1914," *Women's Studies* 1 (1972): 24–25.
39. Josephine Donovan, *New England Local Color Literature: A Women's Tradition* (New York: Ungar, 1983), 110.
40. See Elizabeth Ammons, "Going in Circles: The Female Geography of Jewett's *Country of the Pointed Firs*," *Studies in the Literary Imagination* 16 (Fall 1983): 83–92; and Sandra A. Zagarell, "Narrative of Community: The Identification of a Genre," *Signs* 13 (Spring 1988): 498–527.
41. June Howard, "Introduction: Sarah Orne Jewett and the Traffic in Words," in *New Essays on The Country of the Pointed Firs*, ed. June Howard (New York: Cambridge UP, 1994), 4.
42. Marjorie Pryse, "Sex, Class, and 'Category Crisis': Reading Jewett's Transitivity," in *No More Separate Spheres!* ed. Cathy N. Davidson and Jessamyn Hatcher (Durham: Duke UP, 2002), 150.
43. Heather Love, "Gyn/Apology: Sarah Orne Jewett's Spinster Aesthetics," *ESQ: A Journal of the American Renaissance* 55 (2009): 315. Love further suggests, "Jewett authors some truly devastating accounts of isolation, abandonment, and regret. She chronicles experiences that feminist, lesbian, and queer critical frameworks have not allowed us to see: the feelings of loss, disappointment, and longing that are *internal* to female worlds of love and ritual" (313).
44. Karen Sanchez-Eppler, "Raising Empires Like Children: Race, Nation, and Religious Education," *American Literary History* 8 (1996): 399. In this way, I suggest that Jewett's regionalism, while characteristically nostalgic and invested in enshrining the past, is deeply interested in the American future and in some ways positions itself as prophetic.
45. See Caroline Gebhard, "The Spinster in the House of American Criticism," *Tulsa Studies in Women's Literature* 10 (Spring 1991): 89. See also Love, "Gyn/Apology," 305–34.
46. Wood, "Literature of Impoverishment," 32. Although I agree with Gebhard that Wood's evaluation of local color fiction pathologizes women, her readings of the theme of decline are useful to this discussion.
47. As Allison Berg notes, "the perception that each woman had a hereditary obligation to advance her own race's destiny, in a process understood to be inherently competitive," was not limited to white women: "The specter of white race suicide and the imperative of black racial uplift made motherhood both a cultural ideal and a racial duty, for black and white women alike." See Allison Berg, *Mothering the Race: Women's Narratives of Reproduction, 1890–1930* (Chicago and Urbana: U of Illinois P, 2002), 4–5.
48. Articulating this prevailing critical view, Dana Seitler argues, "feminism and eugenics during this period were not only compatible but were mutually constitutive, each inextricably rooted in the constitution of the other." See Dana Seitler, "Unnatural Selection: Mothers, Eugenic Feminism, and Charlotte Perkins Gilman's Regeneration Narratives," *American Quarterly* 55 (March 2003): 64. See also Newman, *White Women's Rights;* Bederman, *Manliness and Civilization;* and Alys Eve Weinbaum, *Wayward Reproductions: Genealogies of Race and Nation in Transatlantic Modern Thought* (Durham: Duke UP, 2004).

49. Judith Fetterley and Marjorie Pryse, *Writing Out of Place: Regionalism, Women, and American Literary Culture* (Urbana: U of Illinois P, 2003), 28.

50. Paula Blanchard, *Sarah Orne Jewett: Her World and Her Work* (Cambridge, MA: Perseus Books, 1994), 153.

51. Sarah Orne Jewett, *Deephaven* (1877), in *Sarah Orne Jewett: Novels and Stories*, ed. Michael Davitt Bell (New York: Library of America, 1994), 8.

52. Ibid., 14, 41.

53. Ibid., 82, 81.

54. Sarah Orne Jewett, *The Country of the Pointed Firs and Other Stories* (1896; New York: Penguin Putnam, 2000), 57; hereafter cited parenthetically.

55. Thompson, "Race Suicide," 28.

56. Susan Gillman, "Regionalism and Nationalism in Jewett's *Country of the Pointed Firs*," in *New Essays on The Country of the Pointed Firs*, ed. June Howard (New York: Cambridge UP, 1994), 110.

57. Jewett, *Deephaven*, 44.

58. Ibid., 8, 126.

59. The symbolic appropriation of New England's native inhabitants in this scene, as well as the assumption that they had been exterminated, illustrates Foote's observation that "traces of history and conflict score [the] narrative surface" of the communities depicted in regionalist writing. See Foote, *Regional Fictions*, 19.

60. Jewett, *Deephaven*, 108, 112.

61. Walter Benn Michaels, *Our America: Nativism, Modernism, and Pluralism* (Durham: Duke UP, 1995), 45, 41. Michaels sees this relationship to Native Americans as necessarily modernist and a break from turn-of-the-century regionalism: "identification with the Indian could function at the turn of the century as a *refusal* of American identity," but "it would come to function by the early 1920s as the *assertion* of an American identity that could be understood as going beyond citizenship" (44). *The Country of the Pointed Firs* demonstrates a link between local color and nativist modernism in its oscillation between these uses of Native American figures.

62. See Lovett, *Conceiving the Future*, 92.

63. Howard, "Introduction," 21.

64. See Ron Welburn, "The Braided Rug, Pennyroyal, and the Pathos of Almira Todd: A Cultural Reading of *The Country of the Pointed Firs*," *Journal of American Culture* 174 (Winter 1994): 75–76.

65. Historians John D'Emilio and Estelle Freedman note that "in the early nineteenth century, and in rural areas for many later generations, herbal and home remedies for terminating unwanted pregnancies continued to be passed on through oral tradition." See John D'Emilio and Estelle Freedman, *Intimate Matters: A History of Sexuality in America* (Chicago: U of Chicago P, 1997), 63.

66. Gordon, *Moral Property of Women*, 100.

67. Swayze, "Reluctant Pregnancy," 321.

68. Ibid., 321–25.

69. Sandra A. Zagarell, "*Country*'s Portrayal of Community and the Exclusion of Difference," in *New Essays on The Country of the Pointed Firs* (New York: Cambridge UP, 1994), 44–45, 46. In a more recent treatment of the construction of community in this tradition, Stephanie Foote argues that the instability of the identities of "the stranger" and "the native" is "the defining textual economy of regionalism." In Dunnet Landing, she observes Jewett's "inability to imagine a past not already animated by a heterogeneous population." See Foote, *Regional Fictions* (19, 17).

70. In response to readings of this scene as evidence of "regionalism's complicity in the nation's move toward empire," Fetterley and Pryse counter, "Jewett's text proposes region as a site of resistance to empire and offers the region's values as alternatives to those of the nation." See Fetterley and Pryse, *Writing Out of Place*, 235.

71. Laurie Shannon contends that *Country* is about friendship replacing kinship: "The Bowden reunion goes a long way towards converting 'family' into chosen 'friends,'" although the novel insists that "blood is thicker than water." See Laurie Shannon, "'The Country of Our Friendship': Jewett's Intimist Art," *American Literature* 71 (1999): 253.

72. Elizabeth Ammons, "Material Culture, Empire, and Jewett's *Country of the Pointed Firs*," in *New Essays on the Country of the Pointed Firs*, ed. June Howard (New York: Cambridge UP, 1994), 96.

73. Gillman, "Regionalism and Nationalism," 113.

74. Ammons, "Material Culture, Empire, and Jewett's *Pointed Firs*," 97.

75. Notably, *The Country of the Pointed Firs* was published in 1896, the same year in which the Supreme Court officially decreed, in its decision in the *Plessy v. Ferguson* case, that "one drop of black blood" excludes an individual from the distinction of racial whiteness.

76. Wood, "Literature of Impoverishment," 28.

77. The consumption of this house-shaped cake has been a fruitful episode for critics interested in material culture, including Ammons and, Bill Brown. Brown notes, "This is an image of incorporating the particularity of place into the body itself; an image where person, place, and thing converge in the moment of physical consumption; an image not of occupying a material environment but of being occupied by it. It is the narrator's opportunity not to reach inside an object or space, but to internalize built space itself." See Bill Brown, "Regional Artifacts (The Life of Things in the Work of Sarah Orne Jewett)," *American Literary History* (Summer 2002): 212.

    Ammons observes that Jewett establishes an "architectural vocabulary" in which the houses of "small-town New England" represent the "Yankee values of ingenuity, pragmatism, cautiousness, good humor, and visual simplicity." She argues, "All those tiny, tidy, white, fenced, tree-nailed, and wedged houses staring up and down the coast do articulate a vision of preindustrial matrifocal harmony, health, and happiness. But they also stand for white colonial settlement and dominance." See Ammons, "Material Culture, Empire, and Jewett's *Pointed Firs*," 84, 97. Whereas Ammons reads the cake's communal consumption as the moment when we as readers are asked to "swallow" these meanings along with the narrator and Mrs. Todd, I read it as the most explicit threat of the self-destruction of these meanings.

78. Walker was director of the 1870 and the 1880 United States Census and president of the Massachusetts Institute of Technology from 1881 until his death in 1897.

79. In view of this theory, many New Englanders of the "old stock" increasingly asserted their "right" to control the flow of immigrants into the United States. See Solomon, *Ancestors and Immigrants*, 99–102. On Jewett's personal ties to the Immigration Restriction League, see Zagarell, "*Country*'s Portrayal of Community and the Exclusion of Difference," 41.

80. Frances Amasa Walker, "Immigration and Degradation," *Forum* 11 (August 1891), quoted in Solomon, *Ancestors and Immigrants*, 76.

81. "Our Nation and Our Family," *The Congregationalist* (Boston, MA), March 1, 1888.

CHAPTER 6

1. A Member of Congress [Seth M. Gates], "Slavery in the District: The Escape," *New York Evangelist*, September 8, 1842.

2. Seth M. Gates, "The Long Bridge—The Escape," *Prisoner's Friend: A Monthly Magazine Devoted to Criminal Reform, Philosophy, Science, Literature, and Art*, September 10, 1845: 96.

3. Sarah J. Clarke, "The Escape," *Liberator*, September 20, 1844: 152. John Kemble Laskey, "The 'Long Bridge,'" *Liberator*, August 22, 1845: 136.

4. Frederick Douglass, "No Union with Slaveholders," (Boston, MA: May 28, 1844).

5. Jane Grey Cannon Swisshelm, *Half a Century* (Chicago: Jansen, McClurg, and Co., 1880), 129; Frances Harper, *Iola Leroy; Or, Shadows Uplifted* (1892; New York: Oxford UP, 1988), 98; Norman B. Wood, *The White Side of a Black Subject: Enlarged and Brought Down to Date; A Vindication of the Afro-American Race: From the Landing of Slaves at St. Augustine, Florida, in 1565, to the Present Time* (Chicago: American Publishing House, 1897), 140.

6. In anticipation of the first installment of *Hagar's Daughter* two months later, the January 1901 issue of *The Colored American Magazine* establishes Hopkins's relationship with Brown in a number of ways, including biographical sketches of both authors. In her otherwise third-person sketch of Brown's life and work, she mentions in the first person that her father had introduced Brown in 1844 at an event in Aurora, New York, signaling her family's connections to the famous abolitionist. Her biography mentions Brown in connection with the essay "The Evils of Intemperance and their Remedies" that she describes as her first literary effort. Finally, portraits of Brown and Hopkins appear on facing pages, visually illustrating her association with him, even the sense that he precedes her historically as he appears on the left page and she follows on the right.

7. Lois Brown demonstrates that *Hagar's Daughter* is "indebted to three works by and about William Wells Brown," especially an 1856 biography by Josephine Brown, his daughter, and Brown's own autobiographical account of his work for a slave trader named Walker. Lois Brown, *Pauline Elizabeth Hopkins: Black Daughter of the Revolution* (Chapel Hill: U of North Carolina P, 2008), 346.

8. See Carby, *Reconstructing Womanhood*; Tate, *Domestic Allegories of Political Desire*; and duCille, *The Coupling Convention*.

9. The title revises the biblical story of Abraham's rejection of his son, Ishmael, and his mother, the servant Hagar, an ur-story of illegitimacy and splintered heritage. For a reading of the novel in relation to the Hagar myth, see Janet Gabler-Hover, *Dreaming Black/Writing White: Hagar in American Culture and Literature* (Lexington: U of Kentucky P, 2001). This title also revises Brown's *The President's Daughter*, the subtitle of *Clotel*.

10. Hanna Wallinger suggests that in *Hagar's Daughter*, slavery tears apart the white family in addition to the more traditional representation of black familial separations. See Hanna Wallinger, *Pauline E. Hopkins: A Literary Biography* (Athens: U of Georgia P, 2005), 174.

11. Felipe Smith, *American Body Politics: Race, Gender, and Black Literary Renaissance* (Athens: U of Georgia P: 1998), 65. See Smith's chapter "Meanwhile in Black America" (52–83) for excellent treatments of *Hagar's Daughter*, Charles Chesnutt's *Marrow of Tradition* and *Conjure Tales*, Booker T. Washington's "body of death" rhetoric, Hoffman, and atavism.

12. Frederick L. Hoffman, *Race Traits and Tendencies of the American Negro* (New York: Macmillan, 1896), 176.

13. Ibid., 329. William Benjamin Smith similarly asserts that "during the period of slavery the Negro race in the United States was protected from competition with the Whites. . . . Only since emancipation has genuine competition between the races in this country existed." See Smith, *The Color Line*, 182. Joseph Alexander Tillinghast similarly writes, "The system of slavery served as a means of holding the inferior race to at least a semi-civilized mode of life, despite any propensities to the contrary." See Joseph Alexander Tillinghast, *The Negro in Africa and America* (New York: Macmillan, 1902), 209.

14. Hoffman, *Race Traits and Tendencies*, 176.

15. Paul Brandon Barringer, *The American Negro, His Past and Future* (Raleigh, NC: Edwards and Broughton, 1900), 13.

16. Ibid., 25. The Colored Co-Operative Publishing Company ran an advertisement in the April 1901 issue of *The Colored American Magazine* (in which the second installment of *Hagar's Daughter* appeared) that publicized Hopkins's first novel, *Contending Forces*, alongside a forthcoming work declared to be a direct response to Barringer, titled *Progress or Reversion, Which?*

17. Tillinghast, *The Negro in Africa and America*, 226.

18. In "The Sheriff's Children," a white man who fathered a mixed-race son and scorned his mother must protect him from a lynch mob. Here, Chesnutt questions the value and possible claims of familial relationships that have never been acknowledged. "Her Virginia Mammy" revolves around the secret histories of black ancestry submerged in white Americans' family narratives. See Charles Chesnutt, "The Sheriff's Children" and "Her Virginia Mammy" in *The Wife of His Youth and Other Stories of the Color Line* (New York: Penguin Classics, 2000), 133–44 and 115–32.

19. Charles Chesnutt, "The Wife of His Youth," *The Wife of His Youth and Other Stories of the Color Line*, 106.

20. Ibid., 108.

21. Charles Chesnutt, *The Marrow of Tradition* (1901; New York: Penguin, 1993), 2.

22. Ibid., 9.

23. Ibid., 28.

24. Ibid., 238.

25. Ibid., 86, 119, 181.

26. Ibid., 212, 211.

27. Ibid., 296.

28. Ibid., 235.

29. Ibid., 310.

30. Ibid., 309.

31. Chas. H. Williams, "The Race Problem," *The Colored American Magazine* (September 1901): 355.

32. Ibid., 356.

33. Charleea H. Williams "Recent Developments in 'The Land of the Free,'" *The Colored American Magazine* (August 1902): 285–286.

34. Ibid., 293, 292.

35. Pauline Hopkins, *Contending Forces: A Romance Illustrative of Negro Life North and South* (1900; New York: Oxford UP, 1988), 15.

36. Ibid., 15.

37. Pauline Hopkins, *Of One Blood; Or, The Hidden Self* (1903; New York: Washington Square Press, 2004), 120.

38. Augusta Rohrbach's excellent essay on Hopkins's magazine fiction helpfully describes this narrative mode as "antigenealogy," which disrupts the "monolithic (and

hegemonic) conceptions of race promoted by generic conventions of the novel." See Augusta Rohrbach, "To Be Continued: Double Identity, Multiplicity and Antigenealogy as Narrative Strategies in Pauline Hopkins' Magazine Fiction." *Callaloo* 22 (Spring 1999): 483. Lois Brown also views intertexuality as this novel's primary tactic, examining at length not only allusions to the life and works of William Wells Brown, but also Stowe's *Uncle Tom's Cabin*, Milton's *Paradise Lost*, and Tennyson's *Maud*. See Brown, *Pauline Elizabeth Hopkins*.

39. Pauline Hopkins, *Hagar's Daughter* in *The Magazine Novels of Pauline Hopkins* (1901–1902: New York: Oxford UP, Schomberg Library of Nineteenth-Century Black Women Writers, 1988), 53; hereafter cited parenthetically.
40. William Benjamin Smith, *The Color Line*, 15.
41. Ibid., 10.
42. Wallinger, *Pauline E. Hopkins*, 175.
43. Dana Seitler, *Atavistic Tendencies: The Culture of Science in American Modernity*. (Minneapolis: U of Minnesota P, 2008), 2.
44. Similar scenes of white fear of atavism appear in a number of fin-de-siècle novels, including Charles Chesnutt's *The House Behind the Cedars* (1900) and William Dean Howells's *An Imperative Duty* (1892).
45. Seitler, *Atavistic Tendencies*, 7.
46. Ibid., 20.
47. Lois Brown also observes that in *Hagar's Daughter*, Hopkins "focused deliberately on the lingering manifestations of slavery . . . that challenged notions of a reunited nation." See Brown, *Pauline Elizabeth Hopkins*, 319. Also, on the polytemporality of Hopkins's novels, see Susan Gillman, *Blood Talk: American Race Melodrama and the Culture of the Occult* (Chicago: U of Chicago P, 2003), 40–45.
48. McGill, *American Literature and the Culture of Reprinting*, 5.
49. S.C. Cross, "The Negro Problem and the Sunny South; Or, Prejudice the Problem," *The Colored American Magazine* (July 1902), 193.
50. Ibid., 197.
51. Augusta Rohrbach observes that "in a radical way, Hopkins' use of genre rebukes conventional notions of racial inheritance and identity by turning the argument away from the monolithic (and hegemonic) conceptions of race promoted by the generic conventions of the novel." Augusta Rohrbach, "To Be Continued," 483.
52. A character in Charles Chesnutt's *The Marrow of Tradition* describes the future of the African American race as "a tremendously interesting problem. It is a serial story which we are all reading, and which grows in vital interest with each successive installment." This relationship between race progress and serial narrative progress further illuminates Hopkins's formal tactics in *Hagar's Daughter*. See Chesnutt, *The Marrow of Tradition*, 51.
53. Kristina Brooks, "Mammies, Bucks, and Wenches: Minstrelsy, Racial Pornography, and Racial Politics in Pauline Hopkins's *Hagar's Daughter*" in *The Unruly Voice: Rediscovering Pauline Elizabeth Hopkins*, ed. John Cullen Gruesser (Champaign, IL: U of Illinois P, 1996), 133.
54. Kristina Brooks, "Mammies, Bucks, and Wenches," 134. Also see Sandra Hays Bussey, "Whose Will Be Done?: Self-Determination in Pauline Hopkins's 'Hagar's Daughter,'" *African American Review* 39 (Fall 2005): 299–313.
55. Chesnutt, *The Marrow of* Tradition, 42.
56. Ibid., 42.
57. See Elizabeth Freeman, "Packing History, Count(er)ing Generations," *New Literary History* 31 (Autumn 2000): 728. On the temporal function of dialect in the historical romance, see Pratt, "Dialect Writing and Simultaneity."

58. Chesnutt, *The Marrow of Tradition*, 269.
59. Carby, *Reconstructing Womanhood*, xliii. Wallinger notes that Hopkins "does not go so far as to claim, as William Wells Brown does, that one of the founding fathers, Thomas Jefferson, fathered slave children . . . but her setting in the political society of Washington must be taken as a comment on the intricate relationship between the government and the legacy of the slave system." See Wallinger, *Pauline E. Hopkins*, 179.
60. Booker T. Washington, "Atlanta Compromise" (Atlanta, GA: September 18, 1895).
61. Felipe Smith notes that Washington invokes two bodies in this speech, "the black 'body of death' and the white body politic," and links this notion of separate bodies to the ongoing discourse about race extinction. See Smith, *American Body Politics*, 59.
62. Claudia Tate notes that this "failed romantic consummation aborts the story of ideal family formation." See Tate, *Domestic Allegories of Political Desire*, 200.

CODA

1. My thinking here is inspired in part by Povinelli's assertion: "The genealogical imaginary did not die when the sovereign's head tumbled. Nor was it replaced by intimacy. . . . Sociality seems unthinkable not only without one or the other of these two grids, but without them working as twin pairs, intertwined, twisting, struggling against each other." Elizabeth Povinelli, "Notes on Gridlock," 235.
2. Jurgen Habermas, *The Structural Transformation of the Public Sphere: An Inquiry into a Category of Bourgeois Society* (Cambridge: MIT Press, 1991), 48–49.
3. For an excellent recent iteration of this view of the novel, see Terry Castle, "Don't Pick Up: Why Kids Need to Separate from their Parents," *The Chronicle Review* (May 6, 2012).
4. Judith Roof sheds light on the familial logic of genealogical causality and heteromarital teleology underlying narrative development: "reproductive familial narrative assumes a linear, chronological time where the elements that come first appear to cause the elements that come later. This results in a very reproductive (and almost inevitably familial) understanding of change through time; the past produces the future as parents produce children. Conceived as unidirectional, the linear logic of a temporally bound case-effect narrative creates a perpetual debt to the past." Judith Roof, "Generational Difficulties; or, the Fear of a Barren History" in *Generations: Academic Feminists in Dialogue* (Minneapolis: U of Minnesota P, 1997), 71. See also Patricia Tobin, *Time and the Novel: The Genealogical Imperative* (Princeton, NJ: Princeton UP, 1978).
5. Meredith McGill also addresses the republican association of print with the public good. She analyzes major early American copyright decisions that theorized print "as something that necessarily exceeds the bounds of private property." Meredith McGill, *American Literature and the Culture of Reprinting 1834–1853* (Philadelphia: U of Pennsylvania P, 2003), 64.
6. Michael Warner, *The Letters of the Republic: Publication and the Public Sphere in Eighteenth-Century America* (Cambridge: Harvard UP, 1990), 152.
7. See Leslie Fiedler, *Love and Death in the American Novel* (New York: Stein and Day, 1960).
8. Nancy Bentley, "Creole Kinship: Privacy and the Novel in the New World." *The Oxford Handbook of Nineteenth-Century American Literature* Ed. Russ Castronovo (New York: Oxford UP, 2012) 97–114.

9. In cleaving to the family forms that give it meaning, "the novel tampers with the most intimate continuities." Edward Said, *Beginnings: Intention and Method* (New York: Columbia UP, 1975), 149.

10. Michael Warner, "Irving's Posterity," *ELH* 67.3 (Fall 2000), 785.

11. Ibid., 782.

12. Fanny Fern, *Ruth Hall: A Domestic Tale of the Present Time* (New York: Mason Brothers, 1854), 276.

13. Not surprisingly, Ruth's relationship to print culture is associated with republicanism. She is "intensely patriotic." She "believe[s] in Plymouth Rock and Bunker Hill." In another instance, we see "'the spirit of '76' flashing form her eyes." Ibid., 218, 244. Displaying the discomfort with the novel form that Warner notes in eighteenth-century American literature, this novel lionizes periodical culture, seeming to undervalue its own form to aspire to the status of a republican text.

14. Elizabeth Freeman, "Queer Belongings: Kinship Theory and Queer Theory," in *A Companion to Lesbian, Gay, Bisexual, and Transgender Studies*, eds. George Haggerty and Molly McGarry (Blackwell Press, 2007), 306.

15. Ibid., 299.

16. Laurel Thatcher Ulrich, "Introduction" in *The Art of Family: Genealogical Artifacts in New England*, ed. D. Brenton Simons (Boston: New England Historic Genealogical Society, 2002), 11. Ulrich notes that many of the nineteenth-century Americans who were most invested in researching and recording their families' histories were unmarried or childless.

17. Said traces the etymological roots of authorship to paternity: "a begetter, beginner, father, or ancestor" (*Beginnings*, 83).

18. On the influence of Wittgenstein's familial analogy in genre theory, see David Fishelov, *Metaphors of Genre: The Role of Analogies in Genre Theory* (University Park, PA: Penn State Press, 1989).

19. Dimock, *Through Other Continents*, 74–75.

20. Ibid., 57–58.

21. Ibid., 59.

22. Ibid., 64, 66.

23. Peterson, *Kindred Specters*, 137.

24. Said, *Beginnings*, 139.

25. Ibid., 137, 138.

26. Ibid., 143. Said argues that the project of the novel shifted from the representation of life to reflection on its own form, a move that is mirrored by "the substitution of irresponsible celibacy for fruitful marriage" in the content of the works. Ibid., 148. Although this seems to suggest that the novel becomes increasingly perverse the closer it gets historically to modernism, even the early novel deviated markedly from familial normativity in its fixation on orphans, incest, and other violations of traditional kin relations.

27. Ibid., 149.

28. Ibid., 147. Said refers here to the realist dilation of quotidian details in the work of authors like Gustave Flaubert, but this intriguing suggestion sheds light on works like *The Country of the Pointed Firs*, *Clotel*, and *Hagar's Daughter* that honor the termination rather than continuity of bloodlines.

29. This is why Toni Morrison's *Beloved*, another novel that depicts the lineal transmission of slavery as a fate worse than death, insists that the story it tells is a story that should not be passed on. Indeed, Morrison suggests that family stories

can become a form of hereditary enslavement. See Toni Morrison, *Beloved* (New York: Knopf, 1987).

30. My use of "heteronormativity" here follows Warner and Lauren Berlant's definition of the term as something distinct from heterosexuality, a more thoroughgoing "sense of rightness" that accrues around the family: "A complex cluster of sexual practices gets confused, in heterosexual culture, with the love plot of intimacy and familialism that signifies belonging to society in a deep and normal way. Community is imagined through scenes of intimacy, coupling, and kinship; a historical relation to futurity is restricted to generational narrative and reproduction." Lauren Berlant and Michael Warner, "Sex in Public," *Critical Inquiry* 24.2 (Winter 1998), 554.

INDEX